EARLY CHILDHOOD EDUCATION AND CARE

edited by Patti Owens

Trentham Books

First published in 1997 by Trentham Books Limited

Trentham Books Limited
Westview House
734 London Road
Oakhill
Stoke on Trent
Staffordshire
England ST4 5NP

British Cataloguing in Publication Data
A catalogue record for this book is available from the British Library
ISBN: 1 85856 080 2

Designed and typeset by Trentham Print Design Ltd., Chester
and printed in Great Britain by Wessex Press Group Ltd, Wiltshire.

EARLY CHILDHOOD EDUCATION AND CARE

Contents

Introduction

About this book

This self study book began its life as a set of materials for the University of Hertfordshire's distance education course, the *Certificate in Early Childhood Education and Care*. The team of writers involved all have a commitment to the early years world, and they share a concern at the lack of higher education and training opportunities for people currently working in the field.

The knowledge and understanding of early childhood professionals varies widely. Some will have a background in education, health or social welfare, with perhaps little or no training in work with our youngest children. Others may have a good grounding in nursery education and care, yet feel unable to up-date their professional knowledge at higher education level. As well as this, a significant number of people working with young children will as yet have received no professional education and training at all. And, of course, parents form a large percentage of the early childhood 'workforce', in the voluntary sector as well as at home.

We hope that this book will have something to offer early childhood professionals, those who work with young children between birth and eight years old, and parents who want to learn more about their own children's development, care and early education.

The book is split into four units of study, each with reading material, activities and observations covering the three weeks on that study topic.

Unit 1: The Whole Child

This first unit focuses on the physical, social, emotional and personal development of children from birth to eight years old. You will look at the ways children grow and change during this period, moving on to explore the importance of the family and the wider community, in children's social and moral development. Finally, you will review theories of personal development and enter a discussion about how to foster self-esteem in the children we care for and educate.

Unit 2: Promoting Greater Understanding

This unit focuses on children's language and learning development, at home and in early childhood centres. You will look at your own learning, relating this to the nature of learning in the early years, from there moving into an exploration of theories of cognitive development in young children. Lastly, you will examine your role as an adult in promoting greater understanding in the young children in your care.

Unit 3: A Curriculum for the Whole Child

This unit asks the question: 'What is an appropriate curriculum for young children?' In this wide ranging unit of study you will be asked to consider this question in the light of our understanding of children developing and learning. You will see that there are a range of curricular models to choose from, and some will be more appropriate at different points in children's development, and in different early childhood settings.

Unit 4: Supporting Children with Learning Difficulties and Disabilities

The final unit centres on the education and care of young children with learning difficulties and disabilities. By means of a series of case studies, you will be introduced to the debates concerning 'special schooling' and 'integrated education'. You will be encouraged to consider ways of supporting young children with learning difficulties and disabilities, at home, in early childhood settings and in the early years of school.

Who is this book for?

The book is intended to be a study resource for early childhood carers and educators. Whether you choose to use the book purely for independent personal study, or as a means to gaining an award in higher education, you will find it a rich resource for your personal and professional development, especially if you see yourself as one of the following:

- *Someone who already has a degree qualification in education, health or social welfare, wishing to up-date your understanding of work with young children across the birth to eight age range.*

  For example, you may be a trained teacher who is working in an early childhood unit, with little experience or understanding of children below school age. Or you may be a health visitor or social worker wanting to develop your own skill as an educator of young children.

- *Someone who is managing an early childhood centre or group, such as a playgroup, nursery, or parent-toddler group, where your workforce contains people with different levels of training.*

  These materials would form a basis for a common staff development programme on early childhood education and care. Your staff could compare notes with each other on observations and study activities which are designed to inform good professional practice in the early years.

- *Someone who has a qualification in nursery education, or child care and education, wishing to continue your studies at higher education level.*

  For example you may have completed an award with the NNEB or with CACHE, or have achieved NVQ Level 2 or 3, and wish to go further.

- *Someone who is currently in paid employment with young children on an unqualified basis, wishing to support your own learning in the workplace and improve the quality of the experiences you provide for young children.*

  For example, you may be a childminder or nanny, a voluntary worker or a modern apprentice in an early childhood centre.

- *Someone who has an interest in the development, education and care of children between the ages of birth and eight years, without necessarily working with children professionally.*

  Parents of young children, parent groups or community groups will find the book a valuable source of ideas and activities designed to increase your awareness of the ways in which children develop and learn, and the part you can play in this process.

Personal study or gaining an award?

You may wish to register for a higher education award, the University of Hertfordshire's *Certificate in Early Childhood Education and Care*, using the study materials in this book as the main distance education text for the course. If this is your intention, please contact the University at the address given at the end of this introduction. You will then be allocated

Unit 1: The whole child

Patti Owens

Contents

Unit I: Week One
Children growing and changing

Objectives

This week's study will ask you to consider some major themes in the study of child development. By the end of the week you should:

- be engaging with the 'Nature versus Nurture' debate

- know the difference between the biological, environmental and transactional approaches to children's development and learning

- see the importance of both describing and attempting to explain development

- understand how observation provides the 'evidence' for theories about children's development

- have gained a broad picture of children's physical development

- have some idea of the reasons for studying physical development and the connections with other aspects of children's development and learning.

Activities

This week you will need to arrange about one hour in total for observations, some of which should be focused on children under five years old, preferably in an early childhood centre such as a nursery or playgroup. You will be asked to do two 10-15 minute observations, plus time to write up your notes and comment on what you have observed.

About this unit

Studying child development means coming to know about all the ways in which young children grow and change. In this book you will be studying children's affective development: how a child develops in emotional and social terms, building a sense of themselves as a person.

Sometimes it is helpful to focus on one particular area of development, but we must never lose sight of the whole child as a young person. So I begin this unit with a section on physical development, later on making connections with social and emotional development. When I discuss moral development I link it to the social life of the child as well as their capacity to understand and use language. Look out for these interconnections as the unit progresses. In this unit I will draw upon examples and observations from the wide variety of situations in which children of this age find themselves. These include:

• at home with their family

• at a parent-toddler group or playgroup

• with their childminder or nanny

• at a combined nursery centre (staffed by workers from teaching, social services and health backgrounds)

• in a nursery school, nursery class, or an early years unit in a primary school

•   in a reception or primary class.

As we advised you in the introduction, you will need to have access to children across the birth to eight years age range if you are to get the most out of this module. That way you will be able to make your own observations as well as reading mine, and your study will be enriched. At the end of each week of study you will also find suggestions for further reading.

In this unit, where the intention is to enrich and extend your understanding of children's physical, social, emotional and personal development, there are lots of topics I could have chosen to discuss. In this relatively short text we could not hope to cover everything. It may be that some topics you expected to find here are left out, and others are included that you did not expect to see. I have tried to select themes in child development that will interest you and encourage you to re-evaluate your professional understanding of young children. Whether as parent, carer or educator, we have a responsibility to understand something of the emotional, social and personal development of children. In this way we can engage fully in the process of education and care, treating children with the respect they deserve.

In the course of this unit I will mention quite a few recent researchers and investigators. The work of people interested in child development continues to inspire new ideas and debates about how children grow and change. The study of child development is not confined to a static set of established theories. It is a living area of investigation – one in which I hope I can encourage you to take part.

The 'Nature versus Nurture' debate

The study of child development involves two big questions:

- What develops?

- How and why does development happen?

The first question encourages us to *describe* as accurately as we can the patterns of development that we observe in children as they grow and mature. Researchers rely on clear observation to build up an understanding of patterns and sequences of development.

One example might be the sequence of physical development commonly observed in infants. A baby learns first to sit unaided, then crawl, walk and finally run. It is important to say here that the pattern may be commonly seen but is not necessarily universal, as any parent of a baby who never crawled will tell you! More seriously, perhaps, identifying a pattern of development is different from stipulating a *rate* of development. In the past the idea of 'stages' in learning, linked rigidly to particular ages, has been responsible for much inappropriate adult intervention. The sequence of development may be similar for most children. The age at which they pass through points on this sequence may differ enormously. Consider the different ages children might be when they take their first step, read their first book or learn to swim.

You may already have started to think about the second big question, 'How and why does development happen?' Maybe you said to yourself, 'Of course children do things at different ages. It all depends who has been caring for them, the kind of home they come from, or what opportunities they have had.' If so, you were engaging with this second question. You were in fact trying to *explain*, not just describe, development.

The attempt to explain children's development has led to the formulation of a range of theories, each taking a different perspective on the developing child. Broadly speaking, these theories divide around the issue of whether 'Nature' or 'Nurture' is the more significant factor in explaining children's development. Are children born with a biologically in-built programme which makes them develop in a particular way (Nature)? Or are they dependent on environmental influences which control the manner and extent to which they develop (Nurture)? I wonder what your position in this debate might be. Try the following activity before reading the rest of my discussion.

to a telephone tutor and sent details of the assignments you need to complete , plus more information on how to study effectively for the award.

Alternatively, you may wish to use this book for independent study either alone or with a group of interested friends or colleagues. To get the most out of the book you will need to have regular contact with young children, preferably in an early childhood centre such as a nursery, playgroup or early years unit. This will enable you to carry out the suggested activities and observations which accompany the reading material contained in the book.

Thus when we refer to your 'workplace', this may be the early childhood centre which you are visiting for the duration of your study. It is, of course, important to discuss your studies with the manager of the centre you are visiting, and to obtain permission to carry out the observations and activities that will support your learning in the workplace.

How to use this book

There are several ways of using the book. You will know which way best suits your purposes.

- If you follow the book through as a course of study, you will be taken through a series of steps in developing your understanding of the education and care of young children. Each week there will be material to read and reflect upon, and suggestions for observations and activities to undertake in your particular early childhood workplace or setting. If you have registered for the *Certificate in Early Childhood Education and Care* you will also have time allocated for the completion of assignments.

- If you are using the book as a resource for staff development in your team or workplace you may find it better to work through one unit at a time, at a slower pace or in a different order. You can then give time for discussion of the topics and comparison of ideas within the team.

- If you are using this book for self study or out of purely personal interest, the pace is of course up to you. If you have an infant or toddler in your care, Units 1 and 2 may perhaps be of special interest to you. When it is time for your child to move into child care or education outside the home, Unit 3 will make you better informed about the range of educational experiences you can expect for your child. If you wish to know more about ways of supporting young children with learning difficulties or disabilities, then Unit 4 will give you information, examples and ideas.

Activities

There are a number of activities spread throughout the unit. In general these are designed to encourage your active participation as a reader and learner. Some activities are introduced like this:

■ Activity X A

These activities will help you understand more about the topic you are currently studying, maybe by getting you to pause and reflect for a while, do some further reading, or consider a case study. Other activities are introduced like this:

■ Activity X B

These are more complex and time consuming. They often require you to do some observations of young children or of practice in an early childhood centre, and to evaluate your observations using some of the theories and ideas discussed in the teaching material.

A note on observing children

At points during the course of your study using this book you will be asked to make an observation of a child, or children. You will be given detailed advice on each occasion, relating to the context and topic of the observation you are asked to undertake.

If you register for the *Certificate in Early Childhood Education and Care* you will be sent a preparatory unit which contains general advice on observation, plus some examples. If you are using this book for independent study, you will find that each unit of study contains observations of many kinds, and in a number of contexts. For those of you who are new to the skills of observing young children, here are some general considerations.

- Always obtain the permission of the child's parent(s) as well as that of the manager of your workplace.

- Be as unobtrusive as possible when taking notes. Think beforehand about *what* you wish to observe; *why* you want to; and *how* you can best carry out the observation.

- Try first to develop skills of recording accurately what happens, and what is said. You may sometimes want to use a tape recorder or camera but often your own notes will be your main source of information. It is as well to allow time to practice observing, and for developing your own 'shorthand' ways of recording information.

- Delay any interpretations and judgements you may have until after the observation is over. Whilst observing, concentrate on *describing* events. Explanations can be tried out in your evaluation later.

- When you evaluate your observation make sure you show your respect for the child and any adult who is involved in the activity you have observed. It is sometimes easy to judge others, and this can in fact be damaging to the child. Evaluations and interpretations are your 'best shot' at trying to guess what is going on, for the moment. One observation can never tell you the whole story about a child, or the adults they are engaging with. A series of observations can give you a fuller picture, as can discussion with parents or colleagues who know the child well.

Acknowledgements

The team of writers who produced this book would like to thank everyone who contributed to the planning and organisation of the materials within it. Thank you to Gill Scrivens, Mary Thornton, Chris Cook, Mary Read and Barry Hill at the University of Hertfordshire who read draft material, and to Dorothy Rouse Selleck of the National Children's Bureau and Anna Craft of the Open University who acted as planning consultants. Thanks to James Ryan who gave advice on style and layout in editing the pilot materials. Special thanks to the students who took the *Certificate in Early Childhood Education and Care* as a distance education course in 1995/6, giving us valuable feedback and contributing examples and observations. Lastly, thank you to John Egglestone for his support for the idea of turning our distance education materials into this book, making it possible for us to reach a wider number of people interested in early childhood education and care.

Information about the University of Hertfordshire's Certificate in Early Childhood Education and Care award

If you wish to obtain information about registering for this higher education award, using the materials in this book as a basis for study, please contact:

The Admissions Officer
University of Hertfordshire
Wall Hall Campus
Aldenham
Watford
Herts. WD2 8AT
Tel: 01707-285766

Whether you register for the award or use this book for independent study, we hope that you will find it helpful in enhancing your own particular contribution to the quality education and care of young children.

■ Activity 1 A

Below is a list of some developmental goals which children usually achieve during their first eight years. Complete the table by saying something about how each factor, 'Nature' and 'Nurture', influences development. Which do you think is the more important factor in each case?

Goal	Nature?	Nurture?
Growing taller		
Doing arithmetic		
Showing love		
Holding a crayon		
Hearing sounds		
Making friends		
Catching a ball		
Feeding themselves		
Learning to walk		
Feeling pride		

❏ Commentary

Here are the notes I made. You may agree on some points and not others. You may have made different comments to mine. Talk to someone else about it if you can. You will probably find that they say something different again. The responses we make are a matter for discussion and debate.

Goal	Nature?	Nurture?
Growing taller	Genes: family height	Quality of diet
Doing arithmetic	'Natural' brain development	Teaching, practice
Showing love	Baby seeks parental love	Carers show emotion
Holding a crayon	Grasping skills	Experience
Hearing sounds	Physical development	Encouragement
Making friends	Human predisposition	Opportunities to do so
Catching a ball	Hand-eye coordination	Practice
Feeding themselves	Desire for food, curiosity	Training by adults
Learning to walk	Consequence of evolution	Practice, support
Feeling pride	Need for rewards	Praise of others

The biological view

If you put more emphasis on 'Nature', on the in-built mechanisms for development that young children seem to possess, you are in sympathy with the *biological view*, which stresses biological factors in children's development. For example, the height to which a child may grow is said to be genetically determined. The genes contributed by each parent at conception are transmitted to the growing child. In this way it is unlikely, though not impossible, that shorter than average parents will produce a taller than average child.

UNIT 1 WEEK ONE

Closely connected with this broadly biological view is the idea of *maturation*, that children will simply develop certain characteristics of their own accord. You might have said this about learning to walk, for instance. The pattern of physical development leading to the human ability to move about on two legs is so widely observed, except where physical development is delayed or impaired, as to be described as an innate capacity. On this view, change is seen as a gradual and consistent 'unfolding' of development based on biological factors. The child first learns to stand, then takes those early wobbly steps, and then gradually becomes steadier until s/he can walk more confidently, before undertaking more complex movements like running, skipping and jumping.

Biological theorists do not stop at physical development. Some researchers have tried to show that other kinds of development are also influenced by innate (in-built) characteristics in the child. Later in this unit you will learn more about some of this work which seems to show that even the development of particular personality traits may be due to biological factors. In Unit 2 you will look at similar ideas concerning children's supposedly innate mechanisms for learning language. Such biological theories are also sometimes called 'nativist' because of their stress on what is apparently 'natural' or 'native' to the human being as a developing organism.

The environmental view

On the other hand, you may well have put more stress on 'Nurture' in your response to Activity 1. In this case you would agree with the *environmental view*. Even in the fairly straightforward case of growing physically taller, you might have said, a lot depends on environmental factors like the quality of a child's diet, the amount of fresh air and exercise they get and so on. In the case of psychological development, similarly, you might have argued that far more depends on the child's environment. For example, the child who is in frequent contact with others from an early age, and has caregivers who encourage independence while maintaining support, is far more likely to make friends easily than the child of shy parents who rarely mix with other people. Even if a baby seems genetically programmed to want human contact – and researchers we discuss next week would argue this – the growing infant needs social activity in order to foster this natural sociability.

On this view, a change in development such as learning to make friends relies on environmental factors to make it occur. Environmental theorists also point to differences of development and behaviour between children which they would say are the consequence of the 'Nurture' the child receives, the environmental influences and the wide range of experiences that affect their growth.

I expect you can see the importance of both biology and environment, 'Nature *and* Nurture', in children's development. In your response to Activity 1 you probably did as I did, sometimes giving more weight to biological characteristics and predispositions and sometimes to environmental features. It is rare nowadays to find anyone thinking that *just* 'Nature' or *just* 'Nurture' is involved. Most researchers think both aspects are important, but they disagree about the significance to give each side of the development story, as you will see. In the meantime perhaps you will keep an open mind on this debate, coming back to these first ideas later on, in the light of your study.

Observing children and describing development

One important aim of observation is to try and *describe* development as accurately as we can. Descriptive observation offers us evidence for any explanation we may want to give. This unit moves from the study of children's physical development towards thinking about emotional and social development. We will consider whether these are things we can observe.

■ Activity 2 A

Read carefully these two observations of the same child. They were taken on the same morning at the early childhood centre she attended. Make some notes on the following questions before reading my comments.

1.   What do these observations tell you about Lauren's physical development?

2.   What can you learn from them about Lauren's social and emotional development?

Observation 1: 9.30-9.55 am
Child: Lauren   Place: Playgroup (morning session)
Sex: Female   Date: 10 October 1994
Age: 4 years 4 months

Lauren goes over to the block corner and asks Shehana (F) and Roy (M) if she can help them build. They say it's OK. They start building and Lauren accidentally knocks some bricks down. She says immediately, 'I can put them back up,' and begins to do so.

Roy says, 'I'll help,' and for a while Lauren watches him build, before handing him a cylinder block.

'This will be the funnel for our train,' says Lauren.

Shehana tells her where to place it. Lauren begins handing blocks to Shehana and Roy as they build. Finally Lauren places blocks around the perimeter of their building.

An adult arrives and asks if Lauren wants to do some cooking. 'Only if Shehana and Roy can come too,' says Lauren.

Observation 2: 11.15-11.25 am
Lauren has become interested in the full-length mirror in the dressing up area. She moves closer to the mirror, looking at her face and smiling. She turns to look back at the block play area where Roy and Shehana are still playing, turns back and smiles. 'Hello, and how are you today?' she giggles, then tries to touch her cheek in the mirror.

She collects some clothes from the dressing-up box and returns to sit in front of the mirror. First she puts on a baby's bib, tying one knot then slipping it over her head. She 'cries' and rubs her eyes with her fists. Then she puts on a curly wig and says to the mirror with a serious face, shaking her head, 'Oh, that baby. He drives me mad! He's always so hungry ... wanting his bottle and everfink.'

Taking the wig off and stroking the bib she still wears, absorbed in her mirror image, she says in a baby voice, 'Ma-ma ... ma-ma' and 'cries' again.

She stops pretending to cry, smiles at her image and runs off to the drawing table, still wearing the bib. 'I'm going to draw my mum feeding her baby,' she tells the adult there.

❑ Commentary

You may have listed the following features:

1. Lauren's physical development
Grasping, carrying, balancing, placing (block play)
Walking, running, lifting
Tying a knot (bib)
Manipulative skills (placing wig on her head, drawing)

2. Lauren's social and emotional development
Wants to play co-operatively
Confident – to try new things, to make amends, to add to the building
Developing the concept of 'friend'
Sense of fun (mimicry, role play)
Likes the look of herself (self-esteem)
Expressing feelings through solitary/pretend play

Did you find it easier to pinpoint one area of development? My guess is that you found the identification of features of Lauren's physical development more straightforward.

Observing physical development

We can usually observe physical development directly as long as the child is given the opportunity to show us. Sad to say, in many Primary school classes containing children of Lauren's age it would not be easy to observe her ongoing physical development. Except for designated 'playtimes' she would be expected to restrict her movements to those that are possible when seated at a work table or desk. This would mean that one very important area of Lauren's overall development was being neglected. Yet the School Curriculum and Assessment Council (SCAA) recommends that one aim of 'pre-school education' is to ensure that young children are able to

> move confidently and imaginatively with increasing control and co-ordination and an awareness of space and others ... use a range of small and large equipment, such as wheeled toys, beanbags, balls and balancing and climbing apparatus, with increasing skill [and] handle small tools and objects such as pencils, paintbrushes and scissors, with increasing control. [Dearing 1995]

The National Curriculum working group on physical education in the early years also had this to say in 1991: Opportunities for physical development in young children lead not only to 'physical competence and development' but also influence 'self-esteem; artistic and aesthetic understanding; problem-solving skills; interpersonal skills; and links with the community and across cultures' (Dowling 1992, p 106). This is borne out by the observations you have just read. If Lauren had not been able to move to the block play activity she might not have had the chance to initiate the period of play with Shehana and Roy. Similarly, if she had no opportunity to play alone for a while she might not have been able to rehearse her concerns about her new brother, if that is what we were observing.

Observing emotional development

We do not *know* that these emotional states are being experienced by Lauren, in the way that we know she can walk, run or build with blocks. We can only make an educated guess about these areas of her 'inner' development. We are helped in doing this by some of the *theories* discussed later in this unit, but it is important to emphasise that they are theories, that is, attempts to interpret the evidence of our observations. They are attempts to *explain*, as well as describe, children's personal, emotional and social development.

For now it is enough to emphasise the dangers of letting our assumptions go unchallenged or falling into generalised statements. For instance, you may have thought that Lauren was motivated by the desire to play with her two new friends, but maybe she had something else in mind. She might have been hoping that when she had finished helping them build the train they would go away and let her build something all by herself. How are we to know with certainty? And think how you might change your view of Lauren's emotional state if you knew that in reality she had no siblings. What interpretation would you give to her actions then? Obviously it helps to observe and get to know a child over a period of time. Even then I know I have to watch out that I do not form too fixed an opinion of a child's development which may prevent me from seeing them as a complex, always changing, human being.

To return to Lauren's physical development, I wonder if you too were impressed by her manual dexterity and independence in tying the bib. It has been my experience that children will often ask for help with a task like that. We turn now to a survey of some commonly observed patterns of physical development in young children.

Physical development from birth to 8 years

Whether you emphasise the biological or the environmental factors in child development, you will probably be able to identify patterns and sequences in physical development. Sometimes people talk of 'milestones' to indicate developmental tasks or goals that children are expected to achieve in a particular order. These can be seen as markers on the road to adulthood, if you like. What age do you think children normally pass through these milestones of physical development? Take some time to think about the ones below.

■ Activity 3 A

What age do you think a child would usually be when achieving these 'milestones'?

> Follows objects with her gaze
> Sits on his own without support
> Crawls
> Stands upright supported by a chair, for instance
> Grips an object, using thumb and forefinger
> Walks unsteadily
> Pushes wheeled toys
> Climbs into a low armchair
> Builds a tower of three blocks
> Climbs up and down stairs
> Throws a ball
> Kicks a ball

❏ Commentary

Your response to this activity will depend quite a lot on your personal experience. Maybe your own children took their first steps at about ten and a half months, in which case you might have said ten to twelve months for 'walks unsteadily'. If you have met a lot of infants in your professional and family life you probably put the age for this milestone a little later, between twelve and fifteen months. You would know that this is the most usual age for children to begin walking.

Rates and patterns of physical development

Most researchers would place all the milestones listed in Activity 3 in the birth to two years age phase. As an example, you could look at a developmental checklist suggested by Richard Woolfson (1991). It is listed as one of the readings at the end of this week's study. Alternatively you may find it helpful to look at checklists used at your local health centre, for instance.

There have been a number of interesting cross-cultural studies, too, that illustrate different *rates* of development in children across a variety of cultures. The developmental *sequence* nevertheless remains fairly constant. Studies have shown, for example, that in some African societies a great deal of emphasis is placed on encouraging the infant to become physically independent. Mothers and other carers frequently massage their babies, help them to sit and stand unaided, and stimulate walking movements from a much younger age than their European counterparts. This has a marked positive effect on motor development, with most infants walking unaided between nine and eleven months (Hopkins and Westra 1988). Such a study suggests that the encouragement a child receives can make a big difference in speeding up physical development. 'Nurture' is on this view very significant. Even so, patterns of physical development are evident. Children in these African families do not walk before they can sit unaided or run before they can walk.

■ Activity 4 A

List some more milestones of physical development that you would place after the age of two years. You may find it helpful to use this chart as a starting point. I have just put in one or two milestones at each stage, based on my own experience with young children. Now put in some of your own.

By 3 years   Climb on a climbing frame; use small tools such as pencils or crayons

By 4 years   Use scissors; ride a trike; complete 20-piece jigsaw

By 5 years   Build with Lego

By 6 years   Swim

By 7 years   Dance, making a simple sequence with a partner

By 8 years   Play rounders

❏ Commentary

Maybe the most useful comment on your own chart would come from another parent or friend, or a colleague at work or in the early childhood centre you are visiting. See what they think of your ideas. You may want to add to, change or comment on your initial list as a result.

Physiological change

We will focus on three themes: physiological development, motor development and sensory-perceptual development. I hope you will be interested in this information as it is,[JMR1] but while you read please also keep in mind the following question, to which I will return:

- **Why do we need to study the physical development of children?**

You will find it helpful to make notes as reasons occur to you while you are reading this section.

Physiological change is fundamental to development. We can see children's bodies change and grow as they get older. Unless there is some genetic difficulty, and as long as there is enough support from the child's environment, it seems that physical growth and maturation will take place.

Perhaps the most visible sequence of change is in the height and weight of the child. As Figure 1.1 shows, infants grow rapidly taller in the first two years of life. The rate then slows down until adolescence, when there is another spurt. Between birth and two years a child will gain between 10 and 12 inches (25-30 cm) and triple her body weight. From then on there is a steady progress towards adolescence, with about two or three inches (5-7 cm) in height and about 6 pounds (2.5-3.0 kg) in weight being added each year.

Changes that occur inside the body, affecting bones, muscles and fat, are just as important as these visible physiological changes. Bones increase in number between birth and adolescence in the ankle, foot, wrist and hand, giving the child a greater degree of steadiness and manipulative ability. In the skull, bones fuse to close the *fontanels*, or gaps between the baby's separate skull bones, usually by about eighteen months. All the bones harden or ossify as the child grows older, giving them firmer support and making bodily organs less vulnerable.

Unlike the bones, muscles are formed at birth but the fibres are small and watery. Babies also have a large amount of *subcutaneous fat* immediately under the skin, increasing until about nine months and then gradually diminishing by about the age of 7.

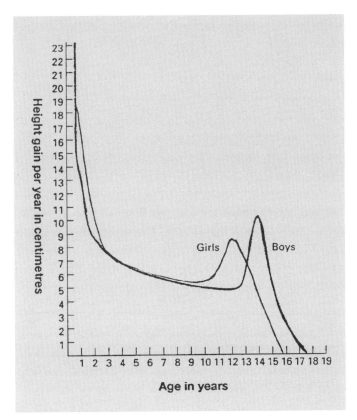

Figure 1.1
You may have noticed changes in muscle and fat when an infant learns to walk, for instance – walking off their 'baby fat'. Or have you witnessed that mysterious change in physical appearance that often occurs between Infant and Junior or Middle school, where a child loses fat and gains height, weight and muscle? These physiological changes are controlled to a large extent by hormones produced in two important glands: the pituitary and thyroid glands. Without this biological factor physical growth would not take place at all, although, as we have seen, environmental features can make a difference to the rate of development.

Motor development

As children change and grow physically, they develop an increasing ability to control their movements. This is known as *motor development*. There are a variety of ways of classifying the different kinds of motor control. You may have heard people talk of 'gross motor skills' to mean large movements such as crawling or walking, and 'fine motor skills' to describe smaller movements such as picking up a fork or unwrapping a sweet. Gross motor skills tend to rely on the child developing bodily strength as muscles and bones are formed. A toddler will not walk steadily until some of that baby fat has been replaced by developing leg and back muscles. Fine motor skills, on the other hand, may rely on muscle and bone formation but they also depend on development of co-ordination between brain and body. To pick up a spoon the (sighted) child must see it and be able to direct his hand to the appropriate spot, before grasping and lifting it. Think of the times when you may have seen a child trying to do this kind of thing but missing the right spot, or failing to grasp at the right moment, or dropping the object unintentionally.

Robert Malina (1982) devised the following way of classifying children's motor development:

- *locomotor development*: moving the body along, such as in running, skipping or jumping

- *nonlocomotor development*: using the body to move other objects or moving without necessarily changing location, as in pushing, pulling and bending

- *manipulative development*: receiving and moving smaller objects, as in grasping a paintbrush, using scissors, throwing, catching or kicking a ball.

You may find Malina's classification helpful when you come to observe children. Remember that one activity can often give the child an opportunity to increase facility in more than one area of motor development. Think of Lauren in Activity 2, for instance. The same period of activity gave her the opportunity to move around (locomotor), move large objects, here building blocks (nonlocomotor), and manipulate smaller objects, here the wig, bib and drawing implements. In doing so she was also making good use of her senses and developing her perceptual abilities.

Sensory-perceptual development

In truth, this area of development is not purely a matter of physical growth and change. In perception both the organs of sense (eyes, ears, nose, etc) and the brain play a part. Through the sense organs we receive information about the world that becomes encoded in a kind of internal message system, which the brain then decodes.

Visual perception

The new-born's visual system is not very developed. Babies cannot show or tell us directly what they are able to see, but research seems to show that they do not see things with much detail or clarity. Interestingly, though, babies can focus relatively well on objects held 8-10 inches away, which is about the distance between a suckling baby and the mother's face. Many studies have also suggested that babies show a marked preference for looking at the human face over any other object of perception.

Visual acuity, or the ability to discriminate visually, gradually increases until full visual acuity is achieved around 10 or 11 years of age. This means that children in our age range will be in the process of developing visual acuity. If we think that 'Nurture' has any significance we will be finding ways to encourage children to use their powers of visual perception. The following activity asks you to reflect on the opportunities you provide in your contact with children for them to 'use their eyes'.

■ Activity 5 A

In each of these observations there is interaction between a baby and an adult. Both observations were made in early childhood centres outside the home. The 'key person' (sometimes called a key worker) is the person assigned to the baby as the primary carer at the centre.

Which observation illustrates adult encouragement for the infant's development of visual acuity?

Child: Gonul   Sex: Female   Age: 3 months

Gonul is lying in her cot, murmuring, moving her hands, arms and legs. Her key person comes in and quickly lifts Gonul from her cot, saying, 'Time for our nappy change, Gonul!' She places Gonul on the changing mat beside the cot and briskly proceeds to change her nappy, thinking all the while that she will be late for lunch.

Child: Darren   Sex: Male   Age: 3 months

Darren is lying in his cot murmuring, kicking his legs and flexing his fingers, which he looks at intently. His key worker comes in and sits down by the cot, waiting for Darren to move his attention from his fingers to his new visitor. 'You look very interested in those fingers, Darren,' says the key worker, and the baby returns her smile and kicks vigorously. Then he shifts his attention to the reflection of sunlight on her spectacles. He blinks and then stares again, smiling and moving his arms rapidly up and down. 'You'd like to wear my specs, would you, Darren?' laughs the key worker. Darren smiles and gurgles, wriggling his body. 'All right then. Would you like me to change that nappy now?' she asks as she lifts him out of the cot, keeping eye contact as she does so, and laying him gently on the changing mat.

❑ Commentary

This is what another reader said:

'Darren's key worker encourages Darren to use his eyes far more than Gonul's does. She notices where his visual attention is as she comes in, and lets Darren decide when to move his eyes to her. She supports this with her words so she is also encouraging Darren to listen. She again notices his change of interest as it shifts to her spectacles, interacting with Darren in a humorous way.'

The second observation also shows how important it is for all those who care for and work with young children to be aware of the quality of their interaction. Maybe in your work you have been more concerned about doing activities with children, and using language effectively in those situations. Of course these aspects are important. If we are interested in educating and caring for the whole child, though, we need to become 'tuned in' to other areas of children's development. As these examples show, this matters just as much at the very youngest end of our age range.

Auditory perception

Infants can hear much more effectively than they can see, so they are said to have better auditory acuity. Typically they can distinguish a wide range of sounds, though not very low-pitched ones, after the first four weeks. This is especially true of the mother's voice. There is some evidence to show that babies might remember their mother's voice from before they were born. Melanie Spence (De Casper and Spence 1986) taped expectant mothers reading stories and then played them back to new-born infants who had 'heard' them while in the womb. Not only did babies appear more content when listening to their mother's voice but they seemed to show a preference for the stories that were taped before their birth. This is interesting, but we must remember that research like this into very young infant behaviour cannot come to hard and fast conclusions. We cannot say for certain what the baby perceives or prefers.

As with visual perception, children's auditory acuity improves as they grow and mature. There are many ways to encourage auditory discrimination in your contact with children. Think, for example, of teaching a young child a traditional song or nursery rhyme. You will be aware that different kinds of sensory-perceptual development can be involved simultaneously. A child learning a song will usually look at you while you sing it, as well as listen to the sounds you make. Often they will clap or beat, so adding tactile experience to their sensory repertoire. This is sometimes called *cross-modal perception*, since our perception of the outside world is gained through the use of all our sense organs working together to bring information to the brain. J.J. Gibson (1979), a researcher interested in the way children develop cross-modal perception, thinks that children do not simply learn to use their senses, nor are they born with an innate ability to develop clear perception. Instead he says that the material world provides 'affordances', or opportunities, for children which evoke abilities they naturally possess. The amazing thing is that out of the myriad messages that bombard our sense organs we are able to select and organise those that will help us to perceive the world around us. This is all the more wonderful when we consider that even new-born human babies have characteristics that enable them to take these 'affordances' and use them to explore their world.

The transactional model of child development

I think Gibson's work is exciting, not least because it sees the developing child as *active*, rather than as just passively receiving the effects of their biology and their environment. This is often referred to more broadly as the *transactional* model of child development. Children play an important part in their own development. They select activities from those on offer in their environment, and in doing so they also have an effect on the behaviour of their caregivers. According to another researcher, Arnold J. Sameroff, in the transactional model of child development:

> the emphasis is placed on the effect of the child on the environment, so that experiences provided by the environment are not independent of the child. The child by its previous behaviour may have been a strong determinant of current experiences. [Sameroff 1991, p. 173]

Think again of baby Darren in the last activity. The 'Nature' model of development would emphasise his 'natural' propensity for showing interest in his surroundings and his

UNIT 1 WEEK ONE

biologically determined ability to focus on particular objects within his field of vision. The 'Nurture' model would stress the importance of aware and sensitive carers like Darren's key worker, in comparison to the poor quality of care shown in baby Gonul's case. In Sameroff's transactional model of development both Nature and Nurture are seen as significant – and *so is the part played by Darren himself in his own development.* In responding to his environment he is changing it, if you like. His interest and response to his key worker's interactions encourage her to continue the stimulation she offers. Darren is an active agent in his own learning and development. We can guess that Gonul would have similarly taken advantage of greater awareness in her key person, had she not been unceremoniously whipped out of her cot and then ignored.

Reasons for studying physical development

Before we finish this week's study I want to return to that question I asked you to keep in the back of your mind as you took notes on this section.

■ Activity 6 A

Why do we need to study the physical development of children?

You may have made some notes on this as you went along. If so, return to them now. If not, think about this question in the light of your study this week, then make some notes. List as many reasons as you can before reading on.

❏ Commentary

I am sure you listed things like:

* making sure a child is growing steadily

* monitoring a child's health

* keeping an eye on their perceptual responses.

These are examples of the kind of everyday monitoring of a child's growth and development undertaken by most parents, early childhood carers and educators. The philosopher Sara Ruddick (1990) says that this watching over the young child is part of the 'maternal work' that can be observed across all cultures. She also thinks of 'mothers' as the women and men who work together to protect, nurture and educate the developing child. So maternal work is shared among biological parents, wider family and friends, and the various agencies involved in supporting the child, directly or indirectly. She would very definitely include you, as someone involved with young children, in this special task.

Physical development and the whole child

You may have listed other kinds of reason for studying children's physical development. Below are four more offered by Helen Bee (1992). See if you agree with her. She argues that physical development is crucial to all other development. It is important to know about physiological changes that are taking place in the child because these in turn affect other kinds of growth and change.

1. *Growth is necessary before learning a new behaviour.*

For example, muscles and bones have to grow strong enough before the infant can learn to stand. This reason links with a biological view of development.

2. *Growth influences, or even determines, the child's experiences.*

An example illustrating this point might be that until babies can crawl or get around a little bit by themselves, everything has to be brought to them, making them heavily dependent on their carers. Once they are mobile they can investigate their environment more fully, in the process experiencing new objects and events. Or again, an older child who learns to ride a bicycle may be provided with the opportunity to range away from home and try out their independence. In both cases the kind of experience that is possible for the child depends on physical growth and development. The second reason therefore makes a connection between biology and environment.

3. *Growth affects the way other people respond to the child.*

The manner of children's physical development affects the way others respond. So the infant who learns to crawl may be given lots of praise and encouragement. This in turn encourages the child to continue her efforts, which stimulates further adult attention. We saw something of this in baby Darren's example.

On a more serious note, a child's appearance can affect the way adults interact with them. Maybe you can think of examples yourself, say, where exceptionally tall children are expected to act older than their age because people are fooled by their physical appearance. At the other extreme a very small child is often treated as 'the baby' by other children and adults. Physical appearance can influence our expectations of children, so we need to take care over this.

4. *Growth affects the child's self-concept.*

The way children develop physically has some effect on their self-concept, or their idea of themselves. Bee remembers how being tall as a young child left a lasting impression on her: she was well into her teens before she managed to overcome her feeling of being 'gawky' and began to see tallness as a useful, or even elegant, quality. Maybe you might recall something like this yourself?

We will return to a discussion of this point later in this module when we look at the development of personal identity in young children. For example, a child in a minority cultural group in the UK develops a self-concept that is at least partly the result of interactions with people who may be very different from her in physical appearance as well as being from the majority white European culture. Just as Helen Bee struggled with seeing tallness as either 'gawky' or 'elegant', many black children struggle with positive and negative images of themselves. As carers for young children, and as educators, we need to be aware of our own role in helping children to develop a healthy self-concept, based in part on an appreciation of their physical being.

Review of the week

Take time to look back over this week's work and consider the following:

-   What interested you most, and why?

-   Are there any activities you need to return to?

-   Have you managed to arrange time to observe in an early childhood centre?

-   How will this week's study influence your ways of interacting with young children?

-   Have you time for more reading on a topic that interests you?

Before moving on to Week 2, make sure you complete the review activity next. Its purpose is to help you consolidate your learning so far and link this to your practical experience with young children. I hope you will also find it interesting.

■ Review activity B

Make two short observations of about 10-15 minutes each.

One should be of an older, possibly school-aged child. You could observe them in the Nursery outdoor play area, at school playtime or in the imaginative play area of a classroom.

The other should be of a younger child. This may be, for instance, an observation of a friend's baby in the home setting, or during a morning spent at your local parent-toddler group or playgroup.

It would be good to have an adult involved in at least one of the observations for part of the time. If this is not possible, please do not worry. Do the best you can with the observations you can make.

Use initials or a false name, rather than the child's actual name. You may wish to return to the advice given in the introduction about making observations. (If you are a student on the University of Hertfordshire's *Certificate in early Childhood Education and Care course*, the Introductory Unit contains more information.) Take each observation in two stages:

1. Make your observation, describing in as much detail as you can exactly what happens and what is said.

2. Take time to think about what you have observed and write a comment using these questions as a framework for each observation:

a) *What does the observation show of the child's physical development?*

    Which of the three aspects of physical development discussed this week (physiological, motor and sensory-perceptual) are observable?

b) *Comment on what you think the observation suggests about personal, social and emotional development.*

    Remember what was said about Lauren in Activity 2. This will help you guard against being too definite in your assertions. Helen Bee's second reason for studying children's physical development is also relevant.

c) *How does any adult interaction you witness encourage the child's development?*

    You might comment on this in relation to physical or affective (emotional, social, personal) development. Try to comment clearly and fairly without being unnecessarily personal or judgmental. On the 'transactional' view of children's development, you will recall that adult interaction is only one feature, though a very important one.

❏ Commentary

You may find it helpful to look at these two observations before you complete your own.

Here is an example observation made by a student working in a Reception class in a Primary school. She observed Abdul Malik (a child in a Year 3 class) at playtime.

Child: Abdul Malik   Sex: Male   Age: 8 years 1 month
Location: In the school playground

Abdul Malik came into the playground with two wooden bats and a small ball. He asked Neil if he wanted to play tennis. When Neil refused and ran off to play football, Abdul Malik looked despondent. Then he spotted Brian, a younger boy, and ran over to him. Brian agreed to play and the two boys found a safe place to play and went on happily for nearly ten minutes. Malik did nearly all the serving and returned the ball confidently every time. When Brian missed or sent the ball sailing off in the wrong direction Malik laughed but then helped him retrieve the ball. At the end of playtime both boys went to the school door, arms on each other's shoulders. As they were about to go in a teacher shouted at them to 'Line up and stop mucking about!' before entering the door.

a) This observation illustrates most obviously Malik's motor development. He is able to manipulate the bat and ball effectively. His hand/eye co-ordination seems well developed too.

b) Malik wants to play with a friend and shows some disappointment when refused. Later on he is keen to stay with his new partner as they go back into school. In this instance playing a game of tennis provides a chance to try out a new friendship.

c) In this case the only adult intervention was a negative one. Instead of recognising the warmth the boys felt for each other after their game, the teacher simply wants them to be prepared for going back into school. Maybe he was feeling harassed after doing fifteen minutes' playground duty! It will make me be a bit more careful about my own responses in future.

Here is another example taken by a student on her first visit to a local private Nursery school.

Child: Female   Age: 4 years 5 months
Date: 13.2.96   Time: 12.50-1.05
Context: Free time in the Nursery (18 children and 3 adults)

S picks up three felt pens from a table. She takes off all the tops. An adult gives her a piece of paper to draw on. She tries to draw with all three pens at once. Puts pens down. Picks up another felt pen and scribbles over the table ...

Joins two children at the wet sand tray. Picks up a handful of sand and drops it all over the floor. Other children tell her to go to another sand tray ...

Goes to the dry sand tray. Teacher intervenes when she tries to take a spade away from another child ...

Returns to wet sand tray and starts shouting. Teacher asks her not to shout but S continues ...

Goes to woodwork area. Picks up a bowl of nails and empties them out over the table. Looks in the box and pulls out a tape measure. Wraps it round her neck and walks off in the direction of the computer ...

Talks to visiting father who is talking to children and teacher at the computer. Teacher shows her how to wind up the tape measure. Sits down at the computer and presses the keys like a piano. Goes off to the playhouse.

a) S shows her developing manipulative skill (Malina 1982). She handles pens, a sand spade and a tape measure, and tries the computer! She moves about quickly and easily from one part of the Nursery to another.

b) From this brief observation S seems to be very self-centred and sometimes annoys other children. She played alone (or in parallel without conversation) nearly all the time I watched her. She showed curiosity about everything that was going on but did not sustain attention for very long on any activity. This may have been due to the fact that it was very near to the end of her session that day. She may well have been tired and/or hungry.

c) At first the only adult interaction S experienced was around negative events – the incident with the spade that led S to start shouting. She did do as she was asked though. Later S responded with interest as she was shown how to wind up the tape measure.

Further reading

Bee, H. (1992) *The Developing Child*, New York: HarperCollins, Chapter 4

Woolfson, R. (1991) *Children with Special Needs: A Guide for Parents and Carers*, London: Faber and Faber, Appendix 1: Developmental Checklist

There is a full list of references at the end of Unit 1.

UNIT 1 WEEK ONE

Unit 1: Week Two
Children, their families and the wider world

Objectives

By the end of this week's study you should:

*   have explored the notions of 'family life' and 'parenting' in the UK and in some world cultures

*   be able to comment on the work of attachment theorists, in particular John Bowlby, as these have led to ideas about the importance of children's earliest relationships with primary carers

*   have begun to examine some of your own ideas about morality

*   have reflected on the theories of Piaget and Kohlberg about children's moral development

*   have begun to think about Judy Dunn's research on pro-social behaviour.

Activities

This week you will need to arrange about one hour in total for observations, some of which will be focused on children under five years old, preferably in an early childhood centre. You will be asked to make two 5-15 minute observations of child/adult interaction, and in addition you will need time to write up your notes and comment on what you have observed.

About this week's study

This week's focus is on the ways young children develop socially, emotionally and morally. How we affect others, and are ourselves affected, depends not just on physical, concrete occurrences but also on what you might call our 'internal' lives – our feelings, intentions, moods and thoughts as well as our actions. In studying *emotional* development we can ask:

*   How does the child come to experience, express, convey and control the full range of emotions?

*   How do the child come to recognise and respond to moods and feelings in others?

Addressing these questions shows us the close link between emotional and *social* development in young children, for it is in forming and maintaining relationships that feelings come to the fore. The question becomes:

*   How does the child come to form healthy relationships within the family and in the wider community?

Moral development, as we shall see, is closely bound up with the child's social and emotional life. I will ask you to think about the question:

*   How does the child develop a sense of right and wrong, in the context of their experience in the family and beyond?

Ideal families and real families

Many people would agree that the family is the most influential context for social, emotional and moral development. Those who look after us and love us as children may be our parents, siblings, grandparents, other relatives or family friends. They may also include professionals such as teachers, doctors, social workers and the like. The family provides the developing child with opportunities to forge intimate relationships. Your idea of family life will no doubt be influenced, as mine is, by your personal and cultural experiences. Let's start with the following three questions:

Activity I A

1. How would you describe the various members of your family and their relations to each other.

2. How would you describe the 'ideal' family, as it is often represented in British culture?

3. What do you think these two families (your own and the 'ideal') have in common? How do they differ?

❑ Commentary

Here is Marian's response (aged 20):

1. 'There's just me and my mum and dad. Neither of them have brothers or sisters. I never knew my grandparents very well. They died when I was just a baby. So we are a very small family I guess.'

2/3. 'The ideal family is one where there are two or three children. I sometimes feel left out when people talk of their brothers and sisters. Mind you, having two parents at home throughout my childhood fits the common îidealî, I think.'

And Jake's (aged 42):

1. 'I was brought up with my aunt and uncle and their four children. My mum went back home when I was a few weeks old and I didn't see her again until quite recently. I saw a lot of my grandparents though. They lived next door to my aunt's house.'

2/3. 'This obviously wasn't ideal in the sense that I never got to know my biological parents. But I was surrounded by love and attention all the same, and I love my cousins as if they were brothers and sisters.'

The 'ideal' family

On BBC Radio 4's lunch time news on 7 July 1994 the Health Minister, Virginia Bottomley, said this:

The best family, as far as I am concerned, is one with mother *and* father and children. I know many families fall short of this ideal but I am rather old-fashioned in this. Children need a mum and a dad, and they need them to be married and to live together.

Her picture of the ideal family implies three elements: being married, living together and sharing parenthood. Whether or not you agree with Virginia Bottomley will depend to some extent on your answer to question 1 in the activity above. If your family was different from her ideal, yet you had a happy childhood, you might want to argue with her assertion. If on the other hand your less than ideal family caused you pain and unhappiness, you might look wistfully at the one she describes.

When we consider the different cultures of the world we see a great diversity of family patterns. Even within the UK in the 1990s, family life is much more varied than Virginia Bottomley's idealised description would suggest. The 'ideal' family of father, mother and children makes up only 25 per cent of households, and includes cohabiting as well as married couples with children. Of families with children nearly one fifth (19 per cent) have only one resident parent. Different patterns of family life exist even within this category of 'lone parent families', with lone fathers making up only 74% of this group; divorced, separated, or single lone mothers 73.6%; and widowed lone mothers 6.3%. (Source: *Guardian*, 1994)

Prajna Das Gupta (in Barnes 1995) has identified five different types of family structure found in the UK today:

- *Conjugal nuclear*. Married couple, with or without children.

- *Non-conjugal nuclear*. As above, but not legally married.

- *Lone parent*. Most are women with a child or children, alone through divorce, separation or widowhood. A small but growing proportion are men.

- *Reconstituted*. Step-families: a combination of two previously lone parent families, or families created by (re)marriage of lone parent(s).

- *Extended*. More than one generation of parents and children living together.

Maybe the description of your own family has more in common with one of these patterns than the supposedly 'ideal' one mentioned by the minister. These examples also remind us that family patterns usually change as time passes. The birth of a new grandchild or the death of a dear family friend can have an impact on family members, including the children. In all the attention that is given to more dramatic events like divorce or marriage separation, we can sometimes forget that these ongoing events and processes in family life also affect the child. They are part of the web of experiences that influence their affective development – part of the environmental 'Nurture' they receive.

Attachment and security

What of the part played by 'Nature' in the emotional and social development of the child? Is there a place for the biological view discussed last week? You may have heard of the work of the psychologist John Bowlby. He argued that emotional development begins in the earliest days of a child's life, when what he called an *attachment bond* is established between the mother and her new-born infant. In healthy maternal relationships, he said, this bond develops quickly and gives the baby a sense of security which forms the basis of their later psychological development. He put forward the following arguments based on his observations (Bowlby 1965):

1. Attachment is an instinctive biological need, a bit like other needs such as the need for food or warmth. So 'babies need their mothers'.

2. Just as bodily malnutrition during the early years can adversely affect physical development, without a secure maternal attachment 'normal healthy mental development' is disrupted.

3. Babies who are separated from their mothers before they are securely attached find it impossible to bond with anyone else. In later life they come to suffer the ill effects of this *maternal deprivation*, or being deprived of their mother's emotional response in infancy. As adults they seem unable to have a close relationship with another adult or their own children.

4. There is a link between maternal deprivation and juvenile crime or delinquency. Bowlby drew this conclusion after studying adolescent boys who were in institutionalised care for being 'thieves'; he found that there was an unusually high incidence of maternal deprivation experience among these boys (Bowlby, 1944).

Bowlby's conclusion that babies need mothers was very influential in the post-war period. Perhaps you can see why. During the Second World War women had been doing much of the paid work that had previously been the preserve of men. They had been lorry drivers, agricultural workers and heavy machinery fitters as well as soldiers and sailors. As men returned from the war they faced unemployment and poverty unless measures could be taken to restore their former work opportunities, so the government of the day was keen to persuade women to return to their traditional role. Many women did not mind going back to the life of home and family, as long as their husbands got jobs as a result. This left a large number of women, though, who were reluctant to give up their new-found freedom. Some historians have argued that these women were pressurised to return to the home by government and media influences of the time (see, for instance, Rowbotham 1973). On this view, Bowlby's ideas were welcomed largely because they supported a political objective. For these reasons and because of criticism of his research methods, Bowlby's original ideas on maternal deprivation are no longer widely accepted. Nonetheless, his notion of attachment has generated a lot of further research.

Bowlby himself modified his views, coming to agree with his colleagues at the Tavistock Clinic in London that the attachment bond could be formed with any single *primary caregiver*, not necessarily or exclusively the child's biological mother. Mary Ainsworth (Ainsworth and Bell 1974) strengthened this idea by proposing that the mother, or primary carer, provides a *secure base* from which the child explores her environment. Ainsworth still put a lot of responsibility on the mother or carer, who was assumed to be a *female* relative or family friend:

- She had to be *sensitive* to the child's needs and be able to anticipate them where appropriate.

- She had to be *responsive* to the child's attempts to explore and form relationships.

- In effect, said Ainsworth, the mother or carer should be *available* to the child in the earliest months.

Her thesis was that the infant needs to learn that their carer will simply be there if needed. If this trust is established in the first weeks of life, the infant develops a sense of safety and security. Paradoxically, this means they are far more likely to venture away from the secure base of care and explore their environment because they are safe in the knowledge that their primary carer is going to be there for them when they get back.

You might well be thinking that this sounds like a version of 'Supermum'. Being sensitive, responsive and always available does sound to some of us like a recipe for turning women into doormats! However, it is important to remember that, unlike Bowlby, Ainsworth is only talking about the first few weeks and months of life, basically until the infant starts to become more mobile and self-reliant.

Some of these criticisms have had the positive effect of raising interest in the father's role in the child's early experiences. White and Woollett (1991, 1992) investigated the ways in which fathers were 'broadening the range of the baby's social interactions'. Contrary to the behaviour of many fathers a generation or more ago, they observed fathers engaging in three important activities with their new-borns:

- holding
- touching
- vocalising.

All of these activities seemed to help them form an attachment bond with the infant. The *mother-infant dyad*, as the maternal infant relationship was called, had been broadened to include the *father-infant dyad*. White and Woollett also noted the significance of three-way *triadic relationships* between both parents and their baby.

Security and continuity of care

Many primary carers from diverse cultural backgrounds seem to know the importance of providing something like Ainsworth's 'secure base', and they make the infancy period one of concentrated time and parental effort. A fascinating example of this theory in action is provided in Jean Liedloff's book, *The Continuum Concept*, in which she recounts her time spent with a group of indigenous South American people in the Amazon rain forest (Liedloff 1986). Along with more recent researchers interested in attachment, Liedloff has argued that it is *security* and *continuity of care* that matter most, not having one particular person as a 'primary carer'. In Liedloff's study all the women in the village community had a role in the care of each new-born. The baby was thus provided with the certainty of comfort and support whenever required, though this could be given by any familiar woman in the village. Care was also continuous; there were no frightening 'gaps' in child care where the baby was left untended.

In Western culture, *continuous* and *secure* care could be exemplified by cases where a child is cared for by biological parents and a childminder at different times of the day. As the child grows older, care may be shared between parents, nursery staff and childminder. The important factor is that all concerned are aware of the importance of security and continuity of care for the child.

Culture and parenting

Some researchers have become interested in the ways that approaches to parenting differ across cultures. From our discussion so far it seems that healthy attachment between child and parent depends on security and continuity of care. But what else is involved in being a parent? Do parents share the same values across cultures?

A number of cross-cultural studies of family interaction and parenting style have shown that while parents and carers all over the world share a set of basic aims and beliefs about the parenting work they do, how they set out to achieve these aims differs very widely. Parents of different cultures disagree about the qualities they would like to see in their growing children and the strategies a family can use to foster these qualities.

All mothers share the following four goals, according to Beatrice Whiting and Caroline Pope Edwards (1988):

- *Survival*: They aim to protect and feed the child.
- *Attachment*: They aim to offer emotional warmth and comfort.
- *Basic health*: They aim to train children in hygiene and get access to medical support when necessary.
- *Social behaviour*: They aim to teach children how to behave and encourage them to be sociable, according to cultural expectations in each case.

The way these goals are put into practice, however, differs a great deal, particularly with regard to the last one, socialisation. A. Nsamenang (1992) asked parents from the Nso community in North West Cameroon, in West Africa, which characteristics they wanted their children to exhibit, and which they did not want. The Nso parents listed as desirable characteristics:

- obedience
- respect and service towards parents
- hard work
- honesty
- intelligence.

UNIT 1 WEEK TWO

They did *not* want their children to be:

- disobedient
- disrespectful
- lazy
- aggressive
- playful
- inquisitive.

How does the Nso list compare with one you might have made? I guess that many of you would be surprised to see 'playfulness' and 'inquisitiveness' on the list of undesirable characteristics. The Nso think that playfulness is similar to being a nuisance. They do not see it as a natural quality in children, it seems. Inquisitiveness is viewed as a hindrance to children's development, partly because the Nso see children as learning by attending carefully to what adults say and do, without any interruption from curious questioners. In the dominant culture of the UK inquisitiveness is seen, on the contrary, as necessary to learning, and an 'enquiring mind' is much praised.

You can see from this example that the social context affects parenting styles and, therefore, the developing child. The 'successful' parent on this view is not one who adopts a particular style, but one who tries to fit their practice into the aims seen as worthwhile by their culture. Think for a minute or two about what this means for the child. The 'inquisitive' child will fare differently in the Nso cultural context than in the UK one. The inquisitive Nso child would be perceived as 'naughty' and parents would probably make efforts to control this quality. The inquisitive British child, by contrast, would be seen as 'normal' and this characteristic would be encouraged. Some researchers have argued that the most significant feature in a child's social and emotional development is the amount of 'fit' between a child's characteristics, the existing cultural expectations and parenting styles used (Lerner 1993).

This can have a particular impact on children and parents who transfer from one cultural setting to another. An example I recall from my days as an Educational Home Visitor working with under-fives might illustrate this point:

> A professional colleague asked me to visit a newly arrived family in my area. She described a single mother who 'did not keep high enough standards of hygiene'. Her four children, all under six years old, were said to be 'neglected' because they did not have any toys to play with. When I visited this family I discovered that they were refugees from a war-torn African country. The mother had witnessed the murder of her husband and mother before fleeing to the UK with her children. In her homeland she had been the wife of a politician and as such had servants to do the domestic chores. The children's grandmother had been their main carer while this mother fulfilled the duties associated with her public role. She herself had been parented by her grandmother, and this was not unusual in her culture. Traditionally, children played together in the compound of the house, making their games and playthings from natural or household objects, so they were not at all familiar with Western toys.

Can you see how my colleague had made a judgement of this family based entirely on her own cultural expectations, plus some stereotypical ideas about 'African' people? In time this family recovered from their grief and shock and were able to make a life in this country. As you can perhaps appreciate, the children were moved from a social context where they were being encouraged to 'fit' one set of cultural expectations, into another where a different set of expectations prevailed. The system of beliefs, attitudes and practices in the UK was quite alien at first, despite the fact that this mother's basic aims were exactly the same as any other mother's. She too wanted to protect, nurture and train her children. Becoming a widow and a refugee in a strange culture disrupted all the means she had to bring this about.

Thinking about this family may have made you wonder what you would have done in those circumstances. You might know from experience how hard it is to deal with economic hardship, or, like this mother, have had to change the way you look after your children because of an unexpected change in your circumstances. Or you may have felt that she should have managed to sort things out for the sake of the children – whatever her personal feelings she should have put her children first. If you did consider any of these issues you were reflecting on *morality*. Ron Dearing's consultation paper, mentioned last week, says that young children should be 'developing a sense of what is right and what is wrong, and why'. For the last half of this week's study, then, we turn to the topic of children's moral development.

What is moral development?

Before we begin to think about children I want you to reflect on how *you* have developed a sense of morality. As an adult, you will have acquired ideas about right and wrong, about how you should treat other people, about what actions are good and bad.

■ Activity 2 A

Complete these sentences, putting something different in each one. Try to be honest: put down whatever comes to mind most strongly.

It is wrong to ....

.... is a bad thing to do.

.... is always wrong.

It is right to ....

.... is a good thing to do.

.... is always right.

❏ Commentary

Did you say something like this reader?

It is wrong to murder.

Stealing is a bad thing to do.

Deliberately hurting another person is always wrong.

Then did you say things like this?

It is right to look after other people.

Praying every day is a good thing to do.

Telling the truth is always right.

Perhaps you did not find it easy to say some things are always right or always wrong. Take truth-telling, for instance. Is it right to tell the truth even when you will end up hurting someone else's feelings? Imagine your best friend has just dyed their hair a different colour and you thought it did not suit them at all. Would you tell them the bald truth, or be tempted to fib a little, to save their feelings? If you decide to fib, that is because you think that, on this occasion, the rule about not hurting other people's feelings is stronger than the one about truth-telling. Adults juggle these moral principles every day. Young children do not usually seem to. They are just as likely to tell your friend that his hair looks funny!

UNIT 1 WEEK TWO

■ **Activity 3 A**

Look back at the things you said in the last activity. Try to say why you think each one of them is good or bad, right or wrong.

❏ **Commentary**

Do your reasons resemble any of these ones given by other readers?

'It is wrong to walk on the flower beds in the park because if everybody did there would be no flowers left.'

'It is good to have friends because you can help each other out in times of trouble.'

These two examples illustrate one way of thinking about why we should, or should not, do something. The reasons here have to do with *consequences*: 'What would happen if ...?'

What others might there be? You will almost certainly have said something like the following:

'... because it is against my religion.'

'... because I've been brought up to think that.'

'... because human beings are different from other species. We have a duty to think things through before we act.'

These three examples illustrate a different way of thinking about why we should or should not do something. They are all based on *rules* or *principles* that people subscribe to or hold dear.

■ **Activity 4 A**

Now say when and where you think you learned about these moral rules, ideas, attitudes and so on.

❏ **Commentary**

Did you say you learned about these things at home; in school; from stories; from things that happened to you; with friends? There might even have been some things that it seems to you that you have always 'just known'.

Some of you will have emphasised the influence of parents, schoolteachers and religious teachers:

'I was taught to think ...'

Some will stress feelings instead:

'I simply could not physically hurt a person. I would feel paralysed.'

Some of you will have considered the shame you might feel if you were caught:

'I can't look someone in the eye and tell them a lie ...'

Some of you will have thought about principles you learned as a child which only made real sense to you later on, like this reader:

'I was always told I must help others as much as I could. This didn't really come home to me though until my little boy became ill. I couldn't have got through without the help I received from other people who came to the hospital with me, and listened to my worries.'

Much of what has been said in the past about young children's moral development has stressed the importance of *understanding* or *knowing* about right and wrong. This can give the impression that morality is something we just think about. If you look back over your responses to the last three activities you will notice that, as well as thinking, *feeling* comes into it in a big way. Our feelings as well as our thoughts are shaped to some extent by our early experiences, particularly in the family. The work done by early childhood educators also forms part of the network that supports the family. As we encourage children's social and emotional development we cannot avoid influencing their moral development too.

Morality is a contentious issue. The reasons people give for saying some-thing is 'right' or 'wrong' can be very diverse. Despite this, as parents, carers and early childhood educators we cannot avoid being moral educators as well. Your values and opinions about right and wrong, and maybe those of the early childhood centre where you work, will affect the way you relate to the children in your care. Some of this will be explicit, as in the policies or ground rules that most centres have adopted. Other aspects will be hidden in the everyday interactions and conversations you have with children. We have a significant influence on children's moral development whether we like it or not. The remaining sections will introduce you to some research on children's moral development as it relates to early childhood education and care.

Children developing a moral sense

■ Activity 5 A

Read the following observation and then try the questions before reading my discussion.

1. What does this observation suggest about children's developing sense of right and wrong?

2. Take each child in turn and try to say what you think they might *understand* and *feel*.

Farid (four years) and his friend Karen (three years) are building a Duplo farm together. It is almost finished and they are very proud of it. Ruksana, Farid's mother, has just finished giving Moriom (fifteen months) her lunch. She puts Moriom on the floor with the other children while she goes into the kitchen to clear things away. Moriom immediately makes for the brightly coloured objects that the older children are playing with. Before they can stop her, Moriom has broken the 'farmhouse' and is proceeding to use the Duplo horse as a teething ring.

'Oh Moriom,' says Karen, 'you pest!' and pushes her over backwards. Moriom sets up a loud wail and Ruksana returns to the scene. By this time both Karen and Moriom are crying. Farid attempts to help the baby sit up again. Seeing his mum looking angrily at him, he says, 'I didn't do nothing, mummy. Honest I didn't.' Moriom stretches her arms towards Ruksana to be picked up. As she does so Ruksana reassures Farid, 'I'm sure that nobody meant to hurt the baby, Farid. Don't worry.'

❑ Commentary

1. Such an everyday occurrence as this provides opportunities for peer interaction which foster children's moral development in the social context of the home or other familiar surroundings. In this example you can see that these children learn a lot from each other, as well as from the adult's reaction to events.

2. Let's take *Farid* first. He seems to know that it is possible to get the blame for something that you did not do. This has made him anxious for the moment. He also understands that something 'wrong' has happened and he is trying to put it right when Ruksana comes back. He shows awareness of Moriom's distress and his mum's concern. On the other hand, like many young children, he had been too absorbed in his own activities to notice Karen getting angry. Now he just wants to make sure that he does not get the blame.

    Now *Karen*. Karen is crying but perhaps you thought the reason for her tears was not clear. She might be crying because she is sorry for having hurt Moriom, because she knows she might be in trouble or simply because the baby is crying. At any rate she seems to show some sympathy for Moriom's distress. On the other hand, she may be more concerned about her broken farmhouse than Moriom's distress and she does not seem to understand that babies don't always mean it!

UNIT I WEEK TWO

And what about *Moriom*? You could go along with the view that says babies are totally self-absorbed. There she is, absolutely uncaring of the havoc she has caused and the proud achievements she has wrecked. She is only interested in her own feelings. On a more positive note, though, she seems to trust and understand that Mum will sort things out. So she has some awareness of what it means to put things right.

Interpreting the evidence

The fact that you can view these observations in a positive or a negative light shows us that the same 'evidence' can be interpreted in many different ways. This seems especially true when what we are trying to observe is the inner world of the child's thoughts and feelings. Please keep this in mind as I introduce you to some theories of children's moral development. Remember these are ways of trying to *interpret* or *explain* observations. They are not 'true' in any cut and dried sense. You must decide for yourself whether any of these ideas help you to understand how children gradually develop a sense of right and wrong.

Morality and understanding

Piaget's moral 'stages'

Some theorists have laid a lot of emphasis on children developing an *understanding* of right and wrong. Not surprisingly, Jean Piaget was one of these. I say not surprisingly, because as you may know he was a psychologist primarily interested in children's intellectual development, and this aspect of his work will be explored in Unit 2.

Piaget divided children's moral development into three stages: the *premoral* stage, the *heteronomous* stage and the *autonomous* stage.

*   He thought that children up to the age of about three or four are *premoral* and have no understanding of right and wrong. He went on to identify two later stages in children's moral development, using research that tested children's responses to stories about 'naughty' children (Piaget 1932). In one story, for example, a child accidentally breaks five glasses while trying to reach a tumbler in the kitchen cupboard. In the parallel story a child breaks one glass just because he feels like it.

*   In the next stage of moral development, which Piaget called the *heteronomous* stage (three to six years), children said that the first child was naughtier because he broke more glasses. Here the child's moral sense comes from their understanding of what their parents see as right or wrong. Morality is viewed by the child as a set of rules imposed by the grown-ups. At this stage, Piaget says, children are *egocentric*, finding it difficult to see the world from another's perspective.

*   In the final *autonomous* stage children would be more likely to see that the first child had no intention to break any glasses, saying instead that the second child was naughtier because they did it deliberately. According to Piaget this is the time when children develop the ability to see things from another's point of view.

Kohlberg's 'levels' of moral development

Lawrence Kohlberg (e.g. 1984) followed Piaget's ideas and methods. He too told children stories which contained a moral problem or dilemma. One of Kohlberg's stories concerned a man whose wife was very ill. The only way he could get the right medicine for her was to steal it. Children were asked what the man should do, and Kohlberg judged their level of moral development from the responses they gave. He suggested that there were three levels of moral development:

*   *Pre-conventional.* People learn about right and wrong first by finding out what everyone else thinks, or discovering what the conventions are.

- *Conventional.* Later on they learn to justify these conventions to themselves and others. This is what you were doing in Activities 2-4.

- *Post-conventional.* If you reach this level, and Kohlberg thought that not everybody does, you might challenge some conventions and put forward new ones, developing a sense of morality that you feel personally comfortable with and can justify when asked.

The level that most concerns us is the pre-conventional one. Kohlberg thought that this lasted until about the age of nine or so. This is most like Piaget's first stage, except that whereas Piaget thought children conform out of respect for adults, Kohlberg saw selfishness and fear as the main factors. He said children were self-interested, wanting only what is best for themselves and to avoid punishment as far as possible.

I think that Kohlberg's is a rather bleak picture of children's morality, even though it has been influential, especially perhaps in school life. You can often see the influence of Kohlberg's ideas in the behaviour policy adopted in a school, for instance. Kohlberg's theory is, in fact, founded on limited evidence as he only studied the responses of school-aged boys before coming to these conclusions.

Gilligan's ethic of care

Not surprisingly, Kohlberg's views have come in for criticism from feminists in particular. One of these was Carol Gilligan (1982). She argued that Kohlberg's research was only relevant to the morality of men and boys. Women whom she interviewed said far more about their *feelings* than about what they *thought*. They also showed much more concern for other people than themselves. She called this an *ethic of care.*

According to Gilligan, women's lives tend to be bound up with the care of others, and young girls learn this from a very early age. In effect, girls are more likely than boys to think that other people's feelings matter more than their own. So Gilligan disagreed with Kohlberg on the issue of self-interest, because girls did not seem to emphasise this in their responses. For instance, when asked whether the man should steal the medicine for his sick wife, as in Kohlberg's example, many more girls than boys said 'Yes' because it was his first duty to help her, not to be worried about getting caught stealing. When Kohlberg heard boys respond that the man should not get the medicine because it was wrong to steal things, he interpreted this to mean that they were at a higher level of moral development because they could quote the conventions. Gilligan argued, on the other hand, that girls thought care for others was more important than keeping the rules. They were not at a lower level of moral development as a result.

The deficit model of child development

Gilligan's research, like Kohlberg's, was based on interviews with adults and older children. Both of them used this evidence to come up with a theory that was meant to apply to young children as well. Along with Piaget, they emphasised two questions:

- How do children come to learn and adopt the moral principles that adults live by?
- How do they come to understand the reasoning behind ideas of right and wrong?

Because they used these questions as the basis of their research they stressed some aspects of children's moral development and neglected others. They emphasised *understanding* about moral issues and neglected the *wishes* and *emotions* that children have. They emphasised a passive view of moral development that sees the child as merely copying adults. They neglected the active role that children play in asking questions of adults, and exploring their feelings about morality. They also neglected the way children develop ideas about morality in their play and conversations together. Think back to the earlier example in Activity 5. These researchers are adopting a *deficit model* of young children's moral development. They focus on what they cannot yet do, rather than on what they *are* able to do. It would obviously not work to tell a two-year-old one of Piaget's stories, or ask them to consider one of Kohlberg's moral dilemmas. Recent researchers have concentrated instead on observing children in everyday situations, usually with their family.

■ Activity 6 A

Read this observation and try to answer the three questions which follow before moving on.

Date: 19.1.93
Activity: Lunch time in the nursery
Group: Key worker (KW) and five children including M (3 years 11 months)
Time: 12.10 to 12.25 pm

M was helping KW to lay the table for lunch. Four other children were reading in the book corner.

KW: *You've come to help me, M? That's kind of you.*

M (smiles): *Where does this one go? Here ... or over here? (Not sure which way to place knife and fork.)*

KW (showing her): *Like this . . . OK?*

M: *This is Sukvinder's plate. She's got the yellow one. And this is mine. It's the red one.*

KW: *That's right, now let's see what is for lunch, shall we? (They both look in the lunch trolley.)*

M: *I hope it's carrots. I like them. My brother doesn't like carrots though.*

KW: *Doesn't he?*

M: *No. But my mum says he has to eat them because they're good for you.*

KW: *Right. Table's laid now.*

M: *I'll get the others. (Runs off.) ... You sit here, Suki ... near the yellow plate. (Shows Sukvinder to her seat.) I'll sit next to you.*

(KW helps children to be seated and dishes out food.)

M: *David's got more carrots than me!*

D: *But I like them.*

KW: *So does M. Here's a few more for you, M.*

M: *Thank you. (Smiles at KW then at David.)*

1. Does M show any awareness of the thoughts, wishes and feelings of others? What makes you think so?

2. Does M seem to have any understanding of general 'rules' about things like possession, responsibility and fairness?

3. Where do you think M gets this understanding from?

❏ Commentary

See if you agree with this nursery nurse's answers to these questions:

1. 'M does show an awareness of other people's thoughts and feelings. She talks about her brother not liking carrots and her mother's insistence that he eat them. She also senses that her key worker is pleased with her offer of help.

2. 'M has some understanding of general 'rules' too. She knows about possession, as she shows when identifying people's plates and places to sit. She knows about fairness, as she shows in her request for an equal amount of carrots. She takes on the responsibility of collecting her friends for lunch.

3. 'Where does she get this understanding from? In this observation the key worker is encouraging M to develop these ideas. She also talks about home and her mother's authority there.'

As you can see from the examples we have discussed, a child's moral development depends on their environment – especially their family and the wider cultural setting – as well as the child's developing ability to understand or think. For children, like adults, emotions are just as important as thoughts in moral deliberation. Family life plus the wider experiences young children have in early childhood centres can offer many opportunities to experience, express and compare these emotions in a safe and contained way.

Young children and pro-social behaviour

Judy Dunn (1988) claims that family life offers children a wealth of opportunity for emotional, social and moral development. In these everyday experiences she observed what she has called the development of *pro-social behaviour*. As the name suggests, this means behaving in a way that is 'in favour' of effective social relationships: seeing other people as important. In the family, she says, moral dilemmas are experienced first hand and at the children's own level of development. This is illustrated in my observation of four-year-old Lisa facing a moral dilemma.

Lisa and Aaron (two years) are completing a jigsaw with their dad. The telephone rings and he goes across the room to answer it. While he is talking Lisa notices that there are some sweets on the table.

'Can we have a sweet, Dad?' she asks.

'Not now, it's nearly lunch time. Wait until after we've eaten, then you can have a sweet,' replies Dad. 'Now let me talk to your mum on the phone for just a minute.'

'Ooooh, Dad . . .'

'No, Lisa – and that's final.'

Lisa turns to look at her dad and notices his back is turned. She reaches out to take a sweet from the dish but then stops and withdraws her hand as Aaron starts to climb up on the chair beside her.

'Sweek, Lisa. Sweek?' asks Aaron.

'No, Aaron,' whispers Lisa. ' We can't have sweets until after dinner!'

Both children clamber down just as Dad replaces the phone and turns back to them. 'Well,' he says, 'let's clear up our puzzle, shall we? And then what shall we have for lunch, do you think?'

Lisa's dilemma concerns whether or not she should take a sweet even though her dad said she could not have one. This is the kind of real life problem young children face. She resolves her problem, in the end, in deciding not to take a sweet despite the temptation. But what else affects her decision? Maybe she knew that taking a sweet would make her dad disappointed or even angry if he saw her. Or possibly being a 'big sister' was a factor in making sure Aaron did not get a sweet either.

Judy Dunn thinks that everyday incidents like this one encourage the child to become more aware of their own feelings. In Lisa's case she probably felt resentful at first, then daring, then maybe protective or bossy towards her brother, then a desire to feel 'good'. Such occasions also encourage a child to be aware of other people's feelings, in this case those of a parent and a sibling. Judy Dunn's observations suggest that earlier research overlooked four big achievements in young children's moral development:

- *Understanding of others' feelings.* In the first few years of life she observed that children begin to show *empathy* for others. Parents who respond to children's attempts to communicate and build trusting relationships where rules are explained and discussed help children to develop empathy. Our examples show that professional educators and carers can also do this.

- *Understanding of others' goals.* It becomes important for children to learn that, like themselves, other people want things as well. This awareness often develops as a result of conflict such as a fight over the ownership of a toy. At other times the experience of social play, especially with brothers and sisters, means sharing a common goal. Farid and Karen were doing this in our earlier example. Conversations between parent and child may also include times when they consider together what other people want. In our last observation Lisa's dad was asking his children to consider what they would all three like for lunch.

- *Understanding social rules.* Dunn observed that children seem to become more aware of what she called 'general rules' by about age two and a half. This is a lot earlier than people like Kohlberg thought. In the familiar surroundings of home, according to Dunn, young children more easily illustrate their grasp of morality in such things as 'telling tales' or talking with a parent about a sibling or friend.

- *Understanding other minds.* An important part of moral development is the ability to 'read' other people. Children seem to focus at first on external features like facial expression or tone of voice. Think of Karen crying in sympathy with baby Moriom earlier, for example. Later on, says Dunn, they begin to notice internal features like other people's moods or feelings, so they know if Mum is in a bad mood, or Granddad is not feeling too well that day.

Can you see how Judy Dunn's research challenges the deficit model of children's moral development? Importantly, unlike those earlier researchers Dunn observed social interactions in everyday situations where children were quite naturally illustrating their developing moral sense. This differs markedly from the earlier research that asked children questions or told them stories as part of a laboratory-based study.

Review of the week

This brings us to the end of this week's study. Take time now to look back over this week's work and see if there is anything further you wish to explore or investigate further.

This week's review task brings together the work you have been doing on the social, emotional and moral development of children. Please complete it before going on to the final week of study for this unit.

■ Review activity B

Judy Dunn identified four kinds of social interaction that she thinks are especially revealing to the observer. They are as follows:

- *Conflicts,* such as disagreement with a sibling, parent or other adult.

- *Pretend play,* especially where children are enacting domestic scenes like putting baby to bed, making tea, shopping or going to the doctor.

- *Conversations about inner states or social rules,* which might be held between siblings and friends, or between children and adults. Discussion of 'inner states' includes talking about how someone else is feeling or what someone likes. Social rules were referred to in our earlier examples.

- *Humorous exchanges,* when a child makes a joke about themselves or another, illustrating their developing sense of social and moral norms. Dunn gives an example of a four-year-old imitating a younger sibling using the potty and having a great laugh with their mother about it.

In your own involvement with children you will often witness, or sometimes take part in, this kind of interaction. Look out for examples of each as you engage with them. There may be one or two that you recall happening. If so, you can use those.

If not, observe two brief examples of social interaction, then comment on them. If you do not usually come into contact with a particular age range, use this as an opportunity to do so, and compare any observation you make there with one you recall from your regular contact with children.

As before, take your work in two stages. First, observe and record the example in detail. Then use these questions to guide your comments on each observation you make.

1. Which of Judy Dunn's four categories of interaction best fits your examples?

2. What does each observation suggest about the social, emotional and moral development of the children concerned?

❏ Commentary

Here is an example taken from Judy Dunn's research (Dunn 1988, pp 90-91). You can see how a very short observation can contain rich material for this question.

Family D (study 1)
Child C, 21 months

C is playing a game of jumping off chair arm to cushion on floor. She jumps and with her shoe accidentally hits sibling, who cries. M comforts sibling. C comes to sibling with concerned expression, strokes her head.

M to sib: Oh, did you get kicked? (To C) You'll have to be more careful with those great shoes, Nan. (To sib) Does it still hurt?

Sib (crying): Yes.

M to C: Say sorry to Clare.

C to sib: Sorry (kisses and strokes her).

M to sib: It was a mistake. She didn't mean to, darling. It was an accident.

1. This example could be described as a minor conflict. Certainly one child is distressed and the parent has to intervene. But did you also notice that the mother is encouraging conversation about the hurt sibling's 'inner state' (what is wrong with her) and about 'social rules' (that she will have to be more careful)?

2. In this example the older sibling is learning that we must be careful not to hurt others, that we can do so by mistake, and that saying sorry is meant to help rectify the situation. The family in this case provides a safe place for the child to develop empathy and understanding for another's feelings.

Your own examples may have the added dimension of social interaction outside the immediate family. It will be interesting to see how Dunn's ideas apply to early childhood centres where professional adults take on this important interactive role.

Further reading

Barnes, P. (ed) (1995) *Personal, Social and Emotional Development of Children*, Milton Keynes/Oxford: Open University/Blackwell, Chapter 3

Dunn, J. (1988) *The Beginnings of Social Understanding*, Oxford: Blackwell, Chapter 7

There is a full list of references at the end of Unit 1.

UNIT 1 WEEK TWO

Unit I: Week Three
Personal identity and self-esteem

Objectives

By the end of this week's study you should:

*   have explored your own sense of identity and self-esteem

*   be familiar with theories about how young children form a sense of personal identity, in particular the three perspectives of temperament, social learning and psychoanalytic theory

*   have begun to reflect on the ways in which you as a parent, carer, or early childhood educator can encourage the development of self-esteem in young children.

Activities

This week you will need to arrange about one hour in total for observations, some of which will be focused on children under five years old, preferably in an early childhood centre. You will not be asked to do specific child observations this week, but you will find it helpful to compare the ideas we discuss with your continuing experience and observation of young children.

About this week's study

You have come to your last week of study on Unit 1. This week I am going to ask you to do some careful reflection, not just on your work with children, but on your own sense of identity and self-esteem. You will benefit from discussion of your responses with a friend or colleague if they are willing.

Pictures of ourselves

Last week you began studying children's emotional, social and moral development. Central to this affective development is the gradual formation of a *personal identity*. This involves the child in responding to a whole range of issues that are peculiar to human experience. There are some questions we carry on asking throughout our lives as we change, grow and develop as people:

*   Who am I?

*   What kind of person am I?

*   What kind of person do I want to be?

When the child is faced with these questions they will, just like adults, look in two directions:

*   *inwards* to their own feelings, thoughts, hopes and fears, and

*   *outwards* to see what other people think of them.

In looking outwards the child's sense of themselves as a person may be confirmed or challenged, in positive or negative ways. The child will be seeking some response, directly or indirectly, to questions like the following:

- Am I OK as a person?

- What do others think of me?

- How do I compare with other people?

- Am I 'good' or loveable? Do others value me?

The child will build their *self-esteem* – their picture of themselves in comparison to others – out of the results of these inward and outward investigations.

I would like you to begin with the picture you have of yourself. Make some notes on the questions below before reading on.

■ Activity 1 A

Try to describe your self, or your personality, as if you were trying to tell someone else what kind of person you are. To get you started, try these on for size. Do any of them fit you? Always or only sometimes? What other characteristics fit you better?

calm	humorous	confident	shy
serious	aggressive	sociable	irritable

❏ Commentary

Here is what a friend told me in response to these questions:

'I am usually quite a calm, steady person. At least people often tell me that. I can be very patient, especially with older people. Sometimes I do lose my temper, particularly if I think someone is trying to bully me. I enjoy being serious and I read a lot but I am also quite a sociable sort of person. I want my own space too, though, where I can just be quiet and by myself occasionally. I think I find it quite difficult to ask other people for help even when I really need it, because I like to be independent and self-reliant. Yet when I am able to help others out I rather like that, feeling proud and motherly, or something. I wish I could relax more as other people seem to. I'm always on the move.'

The self as 'I'

My friend was talking about the kind of person she thinks she is. She uses lots of self-descriptive language to help her do that. Notice words like 'patient' and phrases like 'want my own space'. She has built up a clear picture of herself over the years. This is what many philosophers and psychologists call the *existential self* – the aspect of myself that only I really know about for sure.

My friend's picture of herself also involves the language of *comparison* and value. Notice the way she compares herself with others on several occasions. The qualities she seems to value, like patience and sociability, are also valued by the Western culture she inhabits. This may remind us of the studies of parenting in Week Two where the characteristics parents valued matched those held in high regard by their social group.

Now try this second activity:

■ Activity 2 A

Make a list of all the social groups you belong to, or identify with. How does this make you like or unlike most people you know?

You can start if you like with your gender, religious or cultural background, or work experience.

❏ Commentary

Here is the list my friend made in response to this question:

Black – unlike my neighbours or workmates; like other black people.

Woman – like other women.

Bangladeshi – like many of the children I work with.

Middle class – like workmates; unlike most of the children.

Moslem – like the children but a minority in the UK.

Middle aged – like some parents and workmates; very different from others.

Mother – of grown-up children, unlike most people I know.

The self as 'me'

Did you notice that my friend put 'black' at the top of her list? She said this was because being black was the feature of herself that she was most often reminded of, in her everyday life. Being black made her like a lot of people whom she did not know personally. Being black was also what she felt to be her most obvious group identity in a mainly white society. As well as this she wanted to identify herself as a Bangladeshi woman of the same nationality as the children and families she worked with, yet she also emphasised her difference from work colleagues, who were all white. We all identify ourselves as members of different social groups, which helps us develop a *categorical self* – the *me* that is most influenced by social interaction with others.

The child developing a healthy sense of identity and self-esteem will need to build up a positive yet realistic picture of the kind of person they are, and are becoming. They will also need and deserve encouragement to value those aspects of their identity that connect them with particular social groups. Later in this week's study we will consider how parents, carers and early childhood educators can influence and support this development. For now, we consider how we arrive at all these conclusions about ourselves as people. How does a child develop a sense of personal identity?

Temperament and personal development

In this and the next two sections we will look in turn at three ways of describing and explaining personal development. As you will see, each one responds differently to the 'Nature versus Nurture' debate. Each therefore has a different idea about how young children develop personal identity and self-esteem. As you read about these theories, notice how closely they match your own personal experience and the experience you have gained with young children. The issue is not so much 'Are these theories true?', as 'How useful do these theories seem in helping me understand young children?'

The influence of temperament

Read these two accounts written by an after-school Toy Librarian about two children she knows who attend the toy library regularly.

- *Harbajhan is a one year old with a sunny disposition. He loves being in company and made a fuss of by other children or adults. He plays alone with his toys for periods of up to 25-30 minutes. His particular favourite is an Activity Centre with lots of buttons to press and levers to pull. He is just learning to walk and will take a helping hand from anyone who offers.*

- *Sanjit is a quiet and serious six year old. At school he tends to want to work and play by himself rather than with other children. He enjoys adult conversation and loves working next to his teacher's table. At home he watches TV or reads a lot. His mother describes him as rather a lonely child who prefers being indoors.*

In some ways these two boys are similar. They both enjoy adult company and seem able to concentrate on one activity for a period of time. But did you also notice the differences in their personal style and behaviour? Harbajhan is described as 'sunny' and 'sociable', whereas Sanjit is described as 'quiet', 'serious' and 'lonely'. Harbajhan enjoys being out and about whereas Sanjit prefers being indoors.

These two are in fact brothers, yet there are significant differences of *temperament* between them. Some researchers have become interested in these individual differences between children. They take a biological view, stressing the 'Nature' of the child in development. On this view, every person is born with a tendency to respond to the world in their own special way, making some people 'sunny' in disposition and some 'serious', for example. This is an attempt to explain, among other things, why we see differences in children in the same family. I wonder what you think of this idea that we are each born with particular personal tendencies?

■ Activity 3 A

Read the following two case studies of new-born babies (taken from Berry Brazelton and Cramer 1991, pp 76-79). Then consider these questions:

1. What would a temperament theorist have to say about each of these two babies? What characteristics have they been born with?

2. What do you think are the strengths and weaknesses of the temperament approach?

Case study: Robert

Robert was a well-muscled, well-proportioned baby who was active right after delivery. He weighed nine pounds and was heavy-boned and sturdy. His mother had been prepared for a big baby, but when she first saw him on the delivery table, she said, 'My God, was all that baby inside of *me*?' He had a shock of dark, matted hair, a round face with big, searching eyes, and he looked around the delivery room hungrily. His face and head were slightly pushed to the left because of his position in the womb, and both ears were flattened against the side of his head. His big, soft features were appealingly babyish, more like a one-month-old baby.

As he was placed on his mother's belly for her to inspect him, he quietened down. Before that, he'd been moving arms and legs continuously in slow cycles; his face had been wrinkled as he scanned the room around him. Now, as he lay face down, head on his mother's chest, he made crawling movements with his legs, settling finally with his hand up next to his mouth. His mother picked him up to look at him in the face, his eyes came open, and he looked at her eyes with an eager expression. His face softened as she spoke softly to him, and his body tensed as he looked even more intently at her. She said, 'I think you're seeing my face and hearing my voice already! What a wonderful fellow you are!' She laid him on the bed to inspect him all over. He grasped her fingers with his fists, brought his legs up to his abdomen to push off her hand, and when she pulled him up to a sitting position, he responded with vigorous head control, keeping his head nearly upright and in the midline. As he sat there, again his eyes came open and he surveyed the room.

Everyone in the delivery room was struck with how competent and controlled this alert little boy was, moments after birth. His father leaned over, talking to him in one ear. Immediately, Robert seemed to grow still, turning his head to the sound of the voice, his eyes scanning for its source.

When he found his father's face, he brightened again as if in recognition. His father said, 'Oh, what a great, big handsome boy!' He picked Robert up to handle him. As he was cuddled, Robert turned his body into his father's chest and seemed to lock his legs around one side of his father. Robert reached up to grasp and hold on to his father's gown, looking up into his face. By this time, his father was about to burst with pride and delight. When he put Robert up on his shoulder, the brand-new, still slippery baby nestled against his father, his legs still seeming to hold on, his hands and arms up on his father's shoulder, his head cocked and nestling in the crook of his father's neck. His beaming father pulled him in even closer to contain and cuddle him ... Robert seemed contented at being handled and played with. He was not upset by any of these manoeuvres.

Case study: Chris

Chris was a long, lean baby when born at forty-one weeks, one week overdue. His mother knew she'd not gained for the past three weeks, but the ultrasound showed a perfectly normal baby, and no one paid particular attention to her comment, 'He's slowed down.' At birth, weighing six pounds three ounces, he looked like a famine victim. His skin was loose, peeling on his hands and feet and a bit on his belly. His hair was fine and rather sparse. But the most striking thing about his appearance was his old-man face with a very worried look. As he lay in his crib, his eyes were wide open, staring anxiously off into the room. He lay quietly, but his breathing was deep and relatively noisy. He almost sounded as if he had a cold, and he breathed more rapidly and deeply whenever he was handled, talked to, or stimulated in any way. One had the impression that he wanted to be left alone.

When he was first born, the nurse and obstetrician were concerned about his colour and lack of response. They checked him carefully, wrapping and stimulating him before handing him to his parents. The delay heightened their anxiety, making them wonder, 'What might be wrong?' Assured by the nurse and doctor that he was intact, their hearts nevertheless sank when they saw his wizened face, with ears which protruded and a dome-shaped, nearly bald head. His mother felt like crying and, without expressing it, she began to wonder what she'd done to her baby. Quietly, each began to look for confirmation of his normalcy. 'Poor baby,' said his father, who also wondered if they'd done something to make him appear so pitiful. As he lay wrapped in their arms, he looked peaceful enough. But when he was moved, even slightly, his face wrinkled up into a frightened animal-looking expression, and he let out a piercing, high-pitched wail. They were relieved when the nurses took him away 'to take care of him'.

❏ Commentary

1. A temperament theorist might suggest that each baby has been born with very distinct personal traits, or a tendency to behave in a particular way. The psychologist J.E. Bates (1989) saw three broad areas of behaviour as dimensions of temperament. Let us see how they might apply to Robert and Chris.

   - *Emotional responses.* Robert seems to have a very outgoing and confident demeanour. For a new-born he seems tolerant of being handled and spoken to. Chris, on the other hand, is described as looking anxious and worried. He does not like being moved or handled.

   - *Attentional orientation patterns.* Robert is able to be distracted, particularly by his parents' voices, whereas Chris remains distressed throughout and cannot be calmed.

   - *Motor activity.* Robert seems active and alert, keeping his head erect, grasping and kicking, whereas Chris lies quietly and does not want to be moved.

Bates used these categories to distinguish differences in temperament between children in the birth to four years age range, including babies. The scientist Jerome Kagan (1984) followed this up with another study which showed that during the first year of life temperamental characteristics often change, but after that they become more stable and continuous. On his evidence, if Chris remains a 'worried' and 'anxious' child beyond his first birthday this is likely to become a part of his permanent personal make-up.

2. See how your comments compare with mine. I am sure you will have thought of these and perhaps more.

Strengths of the temperament approach

- Offers an explanation of individual differences between children, especially in the same environment/ family.

- Temperament might be one factor, among others, in forming a personal identity.

Weaknesses of the temperament approach

- Being 'born' a certain way does not mean you have to stay that way.

- Can lead to value judgements like 'Robert is a good baby' and 'Chris is a bad baby'.

- Blames the child for their own character.

- Can be used as supposed justification for racist or sexist attitudes.

Is temperament the only factor?

If temperament was supposed to be the whole story these weaknesses would be very serious indeed. It would follow that our character is fixed from the time we enter the world. Experience seems to argue against this, since we see children and adults growing and changing all through their lives. Think about your own children, or children you have known well over a number of years. Think about yourself as a fifteen year old or a five year old, and how your personality may have changed since then. Even if some characteristics have remained stable, others will have changed, I'll bet.

Did you notice my last objection to the temperament approach? I hope you thought of this. The theory that certain groups of people are born with particular characteristics has often been a source of oppression. Recall the old-fashioned idea that women are naturally less intelligent and more emotional than men, for instance. Or the racist view that people of colour are more prone to 'bad' characteristics such as aggression, childishness or duplicity. If these ideas go unchallenged, life becomes intolerable for some of us.

Luckily, though, most people (including the researchers I have mentioned) take the view that *temperament* and *personality* are not the same things at all. A sense of personal identity and self-esteem are developed over time. I may have particular temperamental traits which affect this development, but they do not finally determine who I am going to become.

Returning to the babies Robert and Chris, their different temperaments at birth do affect their environment, in particular the ways their parents interact with each of them. A child's temperament will make a difference to the experiences they have as they grow up. So a temperament theorist does not have to take a purely biological view of children's development. The environmental factors that a child experiences, and the way the child influences his or her environment, are still important.

Learning to be a person

Social learning theorists (sometimes referred to as behaviourists) say that the child's environment is the most important factor in the way they develop. Children *learn* to be a particular kind of person by interacting with other people and the world around them. On this view temperament takes a back seat.

Albert Bandura (1977) argued that *reinforcement* is crucial to any learning. He meant that we learn best if we are rewarded for our actions. Sometimes the reward is material. Bandura did some experiments where he taught monkeys to press a buzzer in order to get milk from

UNIT I WEEK THREE

a feeding bottle. He also suggested that other non-material rewards, like praise and attention, can reinforce behaviour so that it becomes learned. You could say that school sticker 'reward' systems are a bit like this. Bandura argued that the following factors apply equally well to all types of learning, including learning how we are supposed to think, act and feel:

- *Reinforcement strengthens behaviour.* If, for example, every time a child stamps her feet she get attention from adults, this reinforces the idea that stamping feet goes with getting the attention she wants.

- *Partial reinforcement works best.* Bandura's experiments with monkeys showed that, strangely, reinforcement works best if it does not happen every time. The most long-lasting behaviours are the ones that are only partially reinforced. If our stamping child is given attention seven times out of ten, say, she will continue to use this method for longer than if she got it every time.

- *Children learn most easily from watching a model.* You will have noticed that children often copy the behaviour of people they admire. Modelling is different from copying in the sense that the effects are deeper and longer term. If a child models his behaviour on someone he cares a lot about, he is likely to continue that behaviour long after that person has disappeared from the scene. You will probably be able to think of your own examples of children modelling themselves on an adult, or sometimes another child.

Social learning theorists say that children usually use their parents as their first models, observing them closely and wanting to be like them. They call this the process of *identification.* Later on, people in early childhood centres of various kinds will become further models, providing the child with a variety of ways of being. These theorists think that children *learn* to have the kind of personality that suits them in their current environment. This will be the personality that enables them to meet the expectations first of their parents, then of other adults. If she meets adult expectations, it is likely that the child will get what she wants in emotional terms: love, approval, security and a warm response.

One way to see social learning theory in action is to observe children playing. A key worker made this observation illustrating a game played repeatedly by three children in a combined nursery centre group, over a period of about a week. One imaginative play area had been turned into a 'doctor's waiting room and surgery', and this is the setting for the observation.

Katherine (sitting at the doctor's desk, stethoscope at the ready): Next patient please!

Shofiq (rising from the waiting room bench and taking Celia by the hand): Come along, darling, the doctor won't hurt you, you know. (They go into the surgery and seat themselves demurely.)

Katherine: Yes, what can I do for you today? Aren't you feeling well? (Putting spectacles on the end of her nose and scribbling on a pad on her desk.)

Celia (cries loudly): I don't want a injection!

Shofiq: Sssh! Now behave yourself, you naughty girl!

Celia: But Daddy, I don't want ...

Katherine: Now, now. Stop making all that fuss. I'm not going to give you an injection today. I'm just gonna test your breathing. (Celia stands closer and allows Katherine to 'test' her with the stethoscope.) Isn't that better? (To Shofiq) She seems much better to me. I'll just find some nice medicine in my cupboard, seein' as how you've been such a good girl. Isn't that right, Shofiq?

Shofiq: Yes doctor Katherine. She has been a good girl really.

UNIT I WEEK THREE

Celia: No I'm not, I'm naughty! (Starts crying again.)

Katherine and Shofiq (together): Stop that, you're spoiling it. You have to be good now and have your medicine like a proper good girl.

Perhaps you can see, in this example, evidence of children in a sense 'trying out' different personal characteristics. Katherine obviously enjoyed being the severe and paternalistic doctor, despite the frilly frock and hair ribbons she was wearing. Celia, too, was playing at being 'naughty' in a way that her key worker had not witnessed elsewhere. And Shofiq looked very much like his Granddad who brought him to school, with a similar mildly amused, but caring, expression on his face when he observed his wailing 'daughter'. Each child showed evidence of copying behaviour they had seen in adults and other children. Their conversation enabled interaction which reinforced ideas about good and bad behaviour that they had each heard.

■ Activity 4 A

What do you think of social learning theory? What are the strengths and weaknesses of this approach as a way of explaining the development of children's personal characteristics?

❑ Commentary

You might have said that one *strength* of this approach is that it recognises the impact of role models in the child's immediate social circle. Another strength might be that it matches many of your observations of children's play, where they show they are learning about the value attached to different personal characteristics in their culture. We'll come to *weaknesses* of social learning theory in a while. For now let's look at its positive uses.

The influences of social learning

Nancy Curry and Sarah Arnaud (1984) looked at children's *socio-dramatic play* in five different American cultures, including groups of black and indigenous American children. They found that children's development of a categorical self (the 'me' discussed earlier) was particularly enhanced by this kind of play. In taking on a variety of roles from everyday life they were, if you like, 'playing at society'. Curry and Arnaud found that children were learning and practising themes from within their own culture, including a knowledge of social institutions such as going to work or life in the family, and of course gender roles.

Does social learning theory account for personal development?

If social learning theory does present an accurate picture of the way children develop as people there are serious considerations for the early childhood educator. Let's think back to our 'contented, alert and competent' baby Robert for a minute. Suppose he continues to build upon his happy disposition, thriving in the love and attention of his parents and close family members. Then comes the time for his first visit to the local parent-toddler group, when he is about two and a half years old.

Robert is very excited by all the wonderful activities, shouting to his mum and running about the hall, trying things out. Eventually, digging in the sand tray, Robert accidentally flicks sand in another child's face. This child's carer reacts angrily, saying, 'You stupid boy! Why don't you be careful?' Robert's eyes fill with tears as he moves to his mother, then he watches her face as he hears someone saying, 'That's the trouble with these black children. They are out of control.'

What did you think were the weaknesses of the social learning approach, and do they apply here? Robert has learned from his family that he is loved and valued. This one incident is a shock to him. It is likely that he does not understand the other adult's anger, or their remark, though he will see that his mother is moved by those words. If this kind of supposedly 'minor' incident is allowed to recur, Robert's former positive idea of himself

UNIT I WEEK THREE

will weaken. Instead this new, negative idea of himself as black and out of control will strengthen through the reinforcement of many similar experiences.

One weakness, though, of a rigid social learning approach is that children are seen as passive victims of their experiences, tossed about this way and that by reinforcements and counter-reinforcements. Their sense of self is perhaps too reliant, on this view, on what is learned generally from their social environment. It does not recognise that some people are more important to the child than others, hence they will accept reinforcement from them more readily. In Robert's case this would mean that his family is a strong source of reinforcement for his positive self-image. Scientists like Bandura were able to isolate one kind of reinforcement at a time, under laboratory conditions. Life for the child, unlike Bandura's monkeys, is not like that. So maybe you'll agree with me that social learning, like temperament, can be a very influential factor in personal development, but once again it is not the whole story. The last perspective we will discuss tries to meet some of these difficulties.

Developing a personality

Temperament theorists emphasise biology. The child is born with personal characteristics which then influence the kind of experiences they have, but this influence is unwitting; it is not within the child's control. Social learning theorists, on the other hand, stress the importance of the child's propensity to learn from their environment. The personal attributes they develop are largely the result of learning from the social context of family, community and culture.

There is another perspective which relates better to the *transactional* approach we discussed in Week One. It seeks to describe and explain the development of self – the child's sense of identity and self-esteem – in a manner that acknowledges the child's own role in his or her development. This perspective also makes the assumption that we will find patterns or sequences of personal development to match those found in physical growth and change. As you will see, it also seeks to *explain* many of the patterns we have seen so far in social, emotional and moral development. It is important to say at the outset that there is no one accepted formulation of this transactional approach to personal development. My aim, as before, will be to encourage you to consider how useful these ideas might be in improving your knowledge and understanding of young children.

Psychoanalytic theories

Psychoanalytic theories about human personality development have been very influential during the twentieth century. A number of the key concepts they use have become part of our everyday language. I am thinking of concepts like the *unconscious*, which would have been unintelligible in previous centuries, when people believed that we are always aware of everything that is in our minds and that no thoughts are hidden in this way. Nowadays we speak quite easily of such things as *unconscious wishes and desires* that surface un-expectedly, and of the *unconscious mind* in which we store away uncomfortable or frightening thoughts and memories.

In education, the idea that children *develop in stages* is linked to the psychoanalytic tradition too. Many parents and educators talk readily of children's stages of learning, as if development is like a series of steps which must go in a particular order.

It is important that you clarify your own ideas about these concepts taken from psychoanalytic theory. In everyday use their meaning is often blurred or confused. Try asking two people, for example, what is meant by the 'unconscious mind'. You are likely to get two different answers. Yet we often act as if everyone understands these terms in the same way.

Figure 1.2 Freud's psychosexual stages of personality development

Stage	Age	Erogenous zones	Major developmental need or task	Adult characteristics of children who have become 'fixated' here
Oral	0-1	Mouth, tongue and lips	Weaning	Oral behaviour: smoking, overeating, passivity, gullibility
Anal	2-3	Anus	Toilet training	Exteme orderliness or obstinacy, or the opposite
Phallic	4-5	Genitals	Oedipus complex; identification with same-sex parent	Recklessness, vanity, or the opposite
Latency	6-12	No specific zone; low sexual energy	Development of mechanisms to defend self-image	Fixation does not usually occur here
Genital	13-18 onwards	Genitals	Mature sexual intimacy	Successful integration of previous stages should result in an adult with sincere interest in others, realistic enjoyments, mature sexuality.

In this unit I can only give you an outline introduction to this area of research. Inevitably my account is only one interpretation of psychoanalytic theory. The further reading at the end of this week offers you others if you are interested. As with all of this week's study, you will need to reflect on what is said and if necessary read more widely to deepen your understanding. Talk to other people about these issues if you can.

Freud's stages in personality development

Stages in personality development are said to be connected with patterns of physical growth and change. The psychoanalytic theorists I shall discuss think that stages of personality development correspond to important 'needs' or 'tasks' which children typically experience at certain stages in their lives.

Sigmund Freud is the famous originator of psychoanalytic theory. He said that the personality develops in five *psychosexual* stages, each centring on a particular need (see Figure 1.2).

It is important that the child pass successfully through each stage, otherwise they may become stuck or *fixated* at a particular point in their development. If this happens the child may exhibit *regressive* behaviour, such as thumb-sucking in an older child.

In regressive or fixated adults, personality development has been arrested because unmet childhood needs have been stored up in the unconscious mind (the part of the mind that contains hidden thoughts and feelings). Freud thought that needs, wishes and desires could be pushed into this hidden mind so that the person was no longer aware, or 'conscious', of them. Freud thought such a person would not be fully 'grown up' until they were able to bring those childhood needs back into their conscious mind and deal with them. In most cases, according to him, such a person will need help from a psychoanalyst to achieve this. His 'talking cure', as it was called, consisted of a long series of conversations in which the analyst assisted the person to regain a 'conscious' awareness of all their hidden needs.

As you can see, the formation of a wholesome sexual identity is central to Freud's theory, the most important stage being the phallic one when the *Oedipus conflict* takes place. He thought that boys and girls deal with this differently. Boys, about whom Freud had far more

UNIT I WEEK THREE

to say, become sexually attracted to their mothers, but because these desires are unacceptable they are driven into the unconscious mind. At the same time a boy sees his father as powerful and as having access to the mother. So the boy identifies with his father, trying to be as much like this powerful male as possible. In the process the boy learns to take on what Freud calls an 'inner father' like a kind of conscience.

A parallel process is supposed to occur in girls, though Freud adds this as little more than a footnote. Girls begin by seeing their mother as a 'rival' for father's attention. They cannot, like the boy, identify with the father. So girls, according to Freud, instead identify with their mother.

The successful resolution of the Oedipal conflict marks the beginning of the latency stage, where this same-sex identification is broadened. You may have noticed, as Freud did, how children between the ages of about seven and later puberty seem to seek close friends almost exclusively of their own sex.

Criticisms of Freud

As you might imagine, Freud's ideas have been criticised, particularly in feminist circles. Such criticism has led to modern developments in psychoanalytic theory, particularly as it is meant to apply to girls' personality development. The emphasis has shifted from Freud's psychosexual 'urges' or 'drives' towards opposite-sex parents, to an interest in children's early relationships with the mother. According to researchers like Nancy Chodorow (1978) the mother-child relationship becomes the model for all later relationships. Girls develop the idea that all close relationships should be similar to this all-feminine one, where they see themselves as like their carer in a fundamental way. Boys, on the other hand, have to distance themselves from their mother in order to see themselves as different, and male. The model of relationships for them becomes one where a lack of closeness is the main feature.

Another major criticism of Freud is that he places the drama of the child's developing personality firmly within the *biological* family. Other psychoanalytic theorists have taken a broader line and included the general social and cultural context. Erikson is one of these.

Erikson's psychosocial stages

Erik Erikson (1950/1965) identified eight *psychosocial stages* in develop-ment. Although he broadly agrees with Freud's 'needs' at each stage, Erikson does not warn of fixation. Instead he says that we have to get what we need, or achieve each 'developmental task', if we are to develop the kind of personality that will lead to successful sexual and social relationships later in life (See Figure 1.3).

Can you see some implications of Erikson's theory for your own relationships or work with children? Suppose a three-year-old at an early childhood centre is made to feel guilty about a toileting 'accident'. According to Erikson they run the risk of growing up with a deep-seated feeling of shame which can make them doubt their own abilities. Children moving through the phallic and latency stages will need the opportunity to use their own initiative and develop their own plans. If a nursery or reception class teacher programmes a child's day with set tasks and activities, the child will be denied these opportunities. Erikson thinks this will mean that, as adults, these children run the risk of growing up to be incapable of acting with true self-confidence. Similarly, if insensitive or sometimes cruel adults make a child feel 'inferior', perhaps by publicly criticising their efforts to learn some new skill, the child may take this feeling with them into adult life.

Figure 1.3 Erikson's eight psychosocial stages compared with Freud's psychosexual stages

Approximate age	Successful personality trait to be developed	Tasks and activities of the stage	Comparison with Freud's psycho-sexual stage
0-1	Basic trust versus basic mistrust	Trust in mother and in one's own ability to make things happen – secure attachment	Oral stage
2-3	Autonomy versus shame and doubt	Development of physical skills leading to free choice; toilet training; learning control. Shame may develop if not handled appropriately.	Anal stage
4-5	Initiative versus guilt	Engagement in goal-directed activity; becoming more assertive and aggressive. Oedipus-like conflict may lead to guilt.	Phallic stage
6-12	Industry versus inferiority	Absorb all basic cultural skills and norms	Latency stage
13-18	Identity versus role confusion	Adapt sense of self to physical changes of puberty; make occupational choice; achieve adult sexual identity; search for values	Genital stage
19-25	Intimacy versus isolation	Form one or more intimate relationships; form family groups	
26-40	Generativity versus stagnation	Bear and rear children; focus on occupational achievement, creativity; train next generation	

■ Activity 5 A

Try to say what you think about psychoanalytic theories of personal development. How helpful do you find these ideas? Do they match your experience with children?

❏ Commentary

Like other readers, reflecting on psychoanalytic theories may have given you mixed feelings. Here are some typical initial reactions:

'It does tie in with my experience, and with the way my own children are developing. The 'need' or 'task' at each stage seems about right to me.'

'I don't like the idea of four-year-olds having sexual feelings.'

'I think Freud's right. Some people do get fixated at a particular stage. Take my boss, he's stuck at the anal stage all right!'

'I suppose Freud would say that because I'm gay I must still fancy my mother! I really object to his seeing heterosexuality as the norm. We've moved beyond that now.'

Strengths and weaknesses of psychoanalytic theory

For myself, I do think some aspects of psychoanalytic theory are helpful in our work with children, though I cannot agree with everything that is said. Your response may be very different from mine. If so, that is not surprising since psychoanalytic theorists are trying to describe in generalised terms a process which is uniquely personal and individual. It is hard to pin down 'evidence' that will absolutely confirm any one position.

A strength of psychoanalytic theory is that it attempts to discern patterns in children's development of personal identity and self-esteem. As long as these are not rigidly applied, it may be useful to consider that these sequences in children's 'inner' life parallel outer, more observable physical and social changes. Another strength, in my view, is that it adds another interesting dimension to the complex picture of how we become who we are.

Its major weakness, I think, results from the tone adopted by some major figures in psychoanalytic theory. Freud, in particular, wrote as if psychoanalysis gives us the whole story. His work gives the impression that the relationship between the child and their primary carers is the only thing that really matters. He presented his theory of psychosexual stages as a more or less complete explanation of personality development. He also suggested that a person can be permanently scarred by childhood experiences which have pushed memories and feelings into the 'unconscious mind' – unless, that is, they ask a psychoanalyst to help fish them out in adult life! Although Erikson has perhaps improved on the original Freudian model, you could still argue with these conclusions.

A transactional view of personal development

In the end, perhaps, most of us would adopt a position on children's personal development that combines elements from all three perspectives: temperament, social learning and psychoanalytic theory. Such a transactional approach sees temperament as an important influence affecting the way others interact with the child from the earliest days. It also gives weight to the child's environmental experience which contributes especially to the development of a categorical self – a sense of belonging to social and cultural groups. Lastly, a transactional view recognises that both temperament and social interaction affect the inner, existential self as well as the social one. Further than this, psychoanalytic theory can help us find patterns of development that might go some way towards explaining how each of us might develop our unique personal identity. The last section of this unit will ask you to reflect in a practical way on the ideas we have discussed so far. Before you go on to that you might like to pause for a while and take time to talk to a colleague or friend to see what they think about these views of personal development.

Encouraging children to develop self-esteem

Read these two examples of children describing themselves:

Andrea, four years three months (taped description)

Andrea is big and my sister is little. I got long hair and slides – see? I like Bobby and Rehana. They my friends and we play in Nursery. I can draw my name – look. (Takes observer to see her name on a painting on the Nursery wall.) What else? ... I can skip in a rope out the garden – and ride bikes. We ride bikes when it's sunny out. My mum says I'm a good girl. (Nods and folds her arms.) I watch telly. I like Supertots. I can ... er ... nearly ... read all these books ... we got loadsa books in the Nursery (points). When it's hometime we wash our hands. Sonya can't wash 'er hands. I can wash my hands.

Gemma, seven years six months (written account)

My name is Gemma and I live with my mum, Dad and nan. I am a girl. I like going to school. Because Ms Simms [teacher] is nice and we learn lots of things. Like Maths Games I usually win. In PE we do rounders but Im no good at it. Jane always gets a rounder but not me. I hate spelling tests. Because I carnt remember. Surinder always comes top. She helps me though. Because Im her friend.

You will notice that aspects of these self-descriptions involve expressions of self-worth, or self-esteem. Andrea compares herself favourably with her 'little' sister and Sonya, who cannot wash her own hands. She also stresses all the things she can do. It seems important to her that she *can* do things, even 'nearly', as in the case of reading. She also reports her mother's calling her a 'good girl'.

Gemma, the older child, is also concerned to list her likes and achievements, such as winning maths games. She seems to value her abilities in 'learning lots of things' and having friends. Like Andrea, she compares herself with other children, though for Gemma this can mean that she devalues herself. She says she 'can't do' rounders, or spelling, whereas she thinks that other children can.

Domains of self-esteem

These children are illustrating a point made by psychologists interested in self-esteem. A child's picture of himself or herself is built from two 'domains':

* knowing what they can do, and valuing that

* comparing themselves with others.

Susan Harter (in Vasta *et al* 1992) identified five *domains of self-esteem* in school-aged children. I have adapted these to include younger children.

a) *Learning competence*

   How the child views herself as a learner. Does she usually think, 'Yes I can ...' or 'No I probably can't ...'?

b) *Physical competence*

   How the child approaches physical challenge – riding a trike, learning to swim or playing a team game, perhaps.

c) *Social acceptance*

   How popular the child feels he is with peers. Does he like being with other children? As he gets older, how important are friends?

d) *Behavioural conduct*

   How appropriately the child thinks she behaves. Does she see adults and peers as accepting her behaviour?

e) *Physical appearance*

   How much does the child like the way he looks? Does he think others like the way he looks?

■ Activity 6 A

Sometimes one particular domain can become especially important to a child. Which one, or which ones, seem important to Andrea and Gemma?

❏ Commentary

Andrea seems to mention every domain, but perhaps the most important to her are (a) learning competence and (d) behavioural conduct. This fits with what psychoanalytic theorists say we should expect. Andrea wants to feel that she can do things for herself and learn new skills.

Gemma emphasises (a) learning competence, although in a negative as well as a positive sense. She says more about what she feels she cannot do than what she can. Physical competence (b) looms large as well. And did you notice that the friends she mentions are all female? This would bear out Freud's point about same-sex identification.

The importance of other people

Children's sense of self-esteem is partly influenced by how far they achieve their own hopes and dreams in a particular domain. Gemma's self-esteem is perhaps less secure because she does not perform as well as *she* would like in the domains of learning and physical competence. She also knows this partly through comparing herself with other children.

Susan Harter said that children's overall sense of self-esteem is influenced by the regard that *significant others* have for the child. Another more recent researcher, Rosemary Roberts (1995), also urges us to consider the *important people* in the lives of young children whose job is to offer love, knowledge and acceptance of the growing child. For school-aged children the significant others, or important people, are often other children as well as adults. In building a sense of their own worth, younger children seem to rely much more, it seems, on adults' opinions of them. In the first instance adult members of the child's family will be very influential. As soon as the child comes into contact with other adults, however, their developing self-esteem can either be enhanced or damaged.

■ Activity 7 B

Reflect on your own care and work with children. List some ways in which you try to encourage in children a positive sense of self-esteem. Then make a more detailed record of the ways in which your everyday work reflects this encouragement. You might think of practical examples or use observations to illustrate the things you have listed.

❏ Commentary

Here are some examples showing what other people said in response to this activity. You probably added others. Before reading them, discuss your own notes with a friend or colleague.

One parent said,

> *'I try to accept children for who they are, to respect their individuality.'*

Many psychologists have noted that young children need the acceptance of adults if they are to develop self-esteem. Carl Rogers (1957) called this 'unconditional positive regard'. This means that even though children sometimes make us feel angry or sad this should not affect the way we see them as people. This reasoning is behind the idea that, although a child's behaviour may at times be unacceptable or inappropriate, *the* child is not 'naughty'. Giving a child this label makes them a particular kind of person and does not recognise that all of us act inappropriately some of the time. That doesn't make anyone a 'bad' person, even if they sometimes behave 'badly'.

This nursery officer said,

> *'In our combined nursery centre we have learned a lot about racism in our society. This has helped people to recognise some of the difficulties faced by black children and families in our country.'*

Sometimes it is not just particular adults who find it hard to accept a child. The way our society is organised means that whole groups within it do not receive 'unconditional positive regard'. Racist behaviour and attitudes can undermine black children's sense of self-worth. All of us working in the early years have a responsibility to face our own prejudices and change stereotypical attitudes. Iram Siraj-Blatchford (1994) suggests that a good starting point, particularly for people from the dominant white culture, is to learn about how racist attitudes have developed through history. This history has informed the cultural identity of black children in our care, as well as sometimes giving children from the white culture a mistaken sense of superiority. As we have seen, cultural identity is an important component of the child's categorical self (the 'me' that is the picture of myself I gain from my interactions and experiences with important other people). If we do not acknowledge the effects of racism on children's developing self-esteem we are not supporting their full and healthy development.

Parallel points could be made about how early childhood carers and educators support other aspects of the child's categorical self development. Similarly, an awareness of gender, class and special needs issues is essential if we are to provide the 'good regard' that growing children need and deserve.

A reception class teacher said,

UNIT 1 WEEK THREE

'In my reception class I try to encourage children to try new activities and experiment with new ideas. I am careful to guide them but I do not do things for them all the time.'

As Andrea's and Gemma's self-descriptions illustrated, the development of competence in intellectual and physical achievement does seem important to young children. In a school setting, and in some other early childhood centres, there can be a lot of pressure to speed up the cognitive and linguistic development of the child, without paying enough attention to their social and emotional well-being. This is recognised in Ron Dearing's draft proposals (Dearing 1995) for pre-school education, where we are encouraged to ensure that:

- children are confident and able to establish effective relationships with other children and adults

- work as part of a group and independently

- able to concentrate for sustained periods

- able to explore new learning

- able to seek help where needed.

One way of giving these areas attention is to think about *how* we teach young children, whether formally as trained educators, or more informally in the home setting. This reception teacher showed that she was doing just that. In Unit 3 you will have the chance to explore more fully the curriculum for the early years, and notice the learning opportunities that exist in a number of contexts, across the birth to eight age range.

This playgroup leader said,

'At our playgroup we encourage parents to bring in real objects from home to put in our home corner, like cooking pots, chopsticks, rugs and so on. That way the families feel that their culture is being valued and the children feel more at home.'

This playleader is trying to show the children and families she works with that she values the 'difference' and variety of their cultural backgrounds. Cross-cultural studies have shown the importance for all children of socio-dramatic play. This research also showed that children develop more elaborate play scenarios when using objects familiar to them from their home surroundings. Self-esteem is bound up with a sense that the child's cultural background is valued and that they do not have to minimise or deny this aspect of themselves. In celebrating cultural diversity, we encourage all children to celebrate their own and others' unique identity.

Lastly, a childminder told me,

'I think that the best way to make sure you value the children is to value yourself. I've had to work hard at this as an adult because I used to have a very poor picture of myself, which I have learned to improve.'

This struck me as perhaps the wisest comment of all. I wonder if you thought something similar? For our last exercise, try the next activity.

■ Activity 8 A

List the qualities in yourself that you value. What do you like about yourself? You might say, for instance, 'I'm hard-working' or 'caring'. (Don't be modest! You don't have to show your list to anyone else unless you want to.)

Who do you think were the 'significant others' or 'important people' who encouraged you to value these characteristics? Maybe a parent, sibling, teacher or friend ...

Now do the same for those personal characteristics that you don't like so much. Try to say who the 'significant others' or 'important people' were in these cases. Who was it who helped you to think of these characteristics as unnecessary, unwanted or even 'bad'?

❏ **Commentary**

Obviously, all your responses to these questions will be different. Here are some examples that seem to crop up a lot, so they may be on your list. The 'significant' or 'important' person may of course be different.

Quality I like in myself	*Quality I don't like in myself*
Being caring towards others	Selfishness
Significant other: grandmother	*Significant other:* teacher, priest, parents
Being calm and unflappable	Getting angry or irritated
Important person: employer	*Important person:* father

Valuing ourselves

If we are to value the children in our care, we need to be more aware of our own sense of self-worth. If, for instance, I don't like 'selfishness' in myself, I am liable to use my adult power as an 'important person' to stop children from putting themselves first, even when this might be appropriate.

In my experience this is something that women and girls are very prone to teach each other. How many times have you seen a girl give way to a supposedly more 'selfish' boy, and be praised for that because she is being more 'sensible' or 'grown up' – a 'good girl'?

Taking the example of anger, if I deny myself this necessary and sometimes appropriate emotion, I am likely to find ways of making the children in my care also think that they should never be angry. This can lead to two commonly observed situations:

- The child's anger 'leaks out' in other ways, such as bullying or teasing.

- The child experiences sadness and depression (literally 'pressing down' the emotion they would otherwise be experiencing – in this case anger). What we see may be tearfulness and sometimes manipulative behaviour.

In such cases, as the powerful adult I have denied the child a full experience of the whole range of human emotions, which include sometimes feeling self-centred or angry. As Rosemary Roberts (1995) notes, we tell the child their 'normal bad feelings' are not acceptable. The child then feels that they are not 'acceptable' as a person, with inevitable effects on their sense of themselves – their self-esteem.

So how can you or I learn to integrate all these aspects of our identity – the ones we like and the ones we don't? One way of looking at it is to say that I need to learn to value *all* of myself. Sometimes taking care of myself is more important than caring for others, 'selfish' or not. You could try going through your list of qualities that you don't like, and thinking of a time when it has been an appropriate or good quality to have. So if selfishness is one of yours, consider times when this has been a useful quality because, say, it has protected you from exploitation. Being *self-ish* here means being able to look after yourself appropriately: *valuing your self* as you should.

In this way you might come to see that *all* your attributes are valuable, at least some of the time. Mostly, I expect, you are somewhere between the extremes; maybe a bit selfish and a bit caring, for example. Similarly, growing and developing children will experiment with a whole range of personal qualities. As parents, carers and early childhood educators we can help them to learn, not that one set of personal characteristics is *always* right or *always* wrong, but that it is helpful to be able to call upon a range of personal qualities in response to the changing circumstances we find ourselves in, as we go through life. These are issues I hope you will go on considering.

UNIT 1 WEEK THREE

We have come to the end of this unit now. The review activity this week is designed to help you reflect for a while on what you have been learning, before moving on to Unit 2.

Review of the unit

Before moving on to Unit 2 take time to look back over the week's work as you did in Weeks One and Two, considering how your study may be influencing your care and work with young children. I hope you will continue to reflect on these issues as you move through the rest of the book. The list of references at the end of this unit provide material for those of you who wish to investigate these more fully.

Further reading

Roberts, R. (1995) *Self-Esteem and Successful Early Learning*, London: Hodder and Stoughton

Sylva, K. and Lunt, I. (1982) *Child Development: A First Course*, Oxford: Blackwell, Chapter 5

UNIT I WEEK THREE

Unit I References

Week One

Bee, H. (1992) *The Developing Child*, New York: HarperCollins

Dearing, R. (1995) *Pre-School Education Consultation: Desirable Outcomes for Children's Learning on Entering Compulsory Schooling. Draft Proposals*, London: SCAA

DeCasper, A.J. and Spence, M. (1986) 'Prenatal maternal speech influences newborns' perceptions of speech sounds', *Infant Behaviour and Development*, 9, pp 133-150

Dowling, M. (1992) *Education 3-5*, London: Paul Chapman

Gibson, J.J. (1979) *The Ecological Approach to Visual Perception*, Boston, MA: Houghton Mifflin

Hopkins, B. and Westra, T. (1988) 'Maternal expectations and motor development: some cultural differences', *Developmental Medicine and Child Neurology*

Malina, R.M. (1982) 'Motor development in the early years', in Moore, S.G. and Cooper, S. (eds) *The Young Child: Reviews of Research*, Washington, DC: NAEYC, Vol 3, pp 211-232

Ruddick, S. (1990) *Maternal Thinking: Towards a Politics of Peace*, London: Women's Press

Woodhead, M., Carr, R. and Light, P. (1991) *Becoming a Person*, London and New York: Routledge

Woolfson, R. (1991) *Children with Special Needs: A Guide for Parents and Carers*, London: Faber and Faber

Week Two

Ainsworth, M. and Bell, S.M. (1974) 'Mother-infant interactions and the development of competence', in Connolly, K. and Bruner, J. (eds) *The Growth of Competence*, London: Academic Press

Barnes, P. (1995) *Personal, Social and Emotional Development of Children*, Milton Keynes/Oxford: Open University/Blackwell

Bowlby, J. (1944) 'Forty-four juvenile thieves: their characters and home life', *International Journal of Psychoanalysis*, 25, pp 1-57

Bowlby, J. (1965) *Child Care and the Growth of Love*, Harmondsworth: Penguin

Dearing, R. (1995) *Pre-School Education Consultation: Desirable Outcomes for Children's Learning on Entering Compulsory Schooling. Draft Proposals*, London: SCAA

Dunn, J. (1988) *The Beginnings of Social Understanding*, Oxford: Basil Blackwell

Gilligan, C. (1982) *In a Different Voice: Psychological Theory and Women's Development*, Cambridge, MA: Harvard University Press

Lerner, J. (1993) 'The influence of child temperamental characteristics on parent behavior', in Luster and Okagaki (1993)

Liedloff, J. (1986) *The Continuum Concept*, Harmondsworth: Penguin

Luster, T. and Okagaki, L. (eds) (1993) *Parenting: An Ecological Perspective*, New Jersey: Lawrence Erlbaum

Nsamenang, A. (1992) *Human Development in a Cultural Context: A Third World Perspective*, London: Sage

Kohlberg, L. (1984) *The Psychology of Moral Development*, San Francisco, CA: Harper and Row

Piaget, J. (1932) *The Moral Judgement of the Child*, London: Routledge

Rowbotham, S. (1973) *Hidden from History*, London: Pluto Press

White, D. and Woollett, A. (1991) in Woodhead, M., Carr, R. and Light, P. (eds) *Becoming a Person*, London and New York: Routledge, Chapter 4

White, D. and Woollett, A. (1992) *Families: A Context for Development*, Lewes: Falmer Press

Whiting, B. and Pope-Edwards, C. (1988) *Children of Different Worlds: The Formation of Social Behaviour*, Cambridge, MA: Harvard University Press

Week Three

Bandura, A. (1977) *Social Learning Theory*, New York: Prentice-Hall

Bates, J.E. (1989) 'Concepts and measurements of temperament', in Kohnstamm, G.A., Bates, J.E. and Rothbart, M.K. (eds) *Temperament in Childhood*, Chichester: Wiley

Bee, H. (1992) *The Developing Child*, New York: HarperCollins

Berry Brazelton, T. and Cramer, B.G. (1991) *The Earliest Relationship*, London: Karnak House

Chodorow, N. (1978) *The Reproduction of Mothering: Psychoanalysis and the Sociology of Gender*, Berkeley, CA: University of California Press

Curry, N.E. and Arnaud, S.H. (1984) 'Play in developmental pre-school settings', in Yawkey, T.D. and Pellegrini, A. (eds) *Child's Play: Developmental and Applied*, New Jersey, Lawrence Erlbaum

Erikson, E. (1950, revised 1965) *Childhood and Society*, Harmondsworth: Penguin

Harter, S. (1983) 'The determinants and mediational role of global self-worth in children', in Eisenberg, N. (ed) *Contemporary Topics in Developmental Psychology*, New York, Wiley-Interscience

Kagan, J. (1984) *The Nature of the Child*, New York: Basic Books

Roberts, R. (1995) *Self-Esteem and Successful Early Learning*, London: Hodder and Stoughton

Rogers, C. (1957) 'The necessary and sufficient conditions of therapeutic personality change', reprinted in Kirschenbaum, H. and Henderson, V. (eds) (1990) *The Carl Rogers Reader*, London: Constable

Siraj-Blatchford, I. (1994) *The Early Years: Laying the Foundations for Racial Equality*, Stoke on Trent: Trentham Books

Vasta, R., Haith, M. and Miller, S. (1992) *Child Psychology: The Modern Science*, New York: Wiley

Unit 2:
Promoting greater understanding

Tricia Lilley

Contents

Objectives

This week's study will ask you to consider some key aspects of learning in the early years. By the end of this week you should:

- have begun to reflect on your own experiences as a learner

- know about some of the factors that may affect learning

- be more familiar with some of the principles of practice which are reflected in recent reports

- use observations of children to focus on the nature of their learning.

Activities

This week you will need to arrange about one and a half hours in total for observations of children engaged in learning. If possible, these should be completed in an early childhood centre. You will be asked to do one or two 10-15 minute observations, and you will also need time to write up your notes and comment on what you have observed.

About this unit

The focus for the next three weeks will be on children's cognitive and spoken language development from birth to the age of eight. The term 'cognitive development' refers to the various ways in which we acquire and develop our knowledge and understanding and includes such aspects as language, memory and problem solving. A more detailed explanation is given later in Week Two. You will already have started to think about how children develop physically, socially, emotionally and morally in Unit 1. As you begin to work through this unit you will see again how the different aspects of development are closely linked. Unit 2 begins by looking at your own experiences of learning, helping you to look back on personal experiences as a learner at school or college, in the workplace or at home. I will help you to think about factors that have affected you as a learner, to pick out things that have helped and/or hindered you. You will be able to look more closely at the nature of learning in the early years, exploring some of the theory, maybe building on your existing knowledge as an educator of young children, and also looking at the learning that occurs in your particular early childhood context.

In Week Two we will consider some important research into children's cognitive development and their acquisition of language. You will have an opportunity to explore the work of Piaget and develop further understanding about his theories and their impact on early childhood education and care, in addition to reading more about current research.

In Week Three we will focus on the growth of children's understanding. We will look in more detail at your role as a significant adult supporting children's learning and their cognitive and linguistic development.

I have tried to develop materials that will give you a variety of experiences. As a guide, each week you should expect to spend about three hours on reading, two hours completing the activities and one and a half hours undertaking specified tasks. Whenever I refer to 'workplace', I am making an assumption either that you have some professional contact with young children, or that you are able to visit an early childhood centre on a regular basis whilst working through this book. Of course, much of what is said here can also apply to young children's learning in the home and family situation.

At the end of each week of study you will find one or two suggestions for further reading. A full list of references is included at the end of Unit 2.

Thinking about your own experiences

We have all had a lifetime of experience as learners – in early childhood, during our schooldays, at college, perhaps as a parent, carer or partner. Some of you will have been a learner in an adult educational context, as part of your professional development.

As you work through this unit I will ask you to think back over your experiences as a learner in a range of contexts. We will then look in more detail at some of the recent research about the nature of children's learning.

I want to start by helping you to think about yourself as a learner. Please complete the following task before reading on.

■ Activity I A

Think of two things that you have had to learn recently, one you found easy and one you found difficult – for example, using a new video recorder or a computer, learning to drive or doing some DIY. Identify what helped you to learn and also what made learning difficult for you. Make a list of your ideas, and then read on.

❏ Commentary

Compare your list with these ideas put forward by other readers. Look at how many things you have identified in common.

Factors that have helped my learning	Factors that have hindered my learning
Interest in the topic	Pressure of time
Having a reason for wanting to learn	Poor environment or when I am cold, hungry or tired
Attitude and enthusiasm of the teacher	Boring materials
Time to do it properly	Being talked at
Clear instructions	Being unwell
Interesting materials	
Active involvement	
Talking about it and working with others	

■ Activity 2 A

Now I would like you to think about your workplace, or early childhood centre you are visiting, and the learning that goes on there.

•   What helps your children to learn?

•   What makes learning difficult for them?

❏ Commentary

Here are the notes I have made about some the things that help learners in my workplace. You will probably have a different list of things but may notice some common threads running between the two sets of ideas. If you can, try to talk to someone else about your ideas. See if they share the same view or have different thoughts.

Some of the things that help the learners in my workplace

- Adults being friendly and approachable, setting a positive atmosphere for learning

- Establishing routines and being consistent so that everyone knows what the expectations are

- Encouraging friendships and opportunities for learning together

- Valuing achievements and celebrating success

- Ensuring provision of a range of activities which are interesting and relevant

- Ensuring that the content and context of learning activities reflect the social and cultural backgrounds of the learners

Some of the things that hinder the learners in my workplace

- Some classrooms are cramped and have poor lighting and ventilation.

- Every session is very busy and learners do not always have much time to think, and reflect on what is going on.

- Some days seem very long and the learners get tired by late afternoon.

One reason for asking you to look at the 'workplace' is to help you to make some links between what helps you to learn, and what might help the children in that workplace to learn. Starting from your own experience, drawing on your own knowledge of what it is like to be a learner, may help you to empathise with others.

Asking you to think about yourself first should also highlight the fact that you have a wealth of experience as a learner. You have found some things easy and some things much more difficult to understand, know about, remember or be able to do. This experience is your *personal baggage*, which you carry with you all the time, and it will have a big influence on how you interact with other learners and on the kinds of opportunities you provide for others to learn.

In the same way that you are influenced by your previous experiences, so are the children you work with. They all come to the nursery, day centre, school or family centre with a set of values, beliefs and expectations based on their life experiences to date.

■ Activity 3 A

The following extract provides a rich example of close observation of a young child at school. This may be a familiar scene to you, noticing that a child is unusually subdued, anxious to check the passing of time, preoccupied with his or her own thoughts.

Read the extract and, as you do so, think about what might be influencing the child's behaviour, how his feelings or attitude may affect his experiences of learning.

Phineas (3.11) would not take off his hat and coat and gloves for a long time this morning. He sat, with them on, on the edge of the platform in a very quiet and subdued mood, and did not for a long time join in any of the other children's occupations, nor show any of his usual interests. This occurred every morning for about a week. Several times each morning he asked, 'Is it time to go home yet?' although in the ordinary way he is reluctant to go and far too absorbed in his pursuits to think of the end of the morning. This week he has also been much more easily distracted by the others from any work he has been engaged on, leaving it every few minutes to take up theirs in a listless way, and then coming back to his own.

❏ Commentary

Consider for a moment the possible reasons for Phineas's apparent change of behaviour. Perhaps he had a new hat and coat and did not want to be parted from them, but that would not explain his subdued mood. Or maybe his new clothes were very different from those his friends were wearing, so he felt embarrassed. Being much more easily distracted could have been a sign of tiredness or generally feeling under the weather.

The key thing to note at this point is the importance of knowing the children you work with, so that you are able to notice changes in behaviour or attitude. Once noted, we can spend time exploring possible causes and the ways in which we can support the child. Now read the explanation provided in the original text (Isaacs 1948):

> *After about a week, he returned to his usual self again. This has coincided with the birth of a baby brother (the third child in the family).*

> *The misery of fear and jealousy aroused by the arrival of the new baby had thus awakened all Phineas's deep infantile phantasies, and grave anxiety connected with them. His general enterprise and active interest in the real world was quite inhibited and lost for the time being.*

This example serves to remind us how closely children's social and emotional development is bound up with their learning. Phineas's emotional feelings, his wealth of previous and current experience, played an important part in his learning. You might recognise from the extract some of your own feelings when you are anxious and unable to concentrate.

I have asked you to think about your experiences as a learner so that you can begin to engage with the materials in this unit from your own starting point. Later in the unit I will discuss the importance of finding out what the learner already knows and has experienced. In the next section we will consider the factors that may have an influence on what, when and how we learn.

Factors that may influence learning

So far in this unit you have looked back at memories of your own learning, thinking about things that helped and hindered you as a learner. You have also thought about the personal baggage that everyone brings to every learning situation – the experiences of young children and how these affect their expectations and understanding of their world.

Remember that learning takes place in a range of contexts and for a variety of reasons. Most of us initially look back at learning in school, but do not forget that every day people are learning about the rules of tennis, the Top Ten hits in the charts, the sound of a friend's car coming up the road. Babies learn to recognise the sound of their mother, older children learn how to play games. Retired people learn how to adapt their lives to new situations.

It is also important to remember that there is a big difference between what we assume children are learning as they engage in various activities and what they actually learn. Always look out for the unintended learning and the potential for learning that arises from various experiences.

■ Activity 4 A

Read this observation of a child out shopping with his mother. Make some notes in response to the following questions:

• What do you notice about the nature of this child's learning?

• What do you think he was learning from this experience?

Think particularly about the mother's role and the influence she had on the child's learning.

Observation

On one occasion I went with Simon (5.11) and his mother to the local supermarket. When we arrived, Simon's mother took a shopping basket from the stack, and so did Simon.

Mother: No, we only need one basket, Simon.
Simon: Well I want to carry it.
Mother: You can share it, Simon, you carry it now and David [older brother] can carry it later.

First of all they went to get some bananas. Simon picked up several bunches and put them in the basket.

Mother: No! I only want three, and not too ripe either ... those are too big.

When the bananas had been selected, Simon's mother asked him to get them weighed.

Mother: Simon, will you go and queue up to have them weighed? Wait behind that man ...

Simon continued to carry the basket as more things were added and it soon became quite full.

Simon: David's turn now, it's getting heavy.

David carried the basket until they reached the check-out and then Simon took the things out of the basket and placed them on the conveyor belt. I noted how he positioned the items: he maintained a very neat and ordered arrangement. The bread was placed across the belt, then the sugar, then a row of yoghurts evenly spaced. The bananas and buns were at the end. Simon was evidently pleased with his efforts.

Mother: Meet me round the other side and you can help me pack the shopping.

Simon packed the shopping bag. His mother suggested the order this time.

Mother: Put the sugar in first because it's heavy ... now the bread ... that's right ... bananas last of all so they don't get squashed.

❏ Commentary

In thinking about the nature of the learning that was occurring in this scene you may have commented on the important role of the mother – asking questions, explaining what she was doing, giving reasons for her decisions. You may have recognised the context as an everyday situation which is familiar to many of the children that you work with. Perhaps you made a note of the opportunities for first-hand experience that Simon encountered.

Active construction of meaning

When I began to look at the learning that might occur in this kind of situation, I realised that Simon's shopping trip with his mother had involved him in using and listening to a range of mathematical terms, and participating in weighing, sorting, counting and so on. He was also engaged in manipulating shapes and their position as he set the shopping out on the conveyor belt. This observation reminds us of some of the points made in the first section. Look back at the first activity, where you were identifying things that helped or hindered learning. Colin Conner (1993, p 5) reminds us of these key points:

> Learning requires opportunities for the learner to create an active construction of meaning; learning is dependent on interaction with the learner's past experience; learning is influenced by the context in which it takes place.

In our observation, Simon certainly had opportunities to create an 'active construction of meaning' with lots of practical, first-hand experience. In addition his mother provided a language commentary to support his learning, enabling him to make connections between what he was doing and his developing understanding of the concept of weight. Simon was also able to learn about sorting the shopping in a meaningful context, in a familiar situation

– out shopping with his mother. This in turn enabled him to bring previous experience to bear on the current situation. What do you think he already knew about shopping, putting things on the conveyor belt, the weight of items?

As you begin to explore the nature of early learning and what you already know about learning from your previous experience, you will begin to recognise key themes that appear throughout this unit. These themes can be summarised as principles of practice which relate to the process of learning for the under eights. Some of the foundations which underpin provision for young children were identified by a House of Commons Committee of Inquiry into the Quality of the Educational Experiences offered to three and four years olds in its report entitled *Starting with Quality*, published in 1990. The Committee believed that these principles could be applied in a variety of ways to suit the needs of the children and the context in which they are learning while at the same time providing a common base line for all those who work with the under fives. I would suggest that these principles form the basis of good practice across the age ranges and are certainly as pertinent to eight year olds and beyond as to the age group specified in the report.

■ Activity 5 A

In this activity and the next two I want you to consider a summary of the principles underlying good practice when caring for and educating young children taken from *Starting with Quality*. I have included three sections for you to think about, focusing on young children as learners, the content of learning, and the context of learning. Each section contains some key statements and principles of learning in the early years. When I read the document I found some of the words and phrases particularly powerful, offering vivid examples of good early years practice.

In this activity I would like you to read each statement below with care, then circle or highlight one or two key words in each statement that tell you about how children learn. When you come to review your selection of words and phrases, I hope a valuable list of key ideas and principles will emerge.

Young children as learners

- Although all children follow sequential patterns of development, every child is unique

- All children have competencies which need to be brought out and built upon

- Young children's learning should be embedded in what is familiar

- Play is an essential and rich part of the learning process

- Learning should be a pleasurable and rewarding experience

- Learning should be primarily first hand, experiential and active. Young children need opportunities and space to explore and discover

- Young children are social beings and learning should take place in a social context

- Talk is central to the learning process. It should be reciprocal and often initiated by the child

- Children's independence and autonomy need to be promoted. Children should be encouraged to take responsibility for their learning

- Self-discipline should be encouraged

- Young children need the security of a daily routine which works for them

- There should be opportunities to explore the unexpected

- There should be opportunities for sustained engagement in an activity.

❏ Commentary

In this first section on children as learners, here are some of the phrases and words that I circled:

- 'sequential patterns of development'

- 'embedded in what is familiar'

- 'play'

- 'security of a daily routine'.

These phrases are considered in more detail in Weeks Two and Three of this unit. But as a starting point for my list of principles, the notions of security, sequential learning and starting with the familiar have high priority.

Encouraging independence

In this discussion I want to focus on the notion of *first-hand experience* and the importance of *encouraging autonomy and independence* in young children. When we are developing activities and providing experiences for young children, one of the decisions that we face is how much we will do *for* the child or *with* the child. As we try and answer this question we sometimes underestimate what young children are capable of doing by themselves. This underestimation arises for many reasons; sometimes in a busy home or early childhood centre it is simply a question of time! It is often much quicker and less stressful for parents, carers and staff to 'get things ready', put lots of things out for the children to use and explore, always to mix the paints up in advance. It may also be that our expectations are coloured by our previous experience of preparing activities for young children, or by the policies adopted by our last workplace.

In some of the research that I have been doing recently I have found that many educators unintentionally de-skill children by removing opportunities for them to develop a level of independence appropriate to their current stage of development. I found that four year olds were just as capable of mixing powder paints, selecting the right kind of glue for a given task, pouring a sufficient amount into a pot and getting out items of apparatus as older children, teachers and classroom assistants. What the four year olds needed was to be shown how to do these tasks, and to have space and time to develop their own skills, in a secure environment where it did not matter if they spilled the powder in the early stages of acquiring the skill.

Think about your own workplace. (See my note in the section *About this unit*.) How much space do you give to children to try things out, to take some responsibility for their learning and for getting their own resources ready? Some early years centres have radically changed their approaches, ensuring that resources are accessible and encouraging children to make decisions and become more independent. Often these centres follow an organisational process known as High/Scope. This is a system of planning, monitoring and organising early years centres and nurseries, originally developed in America and is increasingly used here. You will be able to explore the High/Scope model in Unit 3.

■ Activity 6 A

Now have a look at the second section from the report *Starting with Quality* which looks particularly at the content of learning. Once again, I would like you to circle or highlight key words or phrases, bearing in mind that you should be developing a list of principles that have particular meaning for you.

As a point of interest, I have included activities like these, based on marking the text, in devising similar activities to help develop study skills with children. Research has shown that marking the text in this way can become a valuable study skill, picking out pertinent points, making decisions about what you are reading, and importantly, remembering more of what you have read!

The content of learning

- Young children need a broad, balanced and relevant curriculum

- Young children's development should be viewed as a whole, and the curriculum should reflect an understanding of this

- Observation-based assessment is a key to planning an appropriate curriculum for every child

- The process of learning is as important as the content and needs careful consideration in curriculum planning

- Children need certain skills and concepts in order to make sense of, and apply, their knowledge and understanding

- The development of positive attitudes to learning should be a specific aim

- Much knowledge can and should be presented in an integrated, cross-curricular way, depending on the children's experience

- There should be continuity and progression; a co-ordinated approach to planning should be encouraged.

❏ Commentary

In this section I want to focus on just one issue about the content of learning. I think the phrase

- 'the process of learning is as important as the content'

is particularly significant because so much of the current legislation regarding the curriculum for primary-age children is content-driven. By that I mean that much of the content of work in a primary classroom is now laid down in legislation and within the framework of the National Curriculum. There is a danger that this will increase the pressures on early childhood educators to become most focused on ensuring that all the aspects are covered by the children, so that we lose sight of what we know about how children learn – the things we identified earlier as being important, such as first-hand experience, play, independence, sequential patterns of development and so forth.

The process of learning

Take a look at the following example, which helps to illustrate what I mean about process rather than content.

Observing Leita in the playgroup, I watched her move from the carpet area to go and play with the flour tray. She put some of the toys in the flour, ran her finger along the edges of the tray and pushed the flour into the bottom. She appeared totally absorbed in pushing the flour around with her fingers, picking up handfuls and letting it fall into the tray. When her key worker came over to the tray, Leita asked her if she could have some water for the flour. They added a few drops and then some more. Leita still pushed the flour and picked up handfuls but now the flour was sticky and squidged out between her fingers rather than falling in a stream back into the tray. Leita talked to her key worker about the flour, commenting on how sticky it was.

Can you see that Leita had been learning through the *process* of experimenting and playing with the flour? She did not need to know about all the potential learning points that would arise from this activity, but her discussion with an adult helped to focus her attention on the changes that took place when the flour became wet, the difference in texture, the feel of the flour, the smell and so forth. Leita was actively learning through the process of what she was doing. This kind of experiential learning is essential for young children.

This discussion about the process of learning should be of particular concern to those of you who are working with five to eight year olds. I hope you will engage with the debate

UNIT 2 WEEK ONE

and take stock of your own position on this key subject. Those of you who work with the under fives may soon be taking account of the proposed baseline assessments for this age group, which in turn could put increased pressure on you to adopt a content-driven curriculum. These are real challenges to our beliefs about early years education and the rights of the child to have access to a developmentally appropriate curriculum.

The context of learning

We now turn to the context of learning.

■ Activity 7 A

This third section from *Starting with Quality* focuses on the context of learning. Once again, circle or highlight key words that you feel are important. Draw upon your own experiences and your knowledge of the contexts of learning in early childhood centres.

The context of learning

- For young children, every setting is a source of learning; the home is a particularly powerful learning environment

- The content and setting of learning should, as far as possible, reflect the child's social and cultural background

- The child should feel valued and a positive self-concept should be promoted which acknowledges the value of each child's cultural and religious life

- The teaching environment should be open and accessible to the children

- Space for young children to move about and explore is essential

- A variety of learning situations is important

- Certain facilities are essential for the education and care of young children, e.g. access to an outdoor play area, adjacent toilets, space

- Young children need equipment that is appropriate and promotes their learning

- The learning environment should be 'user-friendly', secure, comfortable and stimulating

- A child's growing social competence needs support

- Collaboration with parents in a child's learning is essential

- All those involved in the learning process should be viewed as partners, and should collaborate in planning the curriculum

- The role of the adult is highly significant in the learning process. A favourable ratio of adults to children is critical

- All educators operate within the context of their own values, beliefs and attitudes. They should recognise that these may differ from those of the children they are educating

- Educators of young children need to be open-minded, evaluative, reflective and responsive.

❏ Commentary

In this final section I was particularly interested in the phrases which highlight the importance of the adult's role, and in particular the partnerships that can develop with parents. I wonder if you selected

- 'the role of the adult is highly significant', or

- 'all educators operate within the context of their own values, beliefs and attitudes'.

You may have found the statements about the child's self-concepts or user-friendly environments particularly pertinent. Whatever your choices, I hope this series of activities working with this important document will have highlighted key principles for good practice in early childhood settings.

Partnership with parents

I will be looking at some of the theoretical underpinning which highlights the importance of adult interactions in the final week of this unit. You will also have an opportunity for further exploration of the parent's role when you work on Unit 3. However, at this point I want you to consider for a moment the role that parents already play in your workplace. How much time is given to getting to know the parents? Do you have procedures in place which encourage partnership and collaboration? Do you engage in meaningful consultation with parents about planning, or is there a token consultation with the weekly plan stuck on the window for all to read?

Some of the research that I have been doing has looked at ways in which children develop their mathematical knowledge and understanding outside of formal educational contexts. I spent time with children at home, going shopping, going to parties, at after-school and weekend clubs and going out with their families. I discovered a wealth of opportunities for learning about mathematics, but I also found that the existing attitudes of many teachers need to be challenged. Many teachers believe that as qualified professionals they are the ones who should be teaching mathematics and they fear any increase in parental involvement in this area.

What do you think? Many of you who are working with young children in a professional capacity are also parents. You will have knowledge and experience arising from your work experience and training, and you will also have experience of being an educator in your role as a parent. For example, you will have taught your child to feed herself, go to the toilet and develop her use of speech, and you have probably helped her to learn to read. It is important for early childhood educators to acknowledge parents' role in the education of their children and to make every effort to build links between home and school, nursery or play group to ensure continuity for all the children.

I hope you have now begun to identify some of the common themes that are emerging through this unit. For example, did you notice the emphasis on starting with the familiar – just what I have tried to do in asking you to look at your own experiences as a learner? Did you identify the importance of social interactions and opportunities to talk about learning? Perhaps you recognised examples from your own list of factors affecting learning, jotted down in Activity 1, such as the need for a secure environment in which routines are consistently maintained.

■ Activity 8 A

Now that you have selected key words and phrases from *Starting with Quality*, I would like you to review your whole list. Have another look at the words you have identified and see if you can group them under the following headings:

* Interaction with key worker

* Quality of environment

* Nature of task

❏ Commentary

When I began to classify my selected words and phrases under the various headings, I realised that they form the basis for provision of early childhood education and care. Here is my classification of just some of the points that I identified.

Interaction with key worker	Quality of environment	Nature of task
positive attitudes	reflects social and cultural background	talk
valued	accessible and open	play
collaboration	space	
partners	appropriate equipment	promotes independence
open-minded	security	continuity and progression
highly significant adult		variety of learning situations

Can you see that by grouping my selected phrases in this way I have really drawn attention to my own role as a key worker? I have also set a framework for establishing a positive ethos in the workplace. By identifying key words that relate to the nature of the tasks I would want to provide for the children, I am better placed to articulate my practice and my beliefs about what I am doing and why. I hope you will also have found this to be the case and that you can use some of these points to discuss practice with colleagues and with parents.

You will need to continue to engage with the principles set out in *Starting with Quality* and become increasingly familiar with the key words contained in the statements. In this way you should be able to continually reflect on and monitor your own role and the provision within your workplace. You may also be able to respond in a more informed way to the stream of consultation papers and documentation that is flooding into early years centres and schools at present, as the government attempts to expand provision for the under fives.

In this section I have asked you to begin to think about the factors that will have an effect on the quality of children's learning, factors that will positively support opportunities to learn and also those aspects which may hinder the child. You have read about some of the foundations which should underpin provision for learning, and you have been able to reflect on some common features of the nature of learning which appear in this unit. The next section will give you a chance to take a closer look at your own workplace.

Factors that influence learning in your workplace

Let us now look more closely at what is happening in your workplace. What factors might be affecting learning positively, and what might be hindering the children's learning?

■ Activity 9 B

Please complete the following task (based on materials from Drummond, Rouse and Pugh 1992) during this week. Try to follow the guidelines as you complete a short observation of 10-15 minutes' duration. You will also need time to write up your notes and think about what you have seen.

Observe an incident which involves a child in your workplace learning something. This could be an activity initiated by the child or by an adult; the child might have been painting or playing, talking to you or investigating something. Think about learning in its widest sense! Write down as much information as you can about the incident:

* the context

* the timing (when and for how long)

* the nature of the task

* the possible learning that was taking place.

After making your observations, read your description and think about why you felt this to be an example of learning.

- What were the characteristics that made this into a learning experience?

- Did you spot any factors which helped the child to learn?

- Could you see anything which on reflection may have hindered the child?

Jot down your thoughts and then read the next section.

You may want to do more than one observation if you have the time. Obviously, the more you observe children learning, the richer your own professional response will become.

❏ Commentary

Here is part of a response from a student who completed this activity. She has given some useful background or contextual detail to her observation notes.

Child observed: Lydia
Age: 5 years
Class: Reception
Started school: Beginning of this term (3 weeks ago)
Activity observed: Writing
Timing of observation: 9.30-10.13

Nature of task: Class told story about Martin – young boy who wanted to grow tall. Children talked about the things they could do now and things they could do as baby. The task was to write a sentence trying out their spellings or asking the teacher for help. Then do a picture.

It is always useful to have this kind of background factual information as it enables us to picture the scenario and to begin to draw some tentative conclusions. Did you manage to include this kind of detail in your notes?

The student then goes on to give examples taken from her full observation notes about how Lydia tackled this task.

9.30 am. Lydia held her pencil in her right hand, index finger left hand in her mouth. She leaned across the table to see what the teacher was doing. Talked aloud about the sound of the letter 'r' ... Listened to another child spelling a word and says 'L' for Lydia ... I know how to spell my name ... 'L' for lamp lady ...

9.52 am. Lydia got up to see what the other children were doing across the classroom ... teacher says 'Lydia' and she returned to the table but did not write anything ... stood day-dreaming until the teacher said, 'Sit down, Lydia. I am coming to you.' Lydia still stood by her chair waving her paper in the air. 'What word do you want, Lydia?' asked the teacher. 'Make,' Lydia replied. 'What is the first sound?' 'Lydia replies, 'I know how to write imyî.' ...

10.0 am. Lydia now has two lines of writing. Came and asked me for the word 'sandwiches' and had written 'S W J S' on her pad. I asked her if she could spell 'and' and she wrote down 'sand' immediately. I then said 'wiches'. Lydia replied 'w'. I added 'i' and she completed with 'ch'. Lydia read her sentence to me: 'I could not talk but I could make sandwiches.'

Evaluating the observation

Using this observation, the student suggested that this was an example of learning because it showed how much Lydia was already bringing to the situation, even though she had just started school. The student then suggested that Lydia was learning about story structure and about using her own experiences. Focusing on things which seemed to have hindered Lydia, the student suggested that lack of adult attention at the beginning did not help Lydia to focus on the task. (Other parts of the observation showed that she spent a lot of time wandering around, finding a rubber, crossing out her writing and starting again.) The student interaction with Lydia at the end of the session, helping her to write the word 'sandwiches', refocused the child and enabled her to go on and complete the task.

You will have already identified why you felt your observation was an example of learning. I expect you will have included some comments like those of the student who observed Lydia, or you may have noticed:

• the child's apparent pleasure in undertaking the task

• level of concentration

• ability to talk about what he/she had been doing or to work co-operatively with other children.

Perhaps you also noticed:

• how the practical experience helped them to understand a new concept

• how the key adult made careful use of questions to extend the child's initial ideas

• that the activity took place at a time when he/she were feeling tired and was really lacked concentration and interest.

I wonder whether you chose an incident where the child was engaged in play, not directed by an adult, or whether you identified a specific time when you or another adult had set out to teach the child something. I am really interested in these two aspects and how we can begin to find out what children actually learn from the tasks and activities they engage in. According to John Holt (1989, p xv):

> children, without being coerced or manipulated, or being put in exotic, specially prepared environments, or having their thinking planned and ordered for them, can, will and do pick up from the world around them important information about what we call the Basics.

He adds (p 160) that 'learning is not the product of teaching and teaching does not make learning'. Similarly Mary-Jane Drummond (1994, p 17) reminds us:

> It seems likely that teachers who are primarily interested in their *teaching*, in their strategies, their goals and their lesson plans, may pay less attention to the extent of the possible gap between their intentions, and the actual outcomes, in terms of children's *learning*. Knowing what one set out to do, and looking for evidence that one has done it, may not help one to see what has in fact resulted from one's good, even exemplary, intentions. Unintended learning is not, in any event, easy to recognise; when it runs counter to the teacher's intentions, it may become virtually invisible.

These are really important points for you to consider when you look at learning in more detail. How much of your learning has arisen as a result of your own interests and endeavours quite separately from any 'teaching' you may have received? How closely has some of your learning matched the actual teaching that you received? Sometimes my teachers have only succeeded in confusing me, however hard they have tried and however much they have prepared in order for me to learn. I expect it is the same for you too, and it will be so for the children that you work with.

The nature of learning in the early years

In the final section this week we return to looking at the nature of learning by considering other observations. This will help you to move beyond your own experience and the context of your workplace and to consider some of the wider issues. You have already been introduced to some of the underlying principles of early years education as laid down in the report *Starting with Quality*. Now have a look at some more examples of children learning.

■ Activity 10 A

I would like you to read the following case study and, as you do so, to think about these questions:

•   What previous knowledge do you think Sarah brought to the learning?

•   How do you think her learning was extended?

You will need to make a note of your ideas and responses to the questions.

Sarah (age four years) was playing cards with her mother. The game was called 'The Get-along Gang' and required the players to collect various sets and exchange them for picture cards of greater 'value'. For example, carriages were exchanged for tenders and tenders for train engines and so forth.

Mother: Let's see how many cards we need each. Shall I shuffle them? Now we need four each. Are you going to share them out, Sarah?

Sarah gave us one each.

Mother: That's right, now two.

Sarah carried on until we all had four cards.

Mother: That's it. Have we all got enough now? Put the rest in the middle and turn them over.

Sarah put the remainder down.

Mother: Now, you have to collect three the same and then change them for one of these trains.

Sarah: I've got two already.

Mother: There, take one from the top of the pile.

As they played the game, Sarah was very observant and kept an eye on all the cards, telling her mother if she had one that Sarah wanted. Occasionally, her mother said, 'No, you can't take one yet,' or 'It's not your turn yet.' When Sarah had collected three pictures of the same character or object, her mother said, 'Now you can exchange all those for one of these train pictures.' The winner was the person who exchanged all their pictures for a carriage, a train, a tender and a guards van. Sarah won.

❏ Commentary

I wonder what *previous knowledge* you thought Sarah brought to this learning situation. You may have said that she recognised numbers, or could count and share out the cards. Did you spot the comment by her mother asking Sarah to put the cards in the middle? This could indicate that she also knew some positional language. You may have felt Sarah's learning was *extended* by her mother's use of language and explanation, giving a commentary almost all the time to clarify what was actually happening. Perhaps you said Sarah extended her understanding of taking turns, as her mother said to her a couple of times that it was not her turn yet!

This is what the researcher who undertook this observation wrote:

Sarah had experienced opportunities for counting, division, place value working in base 3, exchange and positioning in a meaningful and familiar way. Sarah was also developing her knowledge and understanding of number through using and also hearing mathematical language in a familiar context. Research evidence supports the notion that where adults provide a commentary of descriptive and contextual language to support the child's actions, they may enable children to gain further meaning from the situation (Vygotsky 1978; Sylva *et al* 1980; Athey 1990). Sarah's mother was using the language of number and division in her interactions with her daughter. This supports the view that if objects have some relevance to the child and the numbers are small, they can be manipulated by young children at an earlier age than previously expected (Hughes 1986).

You can see how the researcher has highlighted a range of aspects of learning that you might not notice at first glance. The observation has also been used to look at a specific area of knowledge and understanding as well as at general issues regarding learning.

Review of the week

We are now at the end of this week's study. During the week you have:

*   looked at your own experiences of learning

*   considered things that might have helped or even hindered you as a learner

*   completed observations of young children, making some connections between the theory and the reality of young children learning.

In the next week you will have a chance to look in more detail at some of the theories of cognitive development and at the early acquisition of language. Take time now to look back over this week's work, and consider the following:

*   What interested you most, and why?

*   Are there any activities that will be useful to revisit now that you have completed this week's study?

*   How will this week's study influence your ways of caring for and educating young children?

Before moving on to Week Two, make sure you complete the review activity below. It should help you to consolidate your learning so far and relate this to your practical experience with young children.

■ Review activity A

Drawing upon your experiences in your own workplace or at an early childhood centre that you know well, use the summary taken from Starting with Quality to consider the following issues. You do not need to do any further observations; just try and think about what you see when you visit the centre in a new light, from a different perspective. The questions and issues that I would like you to focus on are as follows:

*   Look back at the summary section entitled 'The context of learning' that we considered in Activity 7. In what ways have you been able to promote a positive context for learning?

*   Now review the section called 'The content of learning' in Activity 6. How are the decisions made about the content of learning at your chosen early childhood centre?

*   Now look at the section entitled 'Young children as learners' in Activity 5. Consider how far your early childhood centre reflects these principles.

❑ Commentary

I hope you will have been able to reflect on some of the things you have seen or been involved in at your early childhood centre and made some connections with the principles of practice outlined in Starting with Quality. The main focus of this first week of Unit 2 has been to encourage you to look anew at yourself and your workplace, and consider the nature of learning that takes place in that context. In Week Two we will go on to look at the development of language.

Further reading

Drummond, M.J. (1994) *Assessing Children's Learning*, London: David Fulton, Chapter 4: 'Looking at learning: learning to see'

DES (1990) *Starting with Quality: The Report of the Committee of Inquiry into the Quality of the Educational Experiences Offered to Three and Four Year Olds*, London: HMSO, Part 2: 'Material to aid practitioners'

There is a full list of references at the end of Unit 2.

Unit 2: Week Two
Patterns of development

Objectives

This week's study will ask you to look at some of the theories relating to language and cognitive development. By the end of this week you should:

- know about some of the theories of language development

- consider the progression of spoken language from pre-birth to the age of three years

- be able to identify those processes which relate to the term 'cognitive development'

- know about some of the major theorists and models of cognitive development.

Activities

This week you will need to arrange about one and a half hours in total for observations of children engaged in learning. If possible, these should be completed in an early childhood centre. You will be asked to do at least three 10-15 minutes observations, and will also need time to write up your notes and comment on what you have observed.

About this week's study

During this week of study you will be making connections between your own child observations and the models of development that are being discussed. You will begin to consider how these ideas have influenced the way we work with young children in early childhood centres like the one you work in, or are visiting.

Thinking about language development

Most people who work with the under eights or who have children of their own will probably be aware of a child's apparently steady development. They will notice how the child becomes more skilful physically, gradually begins to use language and other communication skills, becomes more confident socially, shows signs of increasing ability to solve problems and to think things through. Last week you were beginning to look at learning from your own point of view and in relation to your workplace. This week we are going to move on to consider how children develop an ability to communicate clearly, in particular through spoken language, and then explore some of the theories of learning in more detail.

In order to begin to understand how children develop their skills in spoken language, we must also take account of how their social, emotional, physical and cognitive development affects their ability to use spoken language effectively. It is not uncommon to hear or read about language being 'acquired' as if it is something 'out there' to be internalised by the child. Language needs to be viewed much more widely, to be seen as a series of actions or behaviours that the child grows into over time, a series of actions that are strongly influenced by all other aspects of development.

The processes involved in the development of spoken language are complex.

■ Activity 1 A

As in Week One, I want you to build on your own experience as a learner and as an educator, this time focusing on language development as a starting point. Jot down some key memories from your own language biography – significant incidents or experiences that have shaped your development as a speaker and as a listener.

Here are some of memories from my own language biography. As you read them, try and think about the possible effects these incidents may have had on my development as a language user.

Speaking memories	Listening memories
From birth to five years	*From birth to five years*
Sitting on the side gate talking to everyone who went by when my brothers had gone to school. Having an imaginary friend who I talked to all the time and played with when I was on my own.	Sitting in the back of the car in the dark and listening to my mum and dad chatting ... their voices always seemed different at night.
From five to ten years	*From five to ten years*
Getting told off by my mum for wandering up to people and chatting to them in the street.	Lying in bed listening to the traffic rushing past ... hearing a car crash into our fence and peeping out the window in the dark.
From ten to fifteen years	*From ten to fifteen years*
Not knowing what to say to other girls in the playground.	Listening to stories on the radio.
Worrying about having to say something in class and planning what I was going to say or ask over and over again in my head.	
Twenty years plus!	*Twenty years plus!*
Worrying about using the telephone and hating it if my dad said I would come to the phone without asking me if I wanted to.	Still liking story tapes and being read to ...

Now try your own language biography using this table. Focus on your memories of speaking and listening. Then read the commentary that follows.

Speaking memories	Listening memories
From birth to five years	*From birth to five years*
From ten to fifteen years	*From ten to fifteen years*
From fifteen to twenty years	*From fifteen to twenty years*
Twenty years plus!	*Twenty years plus!*

❏ Commentary

I wonder how far back you could remember key incidents? You may have found that some of your memories were quite painful to recall; perhaps you had found speaking in front of class difficult, or you were constantly criticised for not listening, or maybe were very shy and did not say much. You may also have included some positive memories, for instance recalling skills that you have recently acquired such as getting to grips with a new language or giving a talk for parents.

You can see from my biography that my main memories appear to indicate a growing anxiety as a speaker as I became older. I appear to have moved from being an apparently confident, constantly chattering child to a shy, quiet and rather insecure teenager. This is not an uncommon pattern, and I have included it to draw your attention to the importance of looking at the whole child and at all aspects of development – social, emotional, physical and cognitive – in order to develop an understanding of what we see and hear and how we can interpret the observations that we make.

The development of spoken language

One of the significant characteristics of human language is its ability to free us from the here and now. Human language enables us to comment on the past, present and future; to describe people, objects, events, contexts. Various theories have been proposed to explain how human language develops, but the process has continued to puzzle psychologists since the seventeenth century.

You will need to become more familiar with these theories as a foundation for your observations and analysis of children's language development. In this unit we can look at only some of the research, but I have listed additional materials at the end of the unit which you can refer to if you would like to explore this subject in more depth.

Lee and Das Gupta (1995) suggest that there are three main theories as to how we develop language, arising from different schools of thought: the *behaviourist, nativist* and *social-psychological* viewpoints. We will explore each of these terms in turn.

The behaviourist viewpoint

This viewpoint takes its lead from the work of John Locke (1632-1704) who believed that children were shaped through their interactions with adults and their peers. They learned responses or behaviours which, if reinforced positively, would become part of their pattern of behaviour. This theory stressed the value of children *imitating* others; in terms of language development, it was believed that children's imitations of adult spoken language were a crucial part of their development. You will recall from Unit 1 that, according to behaviourist theory, personality is formed by the copying, modelling and reinforcement of behaviour.

In the 1950s the American behaviourist B.F. Skinner further developed the theory that language is a behaviour which develops through trial and error: as a young child makes babbling sounds these sounds are associated with real objects or events by an adult who reinforces the connection through praise and encouragement. So social approval, often given by the parent or carer, is seen by behaviourists as a key to the development of language.

The behaviourist theory has had a number of critics. Some have queried how such a theory could explain how children come to use phrases and vocabulary that could not possibly have been overheard or previously spoken by an adult. Others have questioned how children could learn language so well and in such a short time if it was all based on modelling, imitation and reinforcement. What if a child is deaf, or if the child's parents are deaf? How would this affect a child's developing use of language?

Some aspects of behaviourist theory seem to be valid. There is evidence that young children do imitate adults and other children as they begin to develop their spoken language. There is also evidence that behaviour which is reinforced, in this case by responses from carers, may be repeated frequently. The theory offers a partial explanation for us, and we will look in more detail at the stage of *imitation* later in this unit.

The nativist viewpoint

As questions were being raised about the behaviourist research, another view of language development was beginning to flourish. Noam Chomsky (b. 1928), a psycholinguist who is particularly interested in grammar and linguistics, wrote a scathing critique of behaviourism. He believed that the amount of language that a child would be exposed to and could therefore imitate would be relatively small, and he disputed the claim that language was 'acquired' in such a mechanistic manner, whereby the child was 'fed' with words and then reproduced them in appropriate contexts. This was too simplistic and did not explain how children come to say things that they have never heard before.

Chomsky did not believe, as Locke had maintained, that children must learn everything from external sources, that they are like a 'blank sheet' to be filled in with their life experiences. Chomsky suggested that the only way to answer some of the criticisms made of behaviourist theory was to assume that humans have some inbuilt ability and knowledge about language. He called this innate ability the 'language acquisition device' (LAD). This enables children to receive and make sense of language input and to apply the rules of language in a range of contexts without being reliant on imitating adult speech.

■ Activity 2 A

Have a look at these common phrases taken from transcripts of three year olds speaking (adapted from Hearle 1992). Circle the 'mistakes' and try and identify which rules of language the child is trying to apply in each case.

I runned to my mummy.   *I wroted this.*   *We saw sheeps.*

I bringed my packed lunch.   *I catched the ball.*   *My feets are cold.*

I wented to the swings.   *I got two foots.*

❏ Commentary

I expect you will recognise many of these 'mistakes', which are often made by young children as they explore the language and make every effort to apply their knowledge in new contexts. I am sure you will be able to think of other examples. Make a note of them before going on to the next section.

Just by looking at the errors made by these three year olds we can see how much children really know about the rules of spoken language, and how clever they are, constantly using and applying their knowledge of language. There is a great deal of evidence to support the claim that children do make up their own rules and that they apply standard rules to irregular cases, as we have just seen.

For example, children will often make errors when applying different tenses, using:

comed	instead of	*came*
goed	instead of	*went*
catched	instead of	*caught.*

They have knowledge of the rule of adding 'ed' to verbs in order to describe a past event, but they have not had sufficient experience of irregular examples. These 'mistakes', described as *virtuous errors* by Herriot (1971), can provide us with a useful picture of the rules children do know and how we can extend their knowledge and understanding.

It is really important to take great care in talking to children about these virtuous errors. I wonder what you would say to a child who claims she 'wented to school'? Usually, we just repeat the correct version in response to the child, without making it too obvious that we are correcting a mistake. 'Yes, you went to school this morning, didn't you ...' The most important thing is that the child is beginning to use the structures of language to communicate in a meaningful way, and odd words or phrases that are given incorrectly should not distract from this important step in their development.

The social-psychological viewpoint

In addition to the two extremes of the behaviourist and nativist views of language development, there is a middle position which draws from both points of view. In the same way as Skinner's work was criticised, so too was Chomsky's theory of a specific language acquisition device. A growing number of critics suggested that children develop their language alongside a whole range of other skills. They are able to read and interpret cues beyond the spoken word, and they will make sense of gesture, expression, body language, non-linguistic cues and events.

Jerome Bruner (b. 1915), an American psychologist, identified apparent links between the early babblings and pre-verbal communications that occur between the young child and her carer and the child's later use of language. Bruner reminded us that spoken language is only one form of communication. Very young babies will communicate through look, smell, touch and physical closeness. We can usually interpret how a baby is feeling or what his needs might be by listening to him, noticing his smiles or the movements of his body.

These early signals will usually receive some kind of response from the carer, and although many of these interactions are pre-verbal exchanges they do have the structure of conversations. Following this line of thought, it could be said that spoken language emerges as a more effective form of communication than these non-verbal interactions but *not* as the *first* form of communication. We will look at the importance of social interactions later on in this unit.

■ Activity 3 B

For this activity I want you to choose a child from your workplace or from home who is aged three years or younger. Using the information provided in this section on the theories of language development, undertake some observations of your focus child, noting in particular any evidence of the child:

- imitating the language of the parent, carer or key worker

- imitating sounds or taking notice of sounds in their environment

- applying rules of language in particular contexts

- communicating through gesture and/or expression

- clearly conveying meaning to an adult

- initiating communication with an adult.

Make sure you have asked the parent or carer for permission to observe the child and to record their language interactions. You could also ask them for some background details about the child's language development. Here are some examples of questions that you might ask, but you will need to design your own, depending upon the age of the child:

- When did she say her first word?

- What language do you speak at home?

- When did the child first join words together in sentences, etc?

You will probably need to do several observations of this child. Please keep the record for reference. This section of the unit will help you to make some connections between your observations and recognised patters of language development up to three years of age. At the end of the next section there is some further discussion which you will find useful once you have completed this activity, so make sure you have made notes before reading on.

UNIT 2 WEEK TWO

❏ Commentary

Here is part of an observation made by a health visitor, together with her evaluation.

Observation

Charlotte

2 years 5 months

At home

Charlotte is in the sitting room looking at a Ladybird book with her mother and grandmother. 'Nanny' has given her a lollipop which she licks and then puts in a beaker.

Mother: 'Tell Nanny about these animals, darling, while I make us all a drink.'

Nanny: 'What's this, Charlotte?' [Points to page]

Charlotte: 'Cat – go mow, fish go – [opens and closes mouth], sheep – go baa, cow – go moo, chicken – go cuck, pig – go.' [Snorts and dissolves into laughter]

Nanny: 'Well done, Charlotte. Aren't you a clever girl.'

Charlotte: 'Ch'lotte cever girl, Nanny.'

Charlotte licks her lollipop then drops it on the carpet, picks it up and holds it out to her Nanny.

Nanny [pretends to lick the lollipop]: 'Thank you, darling.'

Charlotte [screws up her face]: 'Stick, stick, all stick, stick.'

Nanny: 'What do you want me to do with it, dear? Oh I see. Take the fluff off. There you are, Charlotte.'

Charlotte: 'Fuff all gone, Nanny.'

Mother returns with tray of drinks and some biscuits.

Mother: 'Do you want some juice, Charlotte?'

Charlotte: 'More jus mummy, pease.'

Evaluation: Charlotte has an extensive vocabulary of single words and some short sentences. She often imitates new vocabulary, sometimes incorrectly, and knows many animal sounds. Although she can make herself understood through her increasing store of language, she also communicates through gestures and facial expressions. Occasionally Charlotte initiates a simple conversation but has the ability to understand quite complex adult language and can follow instructions.

The beginnings of spoken language

You have already started to think about your own language biography and some of the theories which attempt to explain human language development. In this section we will look at the progression of language development from pre-birth to the age of three.

Pre-birth to twelve months

Research has shown that babies in the womb respond to both internal body sounds and external sounds. Evidence suggests that pre-birth babies learn to recognise their mother's voice and may also respond to music being played. Those of you who have had children of your own may well recognise some of these points.

We have already seen that very young babies communicate using non-verbal cues, and during the first two months of life they make sounds which relate to their physical condition, so for example they will sneeze, gurgle, burp or cry. From around two months babies produce the vowel sound 'ooooo'. This cooing often encourages the carer to return the cooing sound, thereby initiating the first stages of oral interaction.

By six months of age babies are beginning to play with and use the sounds they make to interact or 'converse' with others in a more specific way. From this period onwards the baby begins to use her communication skills quite deliberately to gain attention and to imitate and play with sounds.

Observations made of babies aged between six and nine months have identified the development of babbling, in which the baby begins to join two syllables together and produce long repetitive strings of syllables such as 'mamamamamama', often for her own amusement when alone. This seems consistent with the view of Chomsky, described earlier, which focused on an inbuilt language acquisition device. While babbling, the baby is also practising articulation and, importantly, producing sounds which the carer or key worker will shape into words for her.

At around nine months the baby begins to respond to adult actions and sounds, imitating them and repeating them with the encouragement of applause or praise from the adult. The baby begins to join sounds together to produce phrases which are very similar to real speech. She begins to respond to her own name and to her immediate carers and family members. This period is sometimes known as a period of 'scribble talk' or 'expressive jargon'.

Twelve to thirty-six months

In the second year of life the young child will continue to develop his understanding and use of specific words. He will also begin to use the context to derive further meaning. Using all the cueing strategies – vocabulary, gesture, facial expression and body language – toddlers can follow simple instructions. The toddler develops an increasing vocabulary, often totalling several hundred words, which he can combine into short 'sentences' of two or three words and use to pose questions.

Between eighteen and thirty months it is common for the child to talk continually to herself and to others while playing, but often much of what she says is unfamiliar even to her carers or key workers. From thirty months onwards the child's vocabulary extends rapidly and she will generally understand many more words than she uses in conversation. There is often evidence of an increasing use of questions, particularly relating to *why* and *who*.

During the period from twelve to thirty-six months there may also be evidence of the child extending his use of the words he has overheard by applying them to alternative situations and contexts. For example, an eighteen-month-old boy began to use the word *more* to mean *water*. 'His mother realised that, when he came to the back door to have his toy watering can refilled, she was asking, 'Do you want some more?'' (Lindon 1993).

Another example is of a sixteen-month-old girl who usually indicated that she wanted to get out of her high chair by trying to climb out and making a series of utterances. As she began to climb out, her mother would usually try and interpret her message by asking 'Do you want to get out?' Some time later, in the same physical context the little girl used the word *out* to seek help in actually climbing *in* to the high chair (Ferrier 1974).

Ferrier suggests that many of the early utterances and attempts to apply rules and vocabulary are idiosyncratic. The pattern of language used by the carer or key worker is largely 'repetitious, context-tied and ritualised' (p 76). This means that everyday activities such as bath time, going to bed and waking up are often greeted with the same phrasing, for example, 'Are we going to play in the water?', 'Night night, darling!' or 'Upsadaisy!' This repetition and contextual information helps the child to begin to make sense of the messages she is receiving.

I am sure you can think of examples like this, where a child has applied a phrase or word learned in one context to another situation. For example, children sometimes begin to call all men 'daddy' or all four-legged animals 'dog'. Think about some examples from your own experience, and perhaps talk to friends or colleagues about their recollections.

■ Activity 4 A

Re-read this section on the beginnings of spoken language and underline or highlight any references to ages and key characteristics of early communication. For example, in the subsection headed 'Pre-birth to twelve months' I suggested that by *six months* babies are beginning to *play with sounds* and to *converse* with others.

Use your selection to make a time line from pre-birth to three years which shows the progression of skills in early communication.

You can use this time line to reflect further on some of the observations you have been making as part of Activity 3.

❏ Commentary

Have a look at the following example showing a record of Charlotte's language development. (You read one of her observations as part of Activity 3). The student used the mother's 'Baby Diary' to track Charlotte's language development in her first year. Compare this time line with the key points you have selected for the first year of life.

From Charlotte's first days *mother used to clap her tiny hands together and say, 'Clap hands, clap hands till Daddy comes home.'*

*When **only a few months old** Charlotte would rock and croon when mother sang. When she was hungry or uncomfortable she murmured 'mum mum' to herself, meaning she was miserable.*

*At **four months** she said 'mum-mum' or 'mam-mam' or 'dad-dad' clearly without associating the sounds with a specific person, object or situation.*

*At **five months** she would sometimes utter these sounds with pleasure, as if she enjoyed making the sound and hearing herself make it.*

*By **six months** she called 'mam-mam' 'dad-dad' when she was wet or unhappy. When mother spoke words of comfort Charlotte would repeat 'mam-mam' as though in gratitude.*

*At nearly **seven months** she started to associate 'dad-dad' with her father and clearly say the sound when he attended to her.*

*By about **seven and a half months** Charlotte was using 'mam-mam' in response to her mother as she always spoke to her saying 'Mama can hear you' or 'Mama has made you clean again', etc.*

*At **eight months** she said 'nan-nan' and would smile and wave her arms and legs in pleasure.*

*At **nine months** she said 'wow-wow' and 'd'tee' (dirty).*

*At **ten months** she added 'dodee' (dolly) and 'teddy'. Sometimes she muddled sounds unless an adult said the correct word first. Then she would correct herself by imitation. She understood many things and would respond to suggestions such as 'Go and find your teddy'. She said 'baby' and because mummy was pleased she called all objects 'baby'.*

*At **eleven months** she could find things not in view.*

*When **almost a year old** she added some new words to her vocabulary, but her understanding of words had greatly increased. Once she had learned to stand and walk her range of exploration was widened and her speech began to develop quickly. She said 'dee-dee' when listening to a clock and made sounds such as 'Bmm, click, yum-yum'. Charlotte called the cat 'mew' although her parents used the word 'pussy' ...*

Learning the rules of language

Before we move on, return to your observation notes for Activity 3 and have a look at some of the following points. First of all, I am going to refer back to the observation of Lydia that was included in the materials for last week. You may remember that she was the girl in the reception class who was doing some writing.

Parts of the observation provide a good example of a child who is able to apply some of the rules of language in a particular context. Lydia knew a lot about spelling, letter sounds, beginnings of words and words within words. Even as a new entrant to her class she was able to apply her previous knowledge to the current task of writing. Remember when she said that she knew how to spell her name, and talked about 'L for lamp lady' and later how she developed S W J S into the correct spelling for sandwiches.

The observer also noted times of Lydia communicating through gesture and expression. The following extract makes the point.

9.37 am. *Lydia stood sucking her index finger, right hand, and watched the teacher writing a sentence for another child. She caught the teacher's eye. The teacher asked Lydia to read what she had written and then asked her to try and spell her next word, which was 'talk'. Lydia did not respond. She joined in to help another child with a word that he needed.*

9.39 am. *Stands up and leans over her writing. Sucks finger again and watches the teacher. Waves her paper at the teacher but does not speak. 'What do you want?' the teacher asks. Lydia reads out her sentence: 'I could not talk.'*

Can you see that by careful observation you can note how skilful Lydia was in expressing needs and showing her feelings with minimal verbal contact. She made use of eye contact, body language and gesture to gain the teacher's attention. She was also able to initiate conversation with an adult, as described last week when she approached the student directly for the spelling of 'sandwiches'. Yet she never approached her teacher in the same direct manner.

The next example shows a younger child than Lydia also using and applying her communication skills:

> When I went to the shops I saw two children by the amusement rides which are outside the supermarket. An older child was already having his ride and a younger sister (not yet using speech to communicate) was using all of her body language, gesture, expression and utterances to indicate by her tone and volume that she too wanted to have a go on this ride.

You will all probably have very different examples and observations, and will hopefully have gleaned some additional information about your particular child's language development. I hope you will continue to make observations of this kind, drawing examples from across the age range.

In the first part of this week's unit, you have extended your knowledge of the various theories of language development, considered the progression of skills from birth to three years of age and begun to undertake some focused observations of a child to help you to clarify your understanding of key points.

In the next section we will look at children's cognitive development, building on what you already know as a learner and as an educator.

What is 'cognitive development'?

In Week One I began the unit by asking you to think about your own experiences as a learner and as an educator. We also started to look in broad terms at the nature of learning and considered some of the factors which influence learning, as well as how children learn.

Drawing on your experience as a learner and your work with young children, you will be aware of the notion that learning never stops, that it is a life-long process. In Unit 1 you considered how children develop physically, emotionally, morally and linguistically, in different ways and at different rates. However, some elements in the processes of learning seem to be common to us all. In this section you will extend your knowledge and understanding of the various processes which constitute cognitive development, and consider some of the theories which attempt to explain how this development takes place.

In this unit so far you have been reading texts, developing understanding, and recalling incidents from your childhood or workplace. You have also engaged in some problem solving, trying to work out how to do some of the activities or record your observations. Sometimes you have reflected on your learning and taken stock to see where you are and what to do next. All these activities have involved you in using a series of cognitive processes.

The term 'cognitive development' refers to all those processes such as language, memory, perception and problem solving which enable us to acquire and develop our knowledge. In the *Oxford Dictionary* 'cognition' is described as 'the action or faculty of knowing'. We will consider how young children develop this faculty of knowing; how they begin to make sense of their world, learn and apply rules, interpret actions and events and apply knowledge in a range of contexts.

One of the most influential psychologists of this century was Jean Piaget. His research, which began in the 1920s, has had an enormous effect not only on the study of developmental psychology but also on what happens in early childhood centres. In the following sections I will summarise some aspects of Piaget's theories about cognitive development, in particular his idea of stages of development, and the principle of children being active and individual learners. We will then go on to consider some criticisms of Piaget's work. Finally we will move on to look at the impact of his research on the education and care of young children, and at some more recent developments in cognitive research. I have listed some additional references at the end of this week's unit for those of you who wish to explore Piaget's work in more detail.

Piaget's model of cognitive development

In brief, Piaget believed that:

- all children are active learners trying to make sense of their world

- all children go though discrete stages of learning and development

- all children learn and think in a different way from each other and from adults

- individual children play a crucial role in their own development.

Assimilation and accommodation

We have already seen how children try to develop their communication skills, interpreting sounds and gestures and applying rules. Piaget believed that as a young child experiences new activities or events and tries to explain or make sense of them he will add or *assimilate* this knowledge or experience into existing ideas or structures. This process is balanced by what Piaget called *accommodation*, where the child is able to adapt to the new experience and engage in higher-order skills of problem solving.

These ideas may be quite difficult to understand at first. The main point to remember is the emphasis on children constantly adding to and adapting knowledge as they engage in each new experience.

■ Activity 5 A

Last week, the first activity asked you to think about something you had recently learned and to identify factors which affected your learning. Think again about something new that you have learned. It could be the same example as in Week One or a different learning situation.

Make a list of all the new things you experienced and assimilated. Look at this example first to help you:

New experience:
Someone showing me how to make play dough.

Assimilation:
I tried to make some and my friend helped me to remember the process. I felt as if I could repeat it then without any help or reminders to put the salt in!

Accommodation:
I replaced the old idea that 'my play dough was always too crumbly' with a new idea that 'I can make smooth, malleable play dough'.

Adaptation:
Now I will be able to use play dough in more contexts, for example in the play corner.

Having read the example, think about how you have subsequently adapted or accommodated new learning into new situations.

❑ Commentary

Some of the students with whom I work are returning to college to undertake further training, having already gained a qualification elsewhere. They all have experience of college life, assignments and getting to know tutors, but they are still assimilating details of the rules, routines and environment of their new college, adding information to their previous experiences. Now, after some weeks at college, I see they can accommodate this learning, adapt it and make use of it in new situations that are put to them during their course.

I hope you have been able to identify similar experiences yourself.

The process of cognitive development

According to Sara Meadows (1986) we are all involved in the twin processes of assimilation and accommodation. Although one aspect may dominate from time to time, these two processes are essential in providing what she describes as 'structures of cognition'. This means that we begin to develop a set of rules, procedures and categories of events which eventually enable us to live our lives in a logical and organised manner. We gradually build up our experience and understanding of the world, constantly taking in new information and relating it to what we already know and adapting knowledge to meet new situations. This activity continues throughout our lives.

Piaget also looked at how this cognitive development proceeds. The model that he proposed is very complex, but I want to highlight four main factors for you to think about as you work through the rest of this unit:

- the maturation of the nervous system and a properly functioning brain (These physiological factors affect the rate of cognitive development, as briefly discussed in Unit 1)

- the importance of physical experience and active involvement of the learner (which we discussed last week)

- the influence of social interaction with peers and adults (We will look at this in more detail next week)

- the overall interaction between assimilation and accommodation, which is also known as *equilibration*

The last term is the most complex, but briefly it includes three phases:

- In the first phase we may be reasonably satisfied with our own understanding or explanation of an experience and so are said to be in a state of *equilibrium*

- But then we may gradually become unsettled or dissatisfied as we see other examples or talk to others. We may then move into a state of *disequilibrium*

- Finally, we manage to reassess the situation, overcome any of the earlier worries or shortcomings of our previous explanations and so reach a more stable state of *equilibrium*.

An example of equilibration is given by Siegler (cited by Lee and Das Gupta 1995), who describes a child who thought animals were the only things that were alive. This is a common belief among four to seven year olds. The girl began to hear other people refer to plants as being alive and she became unsure about how you knew if something was alive. At this point she could be said to be in a state of disequilibrium. Gradually she began to discover similarities between plants and animals in terms of needing certain conditions for growth. Her new knowledge about both plants and animals helped her to achieve a more stable state of equilibrium. She now realised why plants and animals could be said to be alive and was no longer anxious about her original ideas and explanations.

Your own experience, or your observations of the children you care for and work with, will confirm that having your thinking challenged or being presented with a range of alternatives is a vital prompt in moving thinking forward and promoting further development.

Stages of development

Piaget was not just interested in the process of cognitive development, he was also curious about the stages of development that children go through. He believed that all children go through certain periods or stages in their life, and that these stages occur in the same order for every child. You cannot miss out a stage or jump ahead, according to Piaget. He outlined the four stages as follows:

- *The sensorimotor stage*, from birth to around two years. The child explores her world through her physical actions. As she begins to develop language and thought, this stage is said to come to a close

- *The pre-operational stage*, from two years to around seven years. At this stage the child is talking, has started to represent things symbolically and can sort out objects into categories or groups, but is not yet capable of logical thinking. According to Piaget, the child at this stage is also very egocentric, that is, he is unable to see things from anyone else's point of view

- *The concrete operational stage*, from seven years to around twelve years. The child can more easily take on the views of others. She will be able to classify and organise objects, but is still heavily dependent upon immediate concrete experiences

- *The formal operational stage*, from twelve years onwards. The child is now able to manipulate ideas in his mind, begin to reason, formulate and test hypotheses.

For the purposes of this unit we will only consider the first two of these four stages.

UNIT 2 WEEK TWO

■ Activity 6 B

In this activity I would like you to observe a child aged seven or under. Look particularly for evidence of the child as an active learner. Record any evidence which you think could be interpreted as:

- the child trying to make sense of the world

- the child bringing previous experience to bear on the activity

- the child classifying or grouping items

- the child showing evidence of reasoning at this stage.

❑ Commentary

Here is one of my observations:

In the early childhood unit, a girl aged three years ten months was at the writing table. She went to the trays and took a piece of tracing paper and a picture, picked up a bulldog clip and assembled the picture and tracing paper together. She chose a pencil and started to trace. She stopped and held the paper at arm's length to look at it. She put the pencil into the pencil pot and then chose another one. She continued to trace her picture. She lifted up the tracing paper sometimes to see underneath. When she had finished tracing, she pulled the paper out of the clip and put her tracing into her own drawer.

What previous experience was this girl bringing to the activity? What do you think she already knew? Here there seems to be evidence of the girl bringing previous experience to bear on the activity. She did not hesitate but went directly to the materials she wanted and used them effectively. In fact, the day before she had been watching an adult doing a similar tracing activity with a small group of children.

What was she learning from this activity? Ask yourself similar questions about your own observations.

The insights provided by Piaget's research have had a significant and long-lasting influence on early and primary education in this country. Educators began to consider the importance of trying to match the kinds of activities and experiences they provided to children's ability to cope with them, according to their supposed stage of development. His research also promoted the notion of children as active learners, and many teachers began to think about ways of facilitating this active exploration in the classroom.

Alternative views of cognitive development

As with the theories of language development we looked at earlier, Piaget's work was also widely criticised. Other psychologists and researchers believed that by identifying specific stages linked to ages Piaget actually underestimated the abilities of young children. It was felt that his model drew attention to what children could not yet do rather than identifying what they could do at a particular time. During the 1970s and 1980s there was a major shift in thinking about children's abilities and how they learn, which in part arose from the research of Margaret Donaldson and her colleagues (Donaldson 1978). Although she criticised aspects of his work, Donaldson still subscribed to Piaget's model in principle. You will find it useful to read her book entitled *Children's Minds*, details of which are given at the end of this unit.

Donaldson believed that if children were asked to undertake a series of activities or problems within a context with which they were familiar, they would be able to think and reason at a higher level than Piaget had indicated. She suggested that sometimes children could not understand what the adult meant, or could not see any reason for the adult to be asking a particular question. This was quite different from not understanding the content of the task.

Donaldson decided to repeat some of Piaget's tasks but with some changes in the way she administered the tests, paying particular attention to the context of the task. She believed that if adults provided meaningful tasks which made sense to the child and which drew upon his previous experience, he would be able to undertake more complex activities and apply previous knowledge.

Donaldson argued that the knowledge we bring with us to a learning task is of crucial importance, but so too is the context of the experience. She suggested that the meaning of the activity was *embedded* in the situation. For example, young children playing in the play corner will often display their knowledge of reading and writing as they play with the message pad by the telephone or make up a menu card. They might be making marks on a page, but they do know how messages or menus or giving your order to a waiter works. This knowledge is based on their previous experience, and their activity in the play corner is embedded in a familiar context which enables them to use their existing knowledge.

As in the first part of this week's unit, you can see that there are many theories which attempt to explain how we learn and develop. It is important that you also develop your own beliefs and views based on what you have read, observed and experienced as a learner and as an educator.

Continuing research into cognitive development

In the final section of this week's study we look beyond the work of Piaget and consider some of the current thinking about cognitive development. In much the same way as there have been different views about language development, with behaviourist and nativist research constantly being challenged and revisited, there has been a continuing debate about cognitive development.

Many researchers are now arguing that all our cognitive processes and knowledge are essentially inbuilt – part of our genetic make-up. For example, Jerry Fodor (1983) suggests that we all have a set of genetic systems or structures which enable us to make sense of our world. We may still need all the experiences described by Piaget, but we also have innate abilities that enable us to manage and organise the input we receive. This is not a new idea; we have already looked at a similar view put forward by Chomsky. Unit 1 also focused on the *transactional* view as it applies to children's personal, social and emotional development. However, in the last decade, with our increasing knowledge of genetics and the brain, researchers have again taken this idea as a starting point for further exploration.

According to Lee and Das Gupta (1995), part of the neural network in our brain contains subsets of *modules* which enable us to process information that we gather from aural, visual and tactile input. They suggest there is a module that can process language input, another for mathematical or musical input, and so forth. Other researchers believe that our brain operates within various *domains*. These can be quite broad areas of knowledge such as language or science, or they can be specific, concerned with contained areas of knowledge such as the use of verbs in language or understanding force fields in science.

There is still a lot of debate and controversy about these theories, but it is interesting that the research is moving towards a focus on the internal structures of the brain as a means of explaining how we have developed our cognitive and linguistic skills.

Overall we have a set of theories or attempts to explain or interpret children's actions and their development. No one can say for sure how children learn or develop, but knowledge of these theories should inform our thinking, enable us to draw some conclusions for ourselves and encourage us to think about how we promote children's learning and understanding. I believe the key principle to remember is that even if we do have inbuilt mechanisms for learning and language development, children still need to have first-hand experiences, adult support, a positive learning environment and so forth. This relates back to the Nature versus Nurture debate that you explored in Unit 1.

In next week's study you will explore some other theories of cognitive development as we consider the growth of understanding and the role of the adult in that process. You will read research by Vygotsky and Bruner and will return to thinking about the links between language and cognitive development.

Review of the week

We are now at the end of this week's study, during which you have:

- reviewed your own language biography

- considered the development of spoken language from various theoretical viewpoints

- completed some observations of children using, imitating or applying rules of language

- looked at different models of cognitive development and become more familiar with alternative views and recent research.

In the final week of this unit you will have a chance to look in more detail at some of the research about children's learning and ways to promote greater understanding.

Take time now to look back over this week's work and consider the following:

- Which aspects of spoken language have interested you most?

- How might a greater knowledge of the theories of cognitive development influence you in your contact with young children?

Before moving on to Week Three, make sure that you complete the review activity below. It should help to pull together some of the threads from this week and also help you to begin to articulate your own views.

■ Review activity 7 A

In this review activity I want you to take stock of your position, what you think about Piaget's views, and why you agree or disagree with what he has said, before we move on to some alternative views that provide a further challenge to the Piagetian model considered here.

Use the grid provided overleaf to help you to focus on the main points about Piaget's research as *they are described in this unit*. (There are many aspects that I have not touched on this week. You can read about them in more detail in Donaldson's book).

Think about your own views and beliefs and try and give some examples from your own reading or observations which support the points you want to make.

I have included some points to get you started.

❏ Commentary

You will need to revisit much of the information contained in this week's unit as you begin to look more closely at what it means for you and the children in your care. Evidence is widespread as to the effects of Piaget's work on educational provision for nursery and primary age children, as well as the influence he has had on early years practice more generally, for example with parents and play groups. I hope you will continue to develop your own theories and use the knowledge gleaned from your work experience to increase your understanding of how children learn.

Key points noted in reading	I think this is true because...	I am not sure about this because...
Children are active learners...		
Children pass through discrete stages of development at specified ages		
Physical exploration and experience is important		
Young children are egocentric		

Further reading

Donaldson, M. (1978) *Children's Minds*, Glasgow: Fontana

Lee, V. and Das Gupta, P. (eds) (1995) *Children's Cognitive and Language Development*, Oxford: Open University Press/Blackwell, Chapter 2

There is a full list of references at the end of Unit 2.

UNIT 2 WEEK TWO

Unit 2: Week Three
Language and learning

Objectives

In the final week of this unit on cognitive and language development we will explore some of the ways in which adults can build upon a child's early experiences and so promote greater understanding. By the end of the week you should:

- be acquainted with theories of cognitive development which examine the social aspects of learning

- consider the role of adults in supporting learning

- be able to identify some of the similarities and differences between the theories proposed by Piaget, Vygotsky and Bruner.

Activities

This week in Activity 5 you are asked to do some observations for a 'mini audit' of your professional practice, or the practice in the early childhood centre you are visiting. I suggest that you arrange about one hour in total for these observations, if possible in an early childhood setting. This time will allow you to do some short 10-15 minute observations and also have time to write up notes and comments.

About this week's study

During this last week of study for Unit 2 you will be considering the ways in which theories about children's learning can be influential in practice. You will be asked to reflect upon your own role as a professional or parent educator in the light of theories discussed.

The adult's role in promoting understanding

Last week we looked again at Piaget's theories and the influence of his research on models of early childhood education today. We also looked at what some of his critics had to say and at the ways in which our thinking and understanding about learning are constantly evolving. One of the key principles of Piaget's work was his emphasis on the child as an individual and active learner, striving to make sense of the world. This view did not really give much room to the importance of others in the learning process.

A look at some of the work of Vygotsky

Lev Vygotsky was a Russian psychologist, born in the same year as Piaget. He was also very interested in how children learn, but particularly in how knowledge is transmitted or passed on from one human to another. To this end he focused on the part played by language and communication and the effects of social interactions on learning. He criticised Piaget for apparently ignoring the context of situations and the cultural and historical factors that Vygotsky believed would significantly affect a child's learning and development.

In brief, Vygotsky believed that although a child was able to develop some skills and knowledge through personal exploration, it was only by interacting with others, maybe her parents or siblings, that she was able to extend her experience. He emphasised that all children grow up within a social group – their immediate carers, the extended family and the local community. They never grow up in isolation. The ways in which these social groups relate to, behave towards and talk to the child will all serve to shape her knowledge and understanding of her world. Therefore Vygotsky argued that these factors should not be ignored or minimised.

You will remember from last week that Piaget did not dismiss social interactions completely, claiming that it was through discussion with, and observation of, others that a child's stable equilibrium might be challenged and further thought and understanding developed. However, Vygotsky took this notion much further. He suggested that children could often tackle more complex tasks if they had some help or support rather than being left to their own devices. He believed that when children undertook a task independently – for instance, building a tower of bricks – they were performing at what he called an *actual level of development*. With some adult help the child's ability might be stretched slightly, and instead of continuing to build a four-block tower the child might progress to making a taller tower or a series of towers that were connected in some way. He suggested that children had a *zone of proximal development* (ZPD) or, more simply, a 'next' area of development which could only be achieved with the help and support of others.

The zone of proximal development lies between what the child making a tower can do by himself and what he can do with support. Vygotsky believed that the adult's interaction in the task, perhaps showing the child alternative ways to make the tower, or suggesting that the child choose different blocks for the base, would develop the child's experience and knowledge about building towers and provide him with the tools of thinking and learning.

Vygotsky maintained that the adult's interactions and the quality of those interactions were crucial, and he emphasised the importance of *co-operative* or *supported learning* not just between adult and child but also between children. Although Piaget suggested that social interaction was important in helping a child to develop cognitive processes, it was Vygotsky who saw that interaction as central to the development of cognition. Vygotsky also differed from Piaget in highlighting what children *could* do rather than pointing out what they could *not* do. The focus on what children are able to do, starting from where they are and building on that knowledge, underpins the whole of this unit.

■ Activity I A

When I was planning this week's unit I began looking back at key points in my learning as a teacher and realised that I could identify certain people – adults and children – who had played an enormous part in my continuing professional development. These people had intervened or questioned me, or commented on my teaching, and in doing so they provided a structure for me to move forward in my understanding about teaching and learning, enabling me to grow both personally and professionally.

I wonder if you can also identify significant people who have influenced your learning and development, and the effects of their influence on the way you now work or think about young children. Jot down a list of names. Think about why those names have come to mind and how those people have influenced you.

❑ Commentary

Here are some of the people I thought about:

- certain tutors at college who made me think hard about why I was doing what I was doing

- fellow students who encouraged me when teaching experience got really tough

- particular head teachers whom I worked for, who made me think completely differently about how children learn. When I left my first teaching post I thought all schools were the same as that one, and it was not until I moved to another school that I realised how much there was to learn!

UNIT 2 WEEK THREE

- individual children who have asked pertinent questions, who have made me think about the significance of my role, my expectations of them, my attitudes towards them

- parents of children I have worked with who helped me to recognise the importance of partnership with parents

- c olleagues who have encouraged me to go on to further study and research.

You will have a different list, but I am sure you will be able to identify key people who have affected how you work and think and have probably influenced your choice of career – perhaps encouraging you to think about working with young children.

Bruner's views on the role of the adult

We met some of Bruner's ideas about language development last week. He was also very interested in how children learn, and you will notice that some of his ideas are similar to Vygotsky's, while at the same time he acknowledged some of the theories put forward by Piaget. For example, he firmly believed, as did Piaget, that children are actively trying to make sense of their world, but he emphasised the crucial role played by adults in developing children's thinking skills. He also recognised the significance of the context of learning and in this respect held views similar to those of Donaldson.

Bruner has been described as an *interventionist*. He thought we should not wait for a child to reach a particular stage, but that we should 'intervene' to help the child to move forward in her thinking. Bearing in mind the activity you have just done, I would add that this should be a life-long process which does not stop with children! Bruner is famous for saying in 1963 that 'any subject can be taught effectively in some intellectually honest form to any child at any stage of development'. He meant that you can teach most children anything, but the content and the approach need to be at an appropriate level. The child will revisit the content of the lesson several times during her lifetime, each time extending and deepening her understanding.

This view was quite different to Piaget's notion of the child passing through discrete stages of development. In describing a process of revisiting experiences and knowledge, Bruner referred instead to a 'spiral curriculum' where the child initially learns through his actions, then later through images and pictures of the world and finally through the symbols of numbers or words, at which point the child is at last free from the immediate context. Bruner called these stages *enactive, iconic* and *symbolic.*

Can you think of experiences like this in your workplace, where a child revisits something several times? Here are some examples that show how children revisit particular ideas, in this case the concept of shoes!

A toddler is playing with her shoes, pushing them off and trying to put them back on again. She puts one shoe upside down, lays it across the top of her foot, pushes her toe in at the heel end of the shoe, then puts it on her head, swings the shoe round by the lace which has come undone.

She could be said to be at the *enactive* stage, exploring the feel, the use, the properties of her shoes.

An older child draws a picture of herself wearing her new shoes. She tells her teacher about her picture and explains that she got some new shoes at the weekend. She is very pleased with them. Later she adds the rest of her family to her picture and all of them are wearing shoes.

This child could be said to be at the *iconic* stage.

A six year old is helping her sister to get dressed for school and shouts down to her mother, 'I can't find Sara's other shoe!' She continues to give a long commentary on what will happen if Sara does not find the shoe quickly.

This child could be said to be at the *symbolic* stage.

Bruner suggests that one of the key roles of the adult is to provide a structure for the child's learning which will enable her to go beyond the immediate information or experience and so to generate new ideas and ways of looking at the world. Bruner used the term *scaffolding* to describe this process. He used this everyday term to explain how an adult could provide a structure or scaffold of steps and ladders which would enable the child to move on to a higher level of understanding. Bruner emphasised the importance of ensuring that the steps were not too great – enough to challenge the child but always allowing her to progress to the next point.

Bruner and his colleagues identified several components of scaffolding:

- First, gain the attention or interest of the child

- Then simplify the number of actions or responses the child needs to make, thereby making it more likely that the child will be successful

- Maintain the child's interest by giving encouragement and feedback

- Identify the key points of the task, so the child knows whether or not she is 'on task'

- Finally, provide a model for the task: demonstrate how it might be done by giving a similar example or answer.

■ Activity 2 A

Have you supported a child recently by providing some structure or scaffolding to promote her understanding? In this activity I would like you to use the set of components outlined above to write a description of what you did. The following questions should help you to focus your thoughts.

- At what point did you decide to give feedback, to let the child know that he was on the right lines?

- How did you use your comments to encourage further responses from the child?

- What do you think the next step would be for the child?

❑ Commentary

I wonder when you gave feedback to the child? There are various reasons for giving children feedback, many of which seem obvious. Children need to know

- how they are getting on

- whether you are pleased with them

- if they have understood something.

They are usually keen to know what you think about them, whether you like them and so forth. Giving children some information about all these aspects is an important part of our role, but we do not always give much thought to it.

Approaches to supporting learning

Many student teachers I have known complain that they do not know for several weeks how they are getting on with their courses. It takes a long time for them to complete assignments, get them marked and be able to act upon any advice given by their tutor. We do not always take opportunities to scaffold their learning, to sit with them and work through a task, commenting along the way as to their progress. We do not always do this with young children either, but I think it is vital that we do so. Bruner suggested we should use feedback as a means of maintaining the child's interest. What do you think?

Look at these two scenarios and see what you think about the different approaches.

Student A explains to all the children at the beginning of the morning what she wants them to do until playtime. She tells them about three different activities, all of which they are familiar with from previous lessons. She sends them off to work in groups while she hears one child read. She had previously put all the equipment out on each table for them. She is interrupted by the noise levels after ten minutes. She tells the children to be quiet and get on. They should all know what they have to do. The children generally remain off task and distracted. The student manages to hear one more child read to her.

Student B explains to all the children at the beginning of the session what she wants them to do; she asks one or two children to explain the tasks to her so that she can check their understanding of what is expected. She tells the children to get the resources that they need and start the activities. She then calls a child to read with her. She decides to stop the children at intervals, to check how they are doing, she gives further input or instruction, praises the efforts of two or three children, asking them to share what they have done with the rest of the class. This seems to encourage further activity and she continues to share a book with another child.

What were the main differences between these two approaches? What do the two scenarios indicate about the contexts of learning in these two classrooms? Can you see how the second student used intervention strategies skilfully to move children forward and maintain momentum? The input did not always come from her, she encouraged active participation by the children.

Now have a look at this example (adapted from Matthews 1978, pp 181-182) of a conversation between a three year old and an adult. Look at the way the adult uses questions to help the child to solve a problem.

Emma [3.10]: I've made a bunny but he won't fit into his house because his ears are too big. They stick out.

Adult: What could you do to make him fit in?

Emma: The house will have to get a bit bigger.

Adult: Or what else could you do?

Emma: I'll give him some smaller ears. [She removes ears and replaces them with thinner ones which are of a similar length.]

Adult: Is that better?

Emma: No, he still won't fit in.

Adult: What shall we do about that, then?

Emma: I'll make a new house for him, because he still won't fit in.

Teacher: Why won't he fit in?

Emma: I don't know.

Adult: Are these ears [indicating the replacement ones] any smaller than the round ones [original type]?

Emma [measures the two types against each other for comparison]: Yes, but only a little bit. [She then reconstructs the house from a triangle shape to a circle shape into which the rabbit does fit.] Now look at, his house – he fits now, and he can look out.

Now have a look at a second example of an interaction between a child and an adult. Jot down any differences that you notice between this interaction and the first example.

Adult: Which hand are you going to hold your pen in?

[Robert (2.11) picked up the pen in his right hand.]

Adult: That's right. What are you going to draw? How about one of your cars?

[Robert started to draw. He drew a round shape on the paper, moving the pen anti-clockwise.]

Adult: That's right, are you going to put wheels at the bottom? [A little later:] Where are the wheels?

Robert: It hasn't got any, it's an apple.

Adult: Can you draw me a car?

Robert: I can draw another apple. [Continued to draw round and round]

Adult: That's not an apple, that's scribble.

[Robert drew all over his paper.]

Adult: Would you like a drink?

Robert: Yes.

Adult: And a biscuit?

Robert: Yes.

[Robert asked for another biscuit.]

Adult: Just one more then. How many have you had?

Robert: Three.

[When he had finished his drink and his biscuit, Robert did some more drawing.]

■ Activity 3 A

Now that you have read both examples, think about these questions:

- What were the main differences between the two approaches?

- What kind of responses did the questions from the two adults receive?

- In what ways can the adult's use of questions help children to explore their world?

- In what ways can the adults' use of questions limit this exploration?

❏ Commentary

The main feature of the first adult's interactions with Emma seem to be her care and patience. Her choice of questions helped Emma to find a solution to her problem. Did you notice how most of her questions required Emma to really think about an answer? She couldn't easily give a one-word reply. For example, when the adult said 'What could you do to make him fit in?' she was inviting some kind of explanation. This type of question is a very important tool for encouraging thinking. It is sometimes called an *open-ended* or *broad question*. If you asked one or several children this question you could expect to get a range of answers and possibilities. The adult could see from the responses she got how Emma was thinking, what she understood, how she was tackling the problem.

You probably noted the different style of the adult talking to Robert. She also asked lots of questions, but mostly got one-word answers from Robert. The type of questions she asked are sometimes called *closed* or *narrow* questions. You would usually expect to get a one- or two-word answer in response to this kind of question. How much do you think this adult found out about Robert? How do you think her interactions might have made him feel? Her manner seemed very harsh to me, dismissing his drawing because it did not meet her expectations.

Developing effective questioning skills

Developing our skills in using questions and our knowledge of the variety of different questions that we could ask is very important. There are occasions when you need to ask a closed question, to check that a child has understood something, or perhaps recognises a number symbol and so on, but you also need to make sure that you ask more open-ended questions that will encourage the child to think and to solve problems.

Although some might regard Bruner's theory of scaffolding as just another complex theory proposed by a psychologist, it clearly does have relevance to our everyday life, as we have seen in the example of Emma. Many parents, carers and early childhood educators provide this kind of scaffolding all the time as they interact with young children. However, you need to be aware of the cautious response given by some researchers to the notion of scaffolding. Pollard (1990) has suggested that although the adult does have a vital role in supporting children's thinking, the *quality of the questions* asked by the adult and the *skill and sensitivity* needed to make the most of these interactions is not always acknowledged. Pollard suggests that it is not enough just to interact with the child; an adult must also be aware of what the child already knows and what she needs to go onto next.

At this point I would not be surprised if you are saying to yourself, 'So what! I have spent three weeks looking again at all these theories of learning and development, but how will they help me in my work?' It is not at all surprising if you are feeling like this because you have been grappling with some complex information. I do not think for a moment that you will stop in the middle of an activity at work and think to yourself, 'Now is that in line with Piaget or Bruner, and what about Vygotsky?' But I do think that an awareness of the basic theories which underpin some of our current principles of early years education is crucially important for you as you strive to deliver high-quality provision for the children in your care. A knowledge of the various theories of development, and an understanding of the ways in which they can influence early childhood education and care, will enable you to adopt a more informed, reflective approach.

Before we move on, take time to reflect on the material you have just read.

■ Activity 4 A

In Activity 7 last week you used a grid to identify the main points from Piaget's research that were included in the materials, thinking about whether you agreed with them or not. Now make up your own chart to show the main similarities and differences between Piaget, Vygotsky and Bruner.

❏ Commentary

Completing this activity may have reminded you of some of the extracts from the DfE report *Starting with Quality* that we looked at in Week One. The connections between the theories and the principles of practice contained in that document were brought into sharp focus for me. The extracts from the report include reference to the following:

- Although all children follow sequential patterns of development, every child is unique

- Young children's learning should be embedded in what is familiar

- The process of learning is as important as the content

- There should be continuity and progression

- Children need certain skills and concepts in order to make sense of, and apply, their knowledge

- The setting of learning should reflect the child's social and cultural background

- The role of the adult is highly significant

- A variety of learning situations is important.

Can you see how familiar phrases keep appearing both in descriptions of the theory and in practice? Have a look at the chart that I have made about the differences and similarities between Piaget, Bruner and Vygotsky. I have picked out some of their key beliefs and looked to see which are common to all three researchers, showing where each theorist put most emphasis. Compare my thoughts with your own grid and see if you think their ideas match up with the principles contained in the DfE report.

Key features	Piaget	Vygotsky	Bruner
View child as an active learner	✔	✔	✔
Emphasised the importance of social interaction		✔	✔
Interested in the role of language	✔	✔	✔
Focused on what the child is not yet able to do	✔		
Emphasised the importance of the context of learning		✔	✔
Stressed the importance of previous experience		✔	✔
Recognised the need to provide meaningful situations for learning			✔
Believed children go through discrete stages of development	✔		

I believe Piaget, Vygotsky and Bruner have all made a significant contribution to our understanding of how children learn, and I can identify their influence on my own practice. But what do you think? Do you believe that the children in your workplace are learning in discrete stages? Do you recognise the comments about meaningful learning situations? Talk to a friend or colleague about these different views if you can.

■ Activity 5 AB

The main purpose of this activity is to help you to think about what you have been reading and consider ways in which theory about cognitive development might be represented in your workplace.

Using any of statements taken from your own grid or from mine, I want you to do a mini audit of some of the features of practice at your workplace. For example, you might choose these three phrases:

*   focus on what the child is not yet able to do

*   importance of social interactions

*   meaningful situations for learning.

I do not mind which statements you choose to focus on you need to think about which areas would be most useful for you. Complete an audit by observation and/or discussion with colleagues at your workplace. Use these detailed notes and reflections to assess current beliefs and practice where you work.

Here are some questions that might help to get you started. In your workplace do you:

*   notice immediately what a child cannot do when you start to assess her language use?

*   identify strategies that she is using, for example when reading?

*   record difficulties and strengths in daily observations?

*   plan learning opportunities which encourage social interactions?

*   provide meaningful contexts for role play that relate to the children's experiences?

❑ Commentary

Obviously I do not know which aspects you have chosen to focus on in your audit, so I am going to pick one or two that interest me to give you an idea of the kinds of things that might arise from this kind of activity.

The first thing that I noticed when I started looking at my own workplace, talking to colleagues and to students, was how much I took for granted and assumed about my co-workers. I thought they would all think like me! When I looked at the principle of starting with what a child does know, I thought everyone would shout out 'Of course – we all start with what the child knows and brings to the learning!' I found instead that on their first visits to early years centres lots of the students at my college are often overwhelmed by what the children apparently do not know. They express great concerns about the child who 'cannot read a thing' or 'doesn't recognise a single numeral'. They seem to panic over first impressions and make sweeping assumptions about what children do and do not know.

It takes a lot of discussion and sharing of ideas, doing some of the activities you have been doing in this unit, before some students begin to recognise the importance of finding out what a child actually *can* do. Time spent on finding out what a child can read, what English she does understand, how she feels about herself and her work is crucial. It is only by focusing on these things that you will be able to make decisions about what she will need to do next and how you can help her to move forward.

You might be saying, 'Well, a panic reaction is not unexpected from students, but it is different in my workplace where there are more experienced professionals.' This may often be true, but sometimes we do focus on what children cannot do as part of our assessment strategies. Sometimes our observation and assessment of children's learning can point to areas for development, or areas of concern that need to be addressed. You will need to engage with this kind of debate throughout your course. Look at the theories and the practicalities from all angles and viewpoints and gradually develop your own views. Do try to talk to someone about the things you have discovered in your audit.

Developing positive relationships

We have looked at the use of scaffolding, adult interventions and the use of questions as various means of extending understanding and promoting cognitive development. Another aspect of the adult role which I believe to be very important is making relationships with young children. This skill can affect not only a child's cognitive development but also their social and emotional well-being. We will just touch on some of the issues here, but I have suggested some additional reading for those of you who are interested.

Starting with Quality suggested that 'all adults working with under-fives need to ... build relationships of trust with children so that they develop the confidence to take risks in a secure setting and can accept, use and overcome minor failures' (DES 1990, p 12). The adult plays a crucial role in establishing and maintaining positive relationships with young children, as research centred on the home has shown. Think of Judy Dunn's study, for instance, discussed in Unit 1 Week Two. Yet there is less research evidence on the links between successful education and the relationships that exist between children and educators outside the home.

Chris Marsh (1994) has devised a quality framework for assessing relationships that might affect teaching and learning. What follows is a summary of what she sees as the benefits of positive adult-child relationships. As you read the summary, think about some of the relationships that you have had with teachers in the past, and consider how these may have helped or hindered your learning. Marsh suggests that the following framework could be used by early childhood centres to gauge the effectiveness and quality of relationships within each establishment (Marsh 1994, pp 146-151). I have selected a few aspects for the

UNIT 2 WEEK THREE

purposes of this unit, focusing particularly on the quality of interactions, in keeping with the material provided earlier.

- Children need a secure environment built upon sound relationships as a prerequisite to good education

- Adults should be able to view situations from the child's perspective

- Adults should know as much as they can about the children in their care, in order to sense any potential unease, acting upon early signals to pre-empt or minimise any distress

- Adults should value children's contributions and provide positive comments and praise; adults should listen responsively and attentively and provide supportive body language and gestures

- Adults should keep children informed of events and changes which are going to take place.

How do you rate yourself against these statements? Can you see how these issues relate to the whole development of the child – their social, emotional, physical and cognitive development? I think the framework developed by Marsh is a really useful tool for monitoring our effectiveness as 'significant adults'.

The social aspects of learning and language development

So far this week you have looked at the theoretical stances elaborated by Vygotsky and Bruner, and you have begun to consider the role adults can play in supporting and promoting children's understanding through the use of language, questioning and the relationships that develop between child and adult. In the final section of this unit we consider some of the social aspects of learning.

Vygotsky and Bruner were particularly interested in the social aspects of learning and the ways in which knowledge is passed on from one generation to the next. They both recognised the importance of cultural influences on a child's cognitive and language development. Vygotsky drew attention to the social origins of children's language, developed within an environment of immediate family and the wider community.

Research by Haste

Recently researchers have begun to look again at the differences and similarities between Piaget's view of the individual learner and Vygotsky's view of the child exploring her world within a social context. One of those who has been interested in the links between these theories is Helen Haste (1987), a student of Vygotsky. Her research highlighted the importance of cultural experiences. She considered the interrelationship between Piaget's and Vygostsky's theories and in doing so compared individual cognitive development and the value of social interactions with the effects of the contexts and settings in which the learner is placed.

Haste was particularly interested in cultural and historical traditions, and in line with Vygotsky's view she also believed that the immediate environment, society and culture provided a framework for the child's continuing construction of meaning. Smith and Cowie (1991, p 352) have adapted her model of the links between individual, interpersonal and social aspects of learning as shown in Figure 2.1 overleaf. This diagram summarises the main aspects of development that we have considered in the unit. It reminds us that the child is an individual learner, making sense of her world in a context of interpersonal or social interactions with adults and peers and within the framework of the society into which she is born.

UNIT 2 WEEK THREE

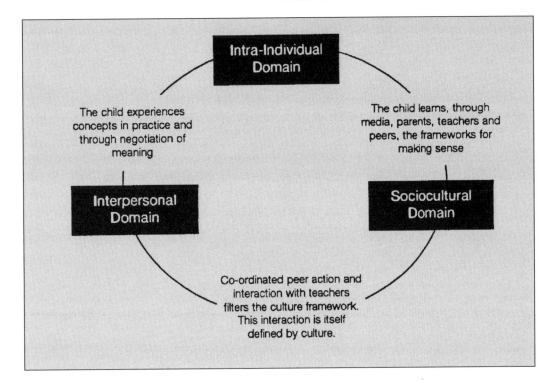

The child experiences concepts in practice and through negotiation of meaning

Intra-Individual Domain

The child learns, through media, parents, teachers and peers, the frameworks for making sense

Interpersonal Domain

Sociocultural Domain

Co-ordinated peer action and interaction with teachers filters the culture framework. This interaction is itself defined by culture.

Figure 2.1

It is important that as early years educators we are aware of the multitude of factors that affect the learning and achievements of the children in our care. Whatever context you work in – school, class, nursery or early childhood centre – the children will be affected by these factors.

Children's learning and development will also be affected by the attitudes and expectations of the educators they meet. In the final section of this unit I want to look at some of the research which challenges certain long-held attitudes, assumptions and deficit models of children from ethnic minority and lower social class groups. I also want to re-emphasise the value of the learning that takes place within the family and community.

Research by Tizard and Hughes, and Wells

Tizard and Hughes (1984) were interested in the language development of young children. Their research looked particularly at the language experiences of children at home and at school; they found that 'working class children were as competent at conceptual and logical thinking as middle class children' (cited by Docking 1990, p 19). Despite this finding, Tizard and Hughes still found nursery teachers who believed that parents did not make any significant or positive contribution to their child's education. The following comments, cited by Docking, indicate some of the common misconceptions held by this group of teachers about parental contributions:

'In an enabling middle-class home, yes, but not round here.'

'To be frank, the children are better off at school.'

These teachers were unaware of how many parents were working really hard to try and teach their children to write and how many were sharing books and reading with their children each day.

This research reminds us that *all* parents, in all types of families, use meaningful and effective language. Parents know about their children's needs and interests and can usually engage in genuine interactions with their children in a way that many teachers are unable to do.

UNIT 2 WEEK THREE

Another researcher, Gordon Wells (1987, 1991), was also interested in language development and how children actually learn to talk. His research showed that 'children learn to talk by engaging in conversations with other people' (Wells 1991). He emphasised the importance of the *quality* of conversations and suggested that variations in the quality of interactions significantly affect the rate of a child's language development. Wells found, just as Tizard and Hughes had done, that all families engage in meaningful use of language. He noted that, although the type of language varied between the families he studied, there was a marked similarity between children in the amount of language they had learned by the time they started school. He suggested that in these pre-school years children are not simply learning to talk. Every conversation they have provides them with evidence and an opportunity to learn *how to talk*, but simultaneously every conversation provides them with an opportunity to learn *through talk* because of course in their talk they meet their culture's view of the world as it is expressed in the language they are speaking (Wells 1991, p 16).

Can you see how important it is for early years educators to be aware of the significance of social aspects of learning? The research by Wells, Tizard and Hughes has highlighted the importance of knowing about the social context in which children spend most of their time. Their studies have drawn our attention to the rich potential for learning that is part of children's everyday lives. Opportunities do exist beyond the range of early childhood centres that make provision for young children's learning. In the same way, in Week One of this unit I highlighted the value of play and of everyday experiences such as shopping in the development of children's cognitive skills.

Research by Gregory and Rashid

More recent research has looked at the differences between home and school language use. Gregory and Rashid (1993) undertook their research with a group of Bangladeshi children aged between five and six in the London borough of Tower Hamlets. Instead of focusing on a deficit model of bilingual children being 'disadvantaged' in terms of their educational achievement, they chose to look at the potential cognitive and linguistic *advantages* of being a bilingual learner at school.

These children attended Arabic and Bengali classes for approximately seven and a half hours each week after they had finished their primary school day. During these community classes the importance of learning to read and write in the mother tongue was emphasised as a sign of belonging to the culture. Children were also taught to read Arabic in order to achieve their ultimate goal of reading the Qur'an. The reading texts provided at the Bengali classes represented life in Bangladesh. Through the use of such materials the children were made aware of the life and culture of Bangladesh. They were encouraged to use the illustrations to interpret the text and to discuss their reading with their teachers.

Have a look at the following example of a text read by the children (Gregory and Rashid 1993, p 8), written phonetically to represent Bengali script:

> Bella Gello
> Hash, murghee gore thullo
> Dade ke oushod doew
> Mamyr hathe dhod-bhat
> kheate beecha mitte
> gore ache baba pulle
> Pathi chapta shatte pitte

This is translated by Gregory and Rashid as follows:

The day has gone,
Put the ducks and chickens in the house,
Give grandmother her medicine.
In auntie's hand there is some rice pudding,
Which is very sweet to eat,
Inside there are different sweetcakes
[The Bengali text then lists some names.]

The researchers point out that the children developed enough literacy skill to read and write this kind of text within three months of starting the classes, yet their attainment in their English school work was in many cases very poor by comparison. The study challenges the commonly heard view that children from ethnic minority groups may get few literacy experiences at home. In fact, like these children, they may have a rich diet of literacy.

Review of the unit

We are now at the end of the week and of this unit. Take some time to look back over the week's work as you did in Weeks One and Two. Think about the things that have interested you most, especially any ideas you want to try out in your workplace.

■ Review activity A

In the final activity for this unit I would like you to undertake a review of the key points contained in this week's study. Consider the ways in which your role as a parent, carer or early childhood educator can be developed to promote greater understanding among the children in your care.

How do you promote children's understanding now? Think of some examples – maybe a story time which encouraged children to reflect on or question some topic, or an activity that led to further exploration.

Consider other ways you can use to promote greater understanding now that you have read this unit. Talk this through with a friend or colleague if you can.

❏ Commentary

In this week's study we have looked at the work of Vygotsky and Bruner, who have helped us understand the importance of the adult's role in developing children's understanding. We have considered the idea of 'scaffolding' as a way of supporting learning, and we have highlighted the adult's use of questions and the quality of conversations with children. In the final section we considered the social aspects of learning and the value of experience gained in the family and in the community. All these elements have a part to play in the work we do to 'promote greater understanding' among young children.

I hope you have enjoyed working through this unit and have found the tasks valuable and illuminating. The field of child development is an exciting and dynamic area, and research is continuing to shape our thinking and inform our practice. I have only been able to touch on one or two aspects in this unit, but I hope you will go on to consider other theories and viewpoints as you continue your studies. The list of further reading provided at the end of this unit should help those of you who would like to continue with these explorations.

Further reading

Barratt-Pugh, C. (1994) 'We only speak English here, don't we? Supporting language development in a multilingual context', in Abbott, L. and Rodgers, R. (eds) *Quality Education in the Early Years*, Buckingham: Open University Press

Drummond, M.J. (1993) *Assessing Children's Learning*, London: David Fulton, Chapter 6

UNIT 2 WEEK THREE

Unit 2 References

Week 1

Athey, C. (1990) *Extending Thought in Young Children: A Parent Teacher Partnership*, London: PCP

Conner, C. (1993) 'Is there still a place for learning in school?', *Cambridge Journal of Education*, No 20, Spring

DES (1990) *Starting with Quality: The Report of the Committee of Inquiry into the Quality of the Educational Experiences Offered to Three and Four Year Olds*, London: HMSO

Drummond, M.J. (1994) *Assessing Children's Learning*, London: David Fulton

Drummond, M.J., Rouse, D. and Pugh, G. (1992) *Making Assessment Work: Values and Principles in Assessing Young Children's Learning*, Nottingham: NES Arnold/NCB

Holt, J. (1989) *Learning All the Time*, Reading, MA: Addison-Wesley

Hughes, M. (1986) *Children and Number: Difficulties in Learning Mathematics*, Oxford: Basil Blackwell

Isaacs, S. (1948) *Intellectual Growth in Young Children*, London: Routledge and Kegan Paul

Sylva, K., Roy, C. and Painter, M. (1980) *Child Watching at Play Group and Nursery School*, London: Grant McIntyre

Vygotsky, L.S. (1978) *Mind in Society*, edited by Cole, M., John-Steiner, V., Scribner, S. and Souberman, E., Cambridge, MA: Harvard University Press

Week 2

Donaldson, M. (1978) *Children's Minds*, Glasgow: Fontana

Ferrier, L.J. (1974) 'Some observations of error in context', reprinted in Lee and Das Gupta (1995)

Lee, V. and Das Gupta, P. (eds) (1995) *Children's Cognitive and Language Development*, Oxford: Open University Press/Blackwell

Fodor, J. (1983) *The Modularity of Mind*, Cambridge, MA: MIT Press

Hearle, P. (1992) 'Language acquisition', in Bain, R., Fitzgerald, B. and Taylor, M. (eds) *Looking into Language: Classroom Approaches to Knowledge about Language*, London: Hodder and Stoughton

Herriot, P. (1971) *Language and Teaching: A Psychological View*, London: Methuen

Lindon, J. (1993) *Child Development from Birth to Eight: A Practical Focus*, London: NCB

Meadows, S. (1986) *Understanding Child Development*, London: Unwin Hyman

Skinner, B.F. (1957) *Verbal Behaviour*, New York: Appleton-Century-Crofts

Week 3

Bruner, J.S. (1963) *The Process of Education*, New York: Vintage

Docking, J. (1990) *Primary Schools and Parents: Rights, Responsibilities and Relationships*, London: Hodder and Stoughton

Gregory, E. and Rashid, N. (1993) 'The Tower Hamlets work: monolingual schooling, multilingual homes', Paper presented to Goldsmiths' Literacy Research Group, Faculty of Education

Haste, H. (1987) 'Growing into rules', in Bruner, J.S. and Haste, H. (eds) *Making Sense,* London: Methuen

Marsh, C. (1994) 'People matter: the role of adults in providing a quality learning environment for the early years', in Abbott, L. and Rodgers, R. (eds) *Quality Education in the Early Years*, Buckingham: Open University Press

Matthews, G. (1978) 'Mathematics', in Fontana, D. (ed) *The Education of the Young Child*, London: Open Books

Pollard, A. (1990) *Learning in Primary Schools*, London: Cassell

Smith, P.K. and Cowie, H. (1991) *Understanding Children's Development*, 2nd edn, Oxford: Basil Blackwell

Tizard, B. and Hughes, M. (1984) *Young Children Learning*, London: Fontana

Wells, G. (1987) *The Meaning Makers: Children Learning Language and Using Language to Learn*, London: Hodder and Stoughton

Wells, G. (1991) 'Language and learning', in Proceedings of conference held at Oxford Polytechnic School of Education, 20 April

Unit 3:
A curriculum for the whole child

Linda Miller

Contents

Unit 3: Week One
What do we mean by 'curriculum'?

Objectives

In Units 1 and 2 you focused on children developing and learning. In this unit you will explore the role of the curriculum in supporting and extending children's learning and development. By the end of this week you should:

- have considered definitions of 'curriculum'

- understand how the diverse range of early years provision affects the curriculum offered to young children

- know about the range of frameworks which can help in planning the early years curriculum

- understand the term 'developmentally appropriate practice'

- have reflected upon the curriculum in your own workplace or another early years setting.

Activities

As in Units 1 and 2, a number of 'A' and 'B' activities are spread throughout this unit. These are designed to encourage your active participation as a reader and learner. In Week One they are based on the text and do not require you to spend additional time in your workplace or another early years setting.

About this unit

In this unit you will be considering frameworks and models of the early years curriculum and how they influence practice, as well as how they arose from diverse philosophies and traditions. You will have the opportunity to develop your own skill in observing young children learning. You will also be asked to observe and evaluate practice in an early childhood centre, focusing in particular on the curriculum offered and the involvement of parents in planning and provision.

The hidden curriculum

In Week One of this unit you will be invited to examine what is meant by the term 'curriculum' and will be introduced to the notion of the 'hidden curriculum'. In Units 1 and 2 you considered the development of the whole child. You will have learned from this work, and no doubt from your own experience, that young children learn from all their experiences and interactions from the moment of birth and even before. The majority of these experiences and activities will be unplanned and take place within the family or other settings where very young children are cared for, maybe in a childminder's or relative's home. This may be long before formal schooling begins. The following observation of five-year-old Katie, who has only just begun primary school, provides an example.

Katie is in the sitting room lying on the floor on her back looking at a book belonging to her older sister. Her mother comes into the room.

Katie: Have you read this book?
Mother: No.
Katie: It's very interesting. It has chapters.
Mother: Do you know what chapters are?
Katie: No.
Mother: Bits of the story.

Katie's mother then bends down to look at the book with Katie and to show her the different sections of the book which make up the chapters.

In this short incident you can see how Katie's mother had the opportunity to catch what Lilian Katz (1995) has called the 'unreturnable moment' – the teachable moment that will not return. Katie's mother made a sensitive response, making good use of the incident to help Katie to expand her knowledge of the new word 'chapter', having made a good guess that Katie was probably unsure of the meaning. This sort of teaching and learning happens on a 'moment to moment' basis (Leichter 1984) between adults and children when they spend time together and know each other well.

Many such moments occur in the everyday life of the home and family, but inevitably some are missed by busy adults going about their daily tasks. This is sometimes referred to as the 'curriculum of the home' or the 'hidden curriculum'.

■ Activity 1 A

Try to recall one or more similar incidents from your own experience.
*   What did the child do or say?
*   How did you respond?
*   What were the conflicting demands on your time?
*   What do you think the child learned from your response or interaction?

❑ Commentary

Did it surprise you that the incident you recalled could be described as curriculum? You have probably realised that this depends upon how you define the term.

Consider another example of the hidden curriculum.

Two-year-old Grace had been playing with the adult toy known as 'Newton's Cradle' in which balls suspended from strings can be set in synchronised motion by knocking the first ball against the remaining line of balls. She had taken this down from a low shelf, and as the object was pretty sturdy she had been encouraged in her play by the four adults in the room. She had a delightful time working out how to make the balls move and enjoying the noise they made. Eventually, tiring of the toy, she made a grab from the same shelves for a rather delicate stone carved elephant brought back from a recent trip to India. There was an immediate cry of alarm from her father, who was a visitor to the house, who told her sharply not to touch. She was told it was naughty. Her bottom lip curled and the game ended, despite the hosts' concern that Grace should not see this as a 'naughty' act.

What is Grace to make of this? That some things you can take off shelves, some things you can't. How is she to know which? No doubt she will learn through experience what she can and cannot touch. Meanwhile the adults might like to think about how this can be made easier for her to learn.

I hope you can see from my examples and your own that the hidden curriculum refers to activities and experiences which are unplanned and which the adult may not be conscious of, but from which children are learning. The term can apply equally to the curriculum in early childhood centres. The ways in which adults respond to aspects of culture or gender can influence what children learn. For example, it is important to plan activities so that both girls and boys are involved in large block and construction play, as this is often an area traditionally dominated by boys.

In settings outside the home which aim to educate and care for young children in groups, capturing the unreturnable moment or waiting for spontaneous learning experiences to present themselves cannot be relied upon, therefore some teaching and learning experiences need to be planned. This unit invites you to explore what a curriculum for the whole child in the early years means. We begin by considering definitions of the term 'curriculum'.

What is 'curriculum'?

Before I offer some definitions for you to consider, I will invite you to contribute your own ideas about this term. As someone who has considerable experience of schools, if only as a pupil, but quite possibly in other roles, you will have your own ideas. Perhaps you had a favourite subject when you were at school or college. You no doubt found some subjects easier than others. Why was this? The people who taught you may have influenced your perceptions of the curriculum offered.

■ Activity 2 A

Write down all the words and ideas that you associate with curriculum. What does the word mean to you? Can you form your ideas into a definition? Write it down.

❏ Commentary

Here is how other people have described the curriculum. Compare their ideas with your own. Note any similarities between the definitions given.

The curriculum for young children includes:

* all the activities and experiences provided for them by adults

* all the activities they devise for themselves

* the language that adults use to them and that they use to each other

* all that they see and hear in the environment around them. [Drummond et al 1989]

the concepts, knowledge, understanding, attitudes and skills that a child needs to develop. [DES 1990]

The creation within the school of a flexible, developing learning environment in which the child will actively pursue his interests with the guidance and support of adults. [NICC, undated]

The curriculum: Includes *all* the activities and experiences (planned and unplanned, formal and informal, overt and hidden) from which a child learns. In its broadest form, the curriculum involves a consideration of the process of learning (how a child learns), the learning content (what a child learns), the learning progression (when a child learns) and the learning context (where and why a child learns). [Ball 1994]

You may be surprised to see some of the ideas included, such as unplanned experiences or the activities which the children themselves devise. Does the inclusion of 'all that they see around them' surprise you? Then again, you may have included ideas which are not in the above definitions.

What ideas about curriculum do these definitions have in common? For example, two of them specifically mention the role of the adult and the context of learning. The learning environment is included in three definitions. How important are these factors? Can you draw upon your own experience in early years settings to support their inclusion?

Try to share your ideas and discuss these definitions with someone else. You may also come across other definitions in your studies which you would wish to include.

UNIT 3 WEEK ONE

Inside and outside the home

What these definitions seem to share is a very broad view of the term curriculum. They include the more formal curriculum such as the National Curriculum which specifies what children should know, understand and do. This covers young children between the ages of five and eight years with whom this unit is concerned. However, they also include the informal curriculum (overt or hidden) which involves learning, for example, about the self and the social world in which we live and which can occur in most settings in which young children may be found. These aspects of learning and developing were explored in the previous two units. A distinction made by Kathy Sylva (in Ball 1994) between the curriculum of the home and education and care in group settings outside the home, is that in the latter the nature of the educational curriculum needs to be made explicit, as does the agreed means for fostering it.

So what does curriculum look like in early childhood centres? Well, this rather depends upon the influences of a number of important factors such as the following, suggested by Blenkin and Yule (1994):

*   the quality of the setting in which provision is made
*   the level of resourcing
*   the qualifications of the adults working in those settings.

There are of course other criteria which could be used depending upon people's values, beliefs and priorities. Provision for early years education in the United Kingdom is diverse and presents a confusing picture. Children are not obliged to begin school until the term after their fifth birthday. In fact the UK is one of the few countries, along with Ireland and the Netherlands, where children begin formal schooling at such an early age. In other countries children may remain in day care settings, kindergartens or other pre-school groups until around the age of seven. In the UK children under five have no curricular entitlement. However, a general and internationally agreed use of the term 'early years' includes children from birth to eight years of age, the age range covered by this unit. In the UK children within this age range will be found in primary schools where they will be taught according to the National Curriculum. If under five, they may be at home or in the home of a childminder, friend or relative. Others will be in a wide range of group settings, some of which may not have an explicitly formulated curriculum. Attempting to consider what curriculum looks like within this very diverse range of settings is a somewhat daunting task. Let us therefore take a closer look at the diversity of early years provision in the United Kingdom in order to consider the implications of this for the curriculum.

The diversity of early years provision

Before reading on, please carry out Activity 3. This will help to 'set the scene' for the issues that are discussed in this section.

■ Activity 3 A

Make a list of all the group settings outside the home which provide care and education for young children within the birth to eight years age range. Note down who you think offers the provision, e.g. LEA, Social Services.

❏ Commentary

Compare your list with this one:

*   childminders
*   local authority day nurseries/family centres
*   private day nurseries, partnership and workplace nurseries
*   LEA nursery schools and classes
*   infant classes

- playgroups
- private nurseries and other schools
- combined nursery centres
- family centres
- out of school/holiday clubs

You may have thought of some forms of provision not included in the list. Did the range and diversity of provision surprise you? Did you realise that early years provision is organised in so many different forms by the public, private and voluntary sector? You can check the providers by taking a look at Figure 3.1, which is taken from the *Start Right* report (Ball 1994).

Responsibility for early years provision is split between two government departments, the Department of Health and the Department for Education and Employment (DfEE). This provision receives limited public funding; in fact the UK has one of the lowest levels of publicly funded pre-school services in Europe (Sylva and Moss, cited in Ball 1994). It is also unevenly distributed; for example, in rural areas there may be little or no choice, so parental choice of early years care and education is not a reality.

You may by now be wondering what this discussion has to do with curriculum. Consult Figure 3.1 and carry out the next activity.

■ Activity 4 A

Figure 3.1 shows the range of provision, which you considered in the last activity, but also lists other important factors.
- Look at who offers the provision
- Look at the length of the day
- Look at cost differences
- Look at the age range of the children
- Look at the ratio of adults to children
- Look at the nature and length of training of the adults.

Now write down how each of these factors might affect the curriculum experienced by young children in the different settings (I gave you some clues above). Explain your reasons for saying this.

❑ Commentary
In your response you may have noted some of the points which I outline below.

The history of early years provision
Figure 3.1 divides the types of provision into those establishments concerned with offering mainly care, those concerned with education and play, and a few such as combined nursery centres that attempt to provide both. You may have questioned why this is so. Tricia David (1990) devotes a chapter to this in her book *Under Five – Under Educated?* Here is a summary of the main points.

During the Second World War women were needed in the workforce, so the Ministries of Health and Education, working together, set up nurseries to provide day care for under fives in working hours. After the war some provision was transferred to the Ministry of Education with a cut in hours and days of provision. Subsequently the two ministries failed to co-ordinate their efforts. The Ministry of Education also failed to implement the requirements of the 1944 Education Act, which had placed the duty to provide nursery education in the hands of the local education authorities (LEAs). Subsequent financial restrictions on education meant that resources were channelled into the statutory sector. Consequently there has been little growth in publicly funded nursery education.

UNIT 3 WEEK ONE

Figure 3.1: Day care and pre-school education, 1991: provisions and costs in Great Britain

Type of Provision	% of children	Hours	Ages	Approximate cost to parents	Provided by	Staffing	Training	Ratios
Day care	**% of 0-4**							
Childminders	7%	All day	0-4	£1.50 per hour £50 per week	Private arrangement	Registered childminders	Variable. No national requirements	1:3 0-5, 1:6 5-7
Local Authority day nurseries/family centres	1%	Some all day, some sessional	0-4 (but few under 2)	Means tested	Local Authority Social Services	Mainly nursery nurses	NNEB/DPQS/BTec SNNB/SCOTVEC Units	1:3 0-2, 1:4 2-3, 1:8 3-5
Private day nurseries, partnership and workplace nurseries	2.5%	All day	0-4	Between £45 - £150 per week depending on age of child and availability of subsidy	Employers, private organisations and individuals	Nursery nurses, some untrained staff	at least half staff must be trained - as above	1:3 0-2, 1:4 2-3, 1:8 3-4
Education and Play	**% of 3-4**							
LEA nursery schools and classes	26%	Termtime: usually 2½ hours a day	3-4	Free	Local Authority Education	Nursery teachers, nursery nurses	Degree and PGCE/BEd, NNEB	1 (teacher):23, 1 (all staff):10/13
Infant classes	21%	Termtime: 9am - 3.30pm	mainly 4	Free	Local Authority Education	Primary teachers, teaching assistant or nursery nurse recommended	Degree and PGCE/BEd, NNEB SNNB/SCOTVEC Units	1:30/40 (better if nursery nurse employed)
Playgroups	60% (1.8 children per place)	Usually 2½ hours for 2/3 days a week, some all day	2½ - 4	£1.70 per 2½ hour session	Parents and voluntary groups	Playgroup leader	Foundation course/diploma in playgroups practice	1:8 3-5
Private nursery and other schools	3.5%	Usually 9am - 3.30pm	2½ - 4	Various fees	Private individuals and organisations	Not specified: often teacher or NNEB	Unknown	1:8 3-4, 1:20/30 5+
Services on which there are no national statistics								
Combined nursery centres	about 50 centres	All day	0-4	Education free, day care means tested	Local authority education and social services, sometime health and voluntary sector input	Nursery teachers, nursery nurses	as for nursery schools/classes and day nurseries	as for nursery schools/classes and day nurseries
Family centres (May include some LA day nurseries)	about 500 members of Family Centre Network (Dec.93)	Usually all day	Vary	Vary	Local Authority social services, health authorities, voluntary sector	nursery nurses, social workers, range of staff	Varied	Depends on nature of centre
Out of school/holiday clubs	700 clubs (Dec.93)	before and after school, holidays	Vary	Vary	Schools, leisure depts, voluntary sector	playleaders, community workers, volunteers	Unknown	1:8 5-7

UNIT 3 WEEK ONE

The influence of philosophy or tradition

The growth of the playgroup movement, recently renamed the Pre-School Learning Alliance (PLA), has been one attempt to fill this gap, as has the more recent expansion in private provision (Sylva and Moss, cited in Ball 1994). You will have noted that playgroups are the largest providers for children aged three to four years. Local authorities are only 'empowered' to provide day nurseries, for which they may charge parents (David 1990). The bringing together of day nurseries, private nurseries, childminders and playgroups under the Department of Health and Social Services (DHSS) umbrella means that educational experiences may not be a high priority, as traditionally health and social services provision has placed an emphasis on *caring* for rather than *educating* the child. This is something that the Pre-School Learning Alliance and the National Childminding Association (NCMA) are currently attempting to address through their training initiatives and publications. So one influence upon the curriculum offered will be the prevailing philosophy or tradition of the establishment concerned.

Educare

A more recent initiative is the development of combined nursery centres, which have attempted to bridge the false care/education divide. These centres are viewed by some as the way forward in offering quality experiences to young children and their families. They may offer, for example, parent education classes in addition to care and education provision for the children (Ball 1994; Whalley 1994).

According to Helen Penn (1995), who as assistant director of education in the Strathclyde region of Scotland was involved in one of the earliest of these initiatives, around 20 LEAs now claim to run a co-ordinated, integrated service for the under fives. This brings care and education together under one administrative roof. These centres offer a flexible combination of day care and nursery education and also support for families. Other authorities have attempted to bridge this gap by having joint working parties or a co-ordinating post funded by both administrative departments.

The curriculum offered in these settings has been described as 'educare' and the workers involved as 'educare teachers' (Penn 1995) or sometimes 'educarers'. This approach is based on the view articulated in the *Start Right* report (Ball 1994) that care and education are inseparable and that young children need both. However, these initiatives have raised some as yet unresolved problems in relation to common training routes and parity of pay for the wide range of workers involved.

Full-time or part-time educare

The length of time that children spend in any one setting will influence the nature of the activities and experiences they encounter. If children are placed in a setting for a whole day from 8 am until 6 pm or later, they will require for at least a good part of the day experiences that have some parallels with home. These include, for instance, time to rest or sleep, to watch television, to help with the preparation of food or to just be with a familiar adult. As we have seen from the above discussion, such experiences can take place within an educational framework. Alternatively, if children are spending just two to three hours in a setting, an emphasis on educational and play-based experiences is appropriate.

The age range of the children

The age range of the children will also be a factor in considering what is an appropriate curriculum. The idea of a key worker or child assignment system, involving a person to whom babies and young children can form an attachment and who can respond sensitively to the child's communications and needs, has been identified as important (Rouse and Griffin 1992). Brenda Griffin (1994), in her chapter which begins 'Look at me – I'm only two', writes about the importance of organising the nursery so that children under three have a place of their own to return to.

Staff training in diverse settings

The type of provision, particularly who the provider is, has implications for the curriculum since this is closely linked to the issue of staff training. You will see from Figure 3.1 that training requirements are very variable. Childminders, who care for more children under the age of four than nurseries, are not required to be trained, although the National Child Minding Association (NCMA) does offer courses. But who will pay for the courses, and when will childminders find it possible to attend them if they are looking after the young children of working parents? The playgroup leader may have followed a short one-year part-time training course (though I acknowledge that sometimes these are trained teachers or qualified nursery nurses taking some time out of their previous work role). However, they earn even less than most childminders, so the questions of payment and time and motivation for training are again raised.

If we look at LEA nursery schools and classes we can see that at least some of the adults are trained to degree level. However, even this is less reassuring than it might appear. Findings from a recent national survey have shown that 65.7 per cent of qualified teachers working with children under eight had received no specific training for working with pre-school children, and in addition 26.5 per cent had no initial training for children under eight (Blenkin and Yule 1994). At the moment this picture seems unlikely to change. The National Curriculum has required those involved in training and educating teachers to focus on subject knowledge. This has reduced the time previously spent on important areas such as child development.

In carrying out Activity 4 you may have asked yourself why private providers would wish to invest in training all their staff when only half are required to be trained. An alarming statistic which emerged from the national survey mentioned above is that around 10 per cent of adults working with young children had no qualifications. This raises a question about what is valued in a society which allows untrained people to work with one of its most precious resources. In what other profession would this be allowed? Would you, for example, be happy if the person who mends your car was similarly untrained? Inevitably the professional skills, knowledge and experience which adults in early years settings bring to their work will have a considerable impact upon children's learning and development and the curriculum offered. I will return to the important role of the adult later in this unit.

Funding and resourcing

Funding or resourcing of provision is of course linked to who provides. Resourcing is bound to be linked to some extent to the quality of the curriculum. Those of you who have worked in pre-school playgroups, as I have, will know about the time and effort spent in sweeping out the village hall after the previous night's Youth Club activities and the energy involved in getting out and putting back the stored equipment each day – taking time which could otherwise be spent in planning for and discussing the curriculum. How many displays did you lose because others using the room did not realise their importance? Life in my purpose-built reception class, funded by the LEA, was quite a different experience.

But what about the more subtle influences of funding on the curriculum? Private providers are reliant upon parental income for their fees. Suppose that parents think that children of two and three should be taught to learn their alphabet or write all the numbers to 20; how does this influence the curriculum experiences offered? To refer back to Brenda Griffin's article, is this what it should be like to be two?

A further threat is posed by the School Curriculum and Assessment Authority's document (SCAA 1996) for a pre-school curriculum for four year olds linked to 'desirable outcomes' for children's learning, which should be achieved by the time they begin school; for example, to write their names and to recognise letters of the alphabet. This could encourage providers to place emphasis on those aspects of the curriculum which are easily visible, but which may not be the most important. I will return to this point later this week.

This curriculum document is linked to the nursery vouchers scheme, in which vouchers will be exchanged by parents for a pre-school place in the state, private or voluntary sector. In the private or voluntary sector these will contribute £1,100 towards fees. State sector places remain free, but local authority budgets have been reduced and LEAs are expected to recoup money through the voucher scheme. Consequently, the initial evaluation of the pilot phase of the scheme suggests that many primary schools are taking an increasing number of four year olds, thus threatening the viability of playgroups and some private sector providers. This in fact reduces, rather than increases parental choice. (Source: *Guardian*, 1997)

There may be other points to consider which I have missed and which you noted when you were working on Activity 4. Perhaps you could discuss these with a friend or colleague. To summarise this section, I have tried to encour-age you to think about some of the influences which may affect curriculum provision in a range of early years settings. The final section for this week's study returns to the question: What does curriculum look like?

What does curriculum look like? Curriculum frameworks

The National Curriculum

You may have experience of the National Curriculum, perhaps from your own work in school settings or from your children's experience of school. No doubt you have followed the implementation of this curriculum through the 1988 Education Reform Act in newspaper and television coverage. It probably bears a strong resemblance to the subject-based curriculum that you experienced at secondary school.

The National Curriculum consists of subjects which children are expected to learn from the age of five. It is organised on the basis of four key stages. For the purpose of this unit we are concerned mainly with key stage 1, covering the five to seven years age range, although of course eight-year-old children are taught within key stage 2. The subjects include English, Mathematics, Science, Technology, History, Geography, Art, Music and Physical Education. For each subject, programmes of study set out what children should be taught and attainment targets set out the expected standard of children's performance.

Since the introduction of the National Curriculum there has been growing concern among people working both with and for young children that it is not an appropriate curriculum for young children. The activity below asks you to think about why this might be so. If possible, draw upon and give written examples from your own experience and debates in the media.

■ Activity 5 A

Try to list the possible reasons for the view that the National Curriculum is not an appropriate curriculum for children between the ages of five and eight. Look back to your work in Units 1 and 2 about how young children learn.

How do these views of learning and development tie in with your own experience of children being taught within the National Curriculum framework? If possible, give examples.

❑ Commentary

This is what other people have said (Blenkin 1994; Abbott and Rodger 1994):

- The child is not placed at the centre of the learning process; learning experiences do not stem from the child's interest and experience but from prescribed subject knowledge

- The National Curriculum focuses upon the product or outcomes of learning – what children must achieve rather the process through which children learn

- There is no place for spontaneity in the planning process or for unplanned or unintended learning outcomes

- The National Curriculum is led by the needs of society, the material demands of the economy and a concern for conformity. This reflects a concern with what children are to become rather than what they are here and now

- The curriculum is defined in terms of subjects rather than what is known about the ways in which children structure their learning

- It favours summative (end point) assessment and paper and pencil tests rather than observation of the ongoing process of learning

- It is having an effect on children under five in early years settings because of the 'downward pressure' on the pre-school curriculum

- It is leading some schools to emphasise sedentary 'table top' activities for children in reception classes.

A wide-ranging debate of these issues is offered in Blenkin and Kelly (1994). Other warnings have been sounded about the negative influences of the National Curriculum upon what is known to be good early years practice, particularly for children under five.

The National Curriculum and children under five

Starting with Quality (DES 1990) is an important report resulting from a government enquiry into the educational experiences offered to three and four year olds. It is commonly known as the Rumbold Report as it was chaired by Angela Rumbold, then a minister within the DES. The report states that there should be no question of a National Curriculum for children of this age, suggesting instead that what is needed is a flexible framework from which curriculum can be developed to suit a range of children in a variety of settings. The report warns against pressures which might lead to over-concentration on formal teaching and the attainment of specific set targets. It goes on to say:

> The educator working with the under fives must pay careful attention not just to the content of the child's learning, but also the way in which that learning is offered to and experienced by the child ... [DES 1990, p 9]

Desirable outcomes for children's learning

In 1995 the DfEE announced a new pre-school education voucher scheme described in the document *Nursery Education Scheme - The Next Steps* (SCAA 1996). Early childhood settings which satisfactorily offer a curriculum for four year olds which works towards learning goals called *Desirable Outcomes for Children's Learning* (SCAA 1996) can claim the vouchers worth £1100 per year. Six learning goals are defined, and can be summarised as follows:

- **Personal and social development**: how children play, work and co-operate with others

- **Language and literacy**: involving skills in talking, listening, reading and writing

- **Mathematics**: use of mathematical language; counting, writing and using numbers

- **Knowledge and understanding of the world**: understanding and exploring the environment

- **Physical development**: involving physical control, mobility, using space

- **Creative development**: expression through sound, dance and imaginative play

In the curriculum document explicit learning goals are set out which are thought desirable for children to achieve by the time they are five. Some outcomes are described in broad terms, as in creative development where 'children explore sound and colour, texture, shape, form and space in two and three dimensions'. Others, however, are more prescriptively described. In mathematics, for example, children are to 'recognise and use numbers to 10'. For all six areas, detailed links with the National Curriculum at age five are made explicit. Fears have been expressed that some of the more prescriptive elements of these learning outcomes may be rigidly interpreted by practitioners, particularly if they are among the large number whose education and training has been minimal. Mary Jane Drummond (1996) questions how such prescribed aims will be achieved by practitioners. In some cases she notes the approach may be 'enriching, educative and respectful of children's powers', though some outcomes may be achieved through less enlightened methods (p 8).

Frameworks for an early years curriculum

You will have seen from the definitions earlier in this unit that curriculum can be defined in a number of ways. It can also comprise varying approaches or frameworks. This unit could not cover them all, but some examples are High Scope/Key Experiences and the approaches of Montessori and Steiner (Drummond *et al* 1989 provides a concise summary of such approaches). Chris Athey's (1990) work on schemas (patterns of thinking and development) has provided new insights which we will consider in Week Two. The remainder of Week One will consist of looking at some approaches and frameworks for planning the early years curriculum.

Areas of experience

I said earlier in this unit that there is no curricular entitlement for children under five. There has, however, been broad agreement among early years educators about an appropriate framework for the early years curriculum, although, as you will see later in this section and in Week Two, ideas about the early years curriculum are still being researched and developed. In 1985 HMI in a discussion document, *The Curriculum from 5-16*, offered a framework covering nine areas of experience and learning. These are:

- aesthetic and creative
- human and social
- linguistic
- mathematical
- physical
- scientific
- moral
- technological
- spiritual.

It also includes four elements of learning:

- knowledge (that is, facts)
- concepts (or ideas)
- skills
- attitudes.

The publication *Aspects of Primary Education: The Education of Children Under Five* (HMI 1989) shows through case studies and examples of good practice how this framework can be used to provide a curriculum that meets the needs of children under five. It has since been endorsed by the Rumbold Report.

UNIT 3 WEEK ONE

One criticism of this framework is that it still reflects the notion of subjects. It also favours a delivery model of curriculum in which the adult passes on to children what Marion Whitehead (1994, p 28) calls 'existing cognitive, cultural tools, for example, literacy or scientific understandings, from a skilful tutor'. However, the Rumbold Report stresses the importance of building on the child's *existing* knowledge, understanding and skills. This puts the child at the centre of curriculum planning, using his or her own knowledge, skills and understanding to inform the educator in planning or facilitating learning experiences. The areas of experience are offered as a means of planning a curriculum which considers breadth and balance of experience.

The Rumbold Report says (p 9) that 'Careful planning and development of the child's experiences, with sensitive and appropriate intervention by the educator, will help to nurture an eagerness to learn as well as enabling the child to learn effectively.' The report also stresses the important role of social relationships and the fostering of positive attitudes towards learning. Play is seen as a vehicle for learning. I have seen Areas of Experience used as a planning framework for the curriculum in many nursery schools. A pictorial and slightly modified version is shown in Figure 3.2, which gives an indication of what children might experience and learn within these areas.

■ Activity 6 A

Consider the following scene:

A group of four children have been playing in the home corner of the playgroup. In the course of their play they have set the table for lunch with four knives, forks, spoons, cups and plates. Coloured utensils (cups, plates, bowls, knives, forks, spoons, napkins) had been provided by the playgroup staff, which led to the opportunity for the children to spontaneously colour match each place setting – blue, green, red and yellow. Rice cakes previously made by the children have been placed on each plate. The children have used language centred around checking if there were 'enough' cakes, looking to see that they all had 'one each', whether they needed 'any more'. One of the children had been shopping with some real money and a shopping list 'written' by another child. He had brought back some empty food packets containing familiar logos such as Weetabix, which were 'read' as they were unpacked.

Now refer to Figure 3.2. Using the Areas of Experience as a framework, write down which experiences you think the children covered in their play. Did one area dominate?

❏ Commentary

You may have decided that the children were engaged in mainly *mathematical* experiences. They were involved in counting, one-to-one correspondence and colour matching, and were using mathematical language such as 'enough' and 'more'. They were experiencing objects of different shape, size and colour. Ideas about money and shopping were involved.

You may also have decided that opportunities for *language and literacy* were present in the form of pretend writing (graphic representation) the shopping list and reading the print (with the help of familiar logos) on the food packets.

Under the heading of *human and social* you may have thought that the children were thinking about others as they checked if everyone had a cake. The child who was involved in shopping was rehearsing what he knew about the adult world and the world of work.

Under the heading *aesthetic and creative* the children were expressing ideas through imaginative play.

Planning within the 'areas of experience' framework

You may feel there are similarities between the areas of experience and the subjects of the National Curriculum, as I have discussed above. However, a crucial difference between these two frameworks is that, in planning through broad areas of experience, the curriculum

Figure 3.2 Graphic representation of the nine areas of experience.
Source: Curriculum Council for Wales (1991)

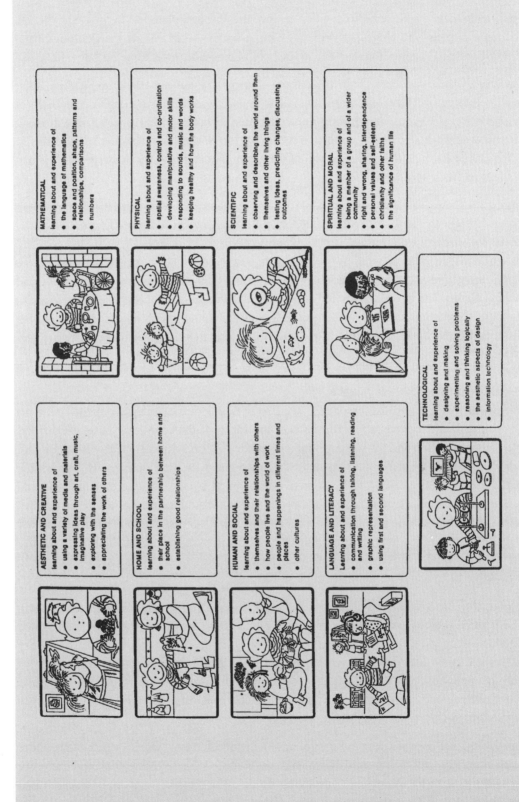

MATHEMATICAL
learning about and experience of
- the language of mathematics
- space and position, shape, patterns and relationships, comparisons
- numbers

PHYSICAL
learning about and experience of
- spatial awareness, control and co-ordination
- developing manipulative and motor skills
- responding to sounds, music and words
- keeping healthy and how the body works

SCIENTIFIC
learning about and experience of
- observing and describing the world around them
- themselves and other living things
- testing ideas, predicting changes, discussing outcomes

SPIRITUAL AND MORAL
learning about and experience of
- being a member of a group and of a wider community
- right and wrong, sharing, interdependence
- personal values and self-esteem
- christianity and other faiths
- the significance of human life

TECHNOLOGICAL
learning about and experience of
- designing and making
- experimenting and solving problems
- reasoning and thinking logically
- the aesthetic aspects of design
- information technology

AESTHETIC AND CREATIVE
learning about and experience of
- using a variety of media and materials
- expressing ideas through art, craft, music, imaginative play
- exploring with the senses
- appreciating the work of others

HOME AND SCHOOL
learning about and experience of
- their place in the partnership between home and school
- establishing good relationships

HUMAN AND SOCIAL
learning about and experience of
- themselves and their relationships with others
- how people live and the world of work
- people and happenings in different times and places
- other cultures

LANGUAGE AND LITERACY
learning about and experience of
- communication through talking, listening, reading and writing
- graphic representation
- using first and second languages

UNIT 3 WEEK ONE

is not offered to young children in the form of subject divisions; different aspects of learning are integrated, as I hope Activity 6 indicated. As you will have understood from the previous two units, young children do not view the world in terms of subject boundaries. Therefore a key feature of good practice in early years settings is the inter-relatedness of these strands of experience.

Traditionally early years educators try to achieve this through planning for projects, themes or topics such as 'growing plants' or 'building a house' (Early Years Curriculum Group 1989). Figure 3.3 shows how one nursery school planned for their topic on butterflies.

Because of their concerns about the effects of a narrow subject-based curriculum upon young children, in 1989 a group of specialists in early years education calling themselves the Early Years Curriculum Group produced a helpful book for early years practitioners. This showed ways of planning within the context of the National Curriculum which adhered to the principles, beliefs and values which underpin good early years practice. I will return to these in Week Two.

Figure 3.4 shows how a cross-curricular topic on the theme of 'Keeping Healthy' has been planned. You can see that it includes opportunities for play, both indoor and outdoor, and for active concrete experiences such as planting bulbs to learn about growth and blowing up balloons leading to thinking about lung capacity. There are opportunities for representing and recording experiences through imaginative play, drawing, writing and making charts. The box in the top left-hand corner of the diagram shows which areas of the National Curriculum can be covered by these activities and which attainment targets the children may be working towards. However, this is done in a way which is not prescriptive or narrowly subject focused; it is developmentally appropriate.

Developmentally appropriate practice

According to Vic Kelly, Professor of Education at Goldsmith's College, London, the term 'developmentally appropriate' indicates that the focus of the early childhood curriculum must be on the child and his/her development rather than on subjects and the acquisition of knowledge. It is for the child that the curriculum must be developmentally appropriate (Kelly 1994). This view of curriculum is underpinned by the notions of childhood and development which were discussed in Unit 1. Such a curriculum, according to Kelly, must be based upon active forms of learning, on enquiry, on discovery and on the process rather than the content of learning. Quoting from the Hadow Report, written in 1931, Kelly argues that the curriculum needs to be framed in terms of activity and experience rather than knowledge to be acquired and facts to be stored.

A powerful American association, the National Association for the Education of Young Children, has voiced similar views in a book which describes developmentally appropriate practice for children from birth to eight years (Bredekamp 1987). They express concern about the diverse growth of early childhood provision (you will see parallels here with your work in Activities 3 and 4) and make a plea for programmes which are based on the notion that children learn most effectively through a concrete, play-oriented approach to the curriculum.

This brings me to a point that I made earlier in this section, which is that ideas about curriculum are still being researched and developed. This is how it should be. Any important area of life is subject to development as understanding increases. Research into practice is part of the early years educator's role.

The Quality in Diversity Project

The Quality in Diversity Project is based at Goldsmith's College, London. It is an important and innovative venture in that it is bringing together practitioners from the statutory,

UNIT 3 WEEK ONE

Figure 3.3 Wall Hall Nursery School Topic Web

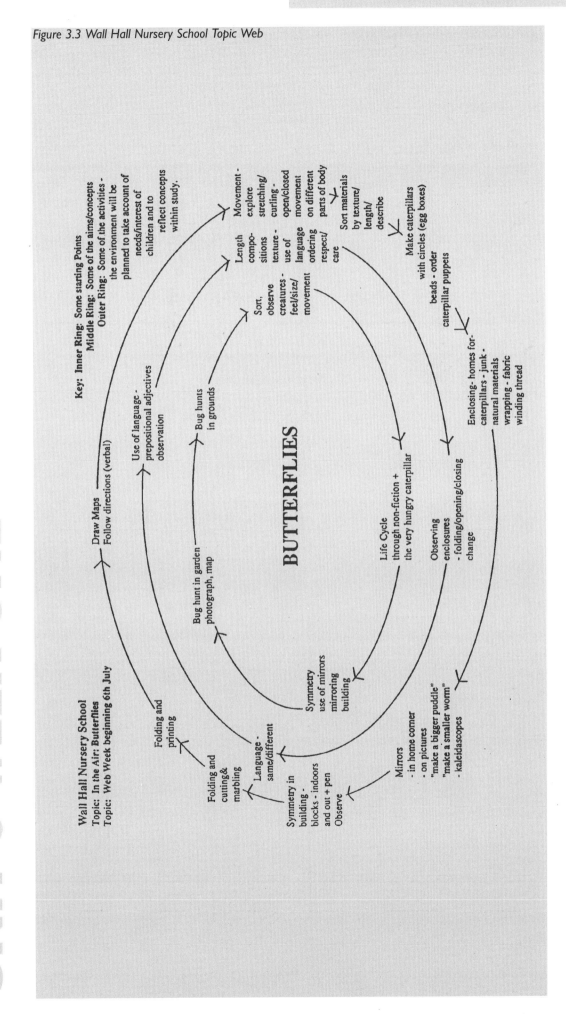

Wall Hall Nursery School
Topic: In the Air: Butterflies
Topic: Web Week beginning 6th July

Key: Inner Ring: Some starting Points
Middle Ring: Some of the aims/concepts
Outer Ring: Some of the activities - the environment will be planned to take account of needs/interest of children and to reflect concepts within study.

BUTTERFLIES

Movement - explore stretching/ curling - open/closed movement on different parts of body

Sort materials by texture/ length/ describe

Make caterpillars with circles (egg boxes)

beads - order caterpillar puppets

Enclosing - homes for caterpillars - junk - natural materials wrapping - fabric winding thread

Length compositions texture - use of language ordering respect/ care

Sort, observe creatures feel/size/ movement

Observing enclosures - folding/opening/closing change

Life Cycle through non-fiction + the very hungry caterpillar

Bug hunts in grounds

Use of language - prepositional adjectives observation

Bug hunt in garden photograph, map

Symmetry use of mirrors mirroring building

Mirrors
- in home corner
- on pictures
"make a bigger puddle"
"make a smaller worm"
- kaleidascopes

Symmetry in building - blocks - indoors and out + pen Observe

Language - same/different

Folding and cutting& marbling

Folding and printing

Draw Maps
Follow directions (verbal)

Figure 3.4. Early Years Curriculum Group

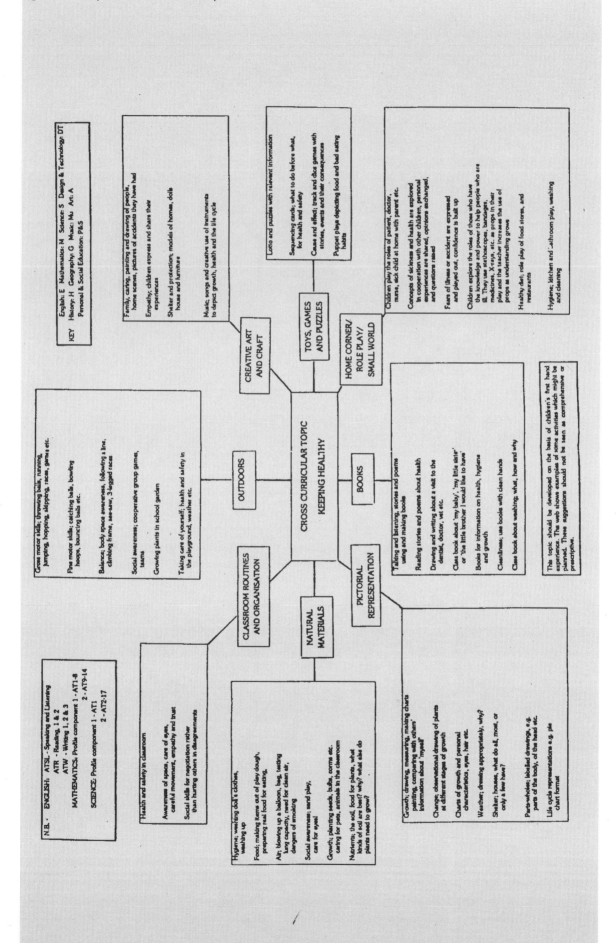

voluntary and independent sectors to seek common views of what is an appropriate curriculum for young children from birth to eight years of age. One of the project's aims is to develop curriculum guidelines which are based upon principles derived from observing and discussing practice in action. These will cover the age ranges 0-3, 3-5 and 5-8 in a way which may be distinctive to particular age groups, but which will also have overarching concerns. The project involves practitioners who are working in settings providing both care and education for young children. The project starts from the premise that children learn from all the experiences, planned and unplanned, that they encounter and that they need adults to plan appropriate learning activities for them. (Look back to the definitions in Activity 2, including your own. You may see similarities with this definition.)

Although the project is in the early stages of development it has begun by considering some basic ideas which it is hoped may become agreed principles underpinning education and care for the under eights. These have been called the 'Foundations for Early Learning' and are proposed as a framework for the curriculum, to be used alongside 'Areas of Experience' as follows.

The Foundations for Early Learning

- *Belonging and connecting*: This involves relationships with children and adults in families, communities and group settings, and learning to be a member of the child's own linguistic, cultural and community group

- *Being and becoming*: This involves the notion that effective learning builds upon self-respect, feelings of personal worth and identity; it includes care of self and the health and safety of the individual

- *Doing and being active*: Effective learning builds upon what children have already achieved. The processes of learning are seen to be important as they contribute to attitudes to learning and achievement

- *Contributing and participating*: This involves learning to be responsible and to make appropriate choices in a group

- *Thinking, understanding and knowing*: In order to learn effectively, children build up their own understanding through active processes such as play, discovery and encounters with world knowledge and culture. They work to make and express their own meanings.

As you will see, this framework offers a different approach to thinking about curriculum which does not divide the curriculum into discrete areas. The approach places practitioners' observations of children learning and develop-ing at the heart of curriculum planning. For example Vicky Hurst, a project researcher, has described how one practitioner's observations of the use children in her setting made of the play material provided led to a change in the way these were offered. Choice of fewer materials and less change of materials were thought to contribute to deeper involvement and concentration. Also important was a different staff role, described as 'keeping quiet and being company for the children' (Hurst 1994, p 40).

Now look back to Activity 6 and the associated reading. Look again at the framework for Areas of Experience. It may seem at first sight that this framework takes quite a different approach from the 'Foundations for Early Learning' framework in that it has clear links with the notion of curriculum as subject based, although the inter-relatedness of this base or framework is stressed. However, I am sure you would agree that both frameworks emphasise the importance of social relationships, the learning environment and the key role of the adults working with young children. The importance of fostering positive attitudes to learning is also stressed in both approaches. The foundations for early learning do seem to be more concerned, however, with the less visible and less tangible aspects of the

UNIT 3 WEEK ONE

curriculum which are so much more difficult to 'measure' or to express in terms of 'outcomes' with which the Government seem to be so concerned in the National Curriculum and in the 'desirable outcomes for children's learning'. This may be why there has been much less focus upon a curriculum for the very youngest children, which is the focus of the remaining work in Week One.

A curriculum for the under threes: educare

Discussion of a curriculum for the under threes does not of course mean the imposition of an 'academic' curriculum, as I hope will be obvious from the work you have done so far in this unit. Dorothy Rouse and Sue Griffin (1992, p 139) provide a helpful definition of the term as they see it relating to this age group:

* all the activities and experiences provided for babies and toddlers by educators

* all the activities devised by the children themselves

* the gestures, vocalisations, and language that educators use to communicate with the children and all language they use with each other

* all that the children see, touch and hear and taste and smell in the environment around them.

Included in their definition are education, care and training. The last of these may at first sight seem a controversial element; however, if you consider the example of Grace and the elephant earlier in this unit, you will see where the need for the adult to say 'no' in certain situations becomes part of the child's social learning.

If you look back again to earlier definitions of curriculum which you have considered, you will see some similarities. You will also see that certain experiences which are present in earlier definitions and frameworks are emphasised for this age group; in particular, the role of early communication skills and sensory experiences. The work you carried out in Units 1 and 2 concerning the learning and development of babies and young children demonstrated the importance of early experiences which are sensitively attuned to the child's needs. This is further emphasised by Rouse and Griffin (p 138) in their identification of two key issues which they consider central to the curriculum for under threes:

* children's needs for relationships with significant responsive adults

* children's needs for developmentally appropriate learning experiences.

You may also recall from Unit 1 how baby Darren's visual skills were facilitated by his key worker in a way which was developmentally appropriate.

■ Activity 7 A

The following examples (adapted from Bredekamp 1987) demonstrate both developmentally appropriate and inappropriate practice in working with the under threes. Make yourself a table using the headings below. Under which heading should each example be placed? Comment briefly for each example on why you think this is so.

Appropriate practice   Inappropriate practice   Comment

1. Space is arranged so that children can enjoy quiet moments of play by themselves. They have space to roll over and crawl safely towards interesting objects placed around them.

2. Pictorial materials depict a variety of ages and ethnic groups in interesting ways.

3. Infants share cots in shifts. Bedding and cot toys are shared.

4. Parents and staff talk daily to share pertinent information about the child.

5. Crying is ignored or responded to on an irregular basis.

6. Objects are restricted to certain locations (for instance, utensils in the home corner). Hoarding, collecting, putting objects in and out of containers and carrying objects around are discouraged.

7. Mirrors are placed where infants can observe themselves, for instance next to the changing area.

❏ Commentary

Here is my list:

1. This is developmentally appropriate practice. Even very young children need time alone under the watchful eye of an adult. However, safe eye-catching objects, some familiar, some new, will encourage visual stimulation and mobility as the child attempts to reach for and move towards them.

2. This can also be considered developmentally appropriate as it indicates the concern of the adults in the setting to recognise a range of cultural identities and practices and the plurality of society.

3. This is developmentally inappropriate practice. Young infants need the security of their own familiar sleeping place, preferably with bedding and toys brought from home. Rouse and Griffin (1992) illustrate this good practice in Italian nurseries where children have floor-level sleeping baskets which they can creep into independently and which contain the child's personal bedding and comfort objects.

4. This is developmentally appropriate practice. Parents and educarers of very young children need to liaise on a daily basis to discuss the child's moods, happenings in the home or group setting and to share all relevant information. Beginnings and ends of days – 'the letting go' – need to be carefully planned (Rouse and Griffin 1992).

5. This is developmentally inappropriate practice. The need for sensitive adults to respond to children's communications contingently (as they occur) was stressed in Unit 1.

6. This is developmentally inappropriate practice. Chris Athey's (1990) research has shown how children develop patterns in their thinking, actions and language through interacting with and using objects in the environment. Elinor Goldscmied's work on 'Treasure Baskets', which is described in Rouse and Griffin (1992), has shown how babies concentrate for long periods on exploring an overflowing basket of natural and household objects. Restricting choice and mobility will have a negative effect on development and learning.

7. This is developmentally appropriate practice. I turn once again to an example from Italian nurseries described by Rouse and Griffin (1992) where babies and toddlers could look in large mirrors from floor to waist height, in order that they could identify themselves as individuals and learn about their own bodies.

Summary

The concept of educare introduced earlier in this unit suggests a need to view teaching and learning and to think about curriculum for the early years in new ways. I hope that this week's work has encouraged you to do this. As Brenda Griffin (1994) has said, allowing children to be 'properly two' (p 180) will subsequently allow them to be 'properly three', and I would add and four and five and six and seven and eight years old. This week you have considered and reflected upon frameworks for planning the curriculum. You have also given some thought to the contexts within which young children learn and develop. In Week Two you will go on to consider provision for learning in a range of early childhood settings.

UNIT 3 WEEK ONE

Review of the week

You have come to the end of this week's study. Take time to look back and consider the following:

• Which curriculum framework do you think is most appropriate for children in early years settings?

• How will this week's study influence the ways in which you interact with young children, given the curriculum framework in your setting - either at home, or in an early childhood centre or school?

• Can you think of examples which show your increased awareness of the 'hidden curriculum' at home and in early childhood centres?

• Can you think of examples of developmentally appropriate practice?

• Is there any particular reading mentioned this week that you think you would like to follow up?

Before moving on to Week Two's study, carry out the review activity. I hope this will help you to reflect upon your learning and thinking about curriculum.

■ Review activity A

1. Use Figure 3.3 as a basis to carry out an activity similar to Activity 6. List the areas of experience which the children will cover through the activities provided within the topic of butterflies.

2. Then comment in the light of other approaches and frameworks discussed in this unit so far, for example Educare and the Foundations of Early Learning. You will have realised by now that some important aspects of learning, such as building a child's self-esteem (Whitehead 1994) are more difficult to plan for.

Here is a short extract from one student's response to this activity which you may find helpful to look at before you begin. The extract follows a discussion of the curriculum frameworks described in Unit 3.

With the approaches and frameworks in mind, the topic 'Butterflies' has been planned for a nursery school, probable age 3-5 years. There are a lot of activities based on hands-on experience. There are bug hunts, painting, marbling, modelling – practical activities that children of this age enjoy. Their imaginative skills are also encouraged with the mirror in the home corner, designing and building houses for the insects and in the use of their bodies in PE. The basic skills of language and literacy are being extended, with the 'Hungry Caterpillar' story making learning fun.

You can see that although Figure 3.3 is not written within the framework of 'areas of experience' this student has been able to identify where these curriculum experiences might take place. In addition she has drawn upon her work in earlier units and noted the importance of learning being concrete, practical, fun and enjoyable.

Further reading

Blenkin, G. (1994) 'Early learning and a developmentally appropriate curriculum', in Blenkin, G. and Kelly, A.V. (eds) *The National Curriculum and Early Learning*, London: Paul Chapman

DES (1990) *Starting with Quality*, London: HMSO, Part 2, pp 35-47

There is a full list of references at the end of Unit 3.

UNIT 3 WEEK ONE

Objectives

As the title states, in Week Two of this unit you will be looking at young children learning, in early childhood centres in particular, and you will consider the adult's role in these settings. By the end of the week you should:

*   have understood the importance of the principles or beliefs which underpin the way we work with young children and the way these influence the learning experiences that are offered

*   have revisited the important role which observation plays in planning for and evaluating children's learning

*   critically consider some ways in which aspects of learning can be recorded

*   be aware of some recent research which looks at children learning.

Activities

The activities are planned to help you to understand more about the topics covered in this week's work. This week you will need about two and a half hours for an observation and record-keeping activity and a small-scale investigation. You may need extra time to think about the activity and write up your notes.

About this week's study

You will be looking at the fundamental question of how we put principles into practice in early childhood education and care. You will be practising your skills of observation in an early childhood centre and critically evaluating what you observe. This is intended to help you to adopt a more reflective attitude towards ways of working with young children.

From principles to practice

One aspect of learning which you looked at in Week One was the curriculum as a framework within which to plan and provide for opportunities for children to learn and develop. A dictionary definition of a framework is 'an essential supporting structure' (Allen 1991). Any structure, if it is to withstand external forces, requires firm foundations. The foundations upon which a sound early years curriculum is based are principles (that is, a set of beliefs, a philosophy) which underpin work in the early years. These principles provide a foundation for thinking and practice.

Margaret Lally (1995) argues that all early years workers should be clear about the principles which underpin their work. Tina Bruce (1991) derived what she saw as twelve principles from the work of pioneers in early childhood education. These have been further developed by the Early Years Curriculum Group (EYCG 1989, 1992) and are summarised below.

Principles which are fundamental to good early years practice

- Early childhood is the foundation on which children build the rest of their lives; it is not just a preparation for the next stage – it is vitally important in itself

- Children develop emotionally, intellectually, morally, physically, spiritually and socially, and at different rates. All aspects of development are equally important and are interwoven

- Young children learn from everything that happens to them and do not separate learning into subjects

- Children learn most effectively by doing rather than being told

- Children learn most effectively when they are actively involved and interested

- Children need time and space to produce work of quality and depth

- What children can do rather than cannot do are the starting points in their learning

- Playing and talking are the main ways through which young children learn about themselves and the world around them

- Children who feel confident in themselves and their own ability have a head-start to learning

- Children who are encouraged to think for themselves are more likely to act independently

- All children have abilities which should be identified and promoted

- The relationships which children establish with adults and other children are of central importance in their development.

Source: Early Years Curriculum Group (1992, p 15)

Read these principles carefully. If possible, discuss them with someone else. See if you can find any links with the work on curriculum in Week One.

Consider principle 3. You will remember that the curriculum frameworks appropriate to the early years reflected a *holistic* approach, that is, they were not rigidly divided into subject headings.

Consider principle 9 in relation to your work on children's self-image and self-esteem in Unit 1. You will see, I hope, that your understanding of such principles and whether they are implemented in practice will govern the ways in which you work with young children.

■ Activity 1 A

Drawing upon your knowledge and experience of a care/education setting with which you are familiar, give:

- at least one example of a situation which demonstrates how some of these principles have been put into practice, and

- at least one example of a situation which demonstrates how some of these principles have not been put into practice.

For example, you may be able to think of a setting which claims either implicitly or explicitly to adhere to principle 8, but where children engage mainly in adult-led table-top activities.

The following example may help you.

Gita is a lively, curly-haired two year old who has happily attended her day nursery for the last year. She attends from 7.30 am to 6.30 pm as both her parents work full time in jobs which are some distance from home. The nursery syllabus claims to provide care and a stimulating environment suited to the children's needs and abilities. Part of Gita's day involves 'work time' where the children are strongly encouraged to sit in small groups, for a short time, with an adult, and carry out directed table-top work. In Figure 3.5 overleaf you can see an offering which is typical of many which Gita takes home for her parents to proudly display on the kitchen walls.

❏ Commentary

Below I offer a commentary in relation to the relevant principles. My comments stem from a personal view that this type of activity – colouring in the adult drawing of a mouse – is not an appropriate or worthwhile activity to be offering to a two year old. Even if the activity were linked to a project about mice, I would question how this could add to her knowledge.

Principle 1. I would argue that already Gita is being prepared for 'the next stage' by being expected to sit at a table-top activity which requires her to colour in an adult drawing of a mouse. It is obvious that at the moment she does not have the fine motor skill with which to carry out this activity. It is not valuing what she is able to do at the moment (we have evidence of what she can do independently from her mark making around the edge of the mouse and close to her name).

Principles 4 and 5. There is little evidence of learning by doing. Although I did not observe this activity I find it hard to imagine that it would have actively involved her or engaged her interest for more than a few moments.

Principle 7. The activity is not building upon what Gita can do now.

Figure 3.5 Gita's mouse

Principle 8. Play was not the key vehicle for learning (although no doubt some talking took place).

Principle 9. The activity offered little scope for thinking or action.

Principle 10. The activity did not build upon her abilities.

Before reading on, return to Activity 1 and make similar notes on your own examples.

Beliefs influence practice

I am sure the staff in Gita's nursery feel they are offering what they claim to offer, and probably for much of the day they do offer a stimulating and caring environment to support her learning and development. Gita goes happily to her nursery, mutual affection and pleasure are shown by both Gita and her key worker, and Gita is able to separate from her parents – all of which suggests that she feels safe and secure. This offers a sound basis for her to explore and use the learning environment that the nursery provides. There is, however, evidence of a 'top-down' approach to the curriculum which your work in Week One suggested was not an appropriate way to plan for young children's learning.

I came across a similar example in a recent curriculum workshop shared by early years educators, where we were shown a task given to a five-year-old child in a reception class. She had been asked to colour in a map of the British Isles; her efforts were very similar to Gita's colouring in of the mouse. We pondered in the workshop what she could have learned from this task. This work would seem to arise from a misinterpretation of the National Curriculum, Geography, Key Stage 1, which requires children to become aware that the world extends beyond their locality. You can probably think of more developmentally appropriate ways for a five year old to do this.

I hope Activity 1 has enabled you to see that there is a link between what adults working in early childhood centres believe in (i.e. the principles upon which they base their practice), their practical arrangements (i.e. the planning of the learning environment, both indoors and outdoors) and their plans for children's learning. It is of course important that the principles underlying practice are derived from research and theory and a knowledge of child development (Bruce 1987). Reasons for practice should not include the concern that parents want to see finished products such as Figure 3.5 or 'work in books', or 'because of the National Curriculum'. Margaret Lally (1995) argues strongly that principles need to be made clear and accessible to all staff in early childhood settings, so that everyone is sharing the same meaning of terms such as 'play', 'learning', 'emergent writing', 'work' and 'structure'. In her work with practitioners she has found that there can be a mismatch between what early childhood educators say they believe and what they actually do with the children. This may be for a number of reasons, such as:

- not having asked questions about why they do what they do

- because they have not worked out the rationale for what they do

- because they are not able to articulate clearly their beliefs about their practice.

■ Activity 2 A

I hope the following questions will help you to think about your own practice and beliefs and their implications for the children with whom you work or have regular contact.

Write your answers down. Set them in the context of your own workplace or an early childhood centre with which you are familiar. Briefly describe the setting you choose. Where possible, support your answers with specific examples drawn from practice.

1. What principles would you say underpin the work of the centre? (You may find it helpful at this point to look back at the principles listed earlier in this section.)

2. What opportunities are available for the staff to discuss their philosophies and beliefs?

3. Is there evidence of a shared philosophy?

4. Do the principles expressed in the written documentation reflect what happens in practice?

5. Are there principles not in evidence which you feel could be included?

❏ Commentary

Your responses and examples will of course have been influenced by the setting you chose. If this was a school-based setting involving children from five to eight years of age, i.e. Key Stage 1 of the National Curriculum, the children will by law have to receive this curriculum. If the early childhood centre or school was claiming nursery vouchers for four year olds, then these children would be working towards 'desirable outcomes for children's learning. You may, however, have been pleased and surprised to find that many of the early years principles outlined in Figure 3.1 were underpinning practice. You may have noted that within a subject framework the children were actively engaged in concrete experiences – learning by doing – and that much playing and talking was involved through a thematic or cross-curricular approach.

Learning by doing, playing and talking

Rosemary Rodger (1994) describes a case study of a group of six children and their teacher in a reception class who are engaged in a topic on 'Ourselves'. This involved the children exploring and using language about their own clothes. In one session focusing on their coats they noticed they were 'soft and furry', 'soft and prickly', 'reversible' (p 19). These and other words produced by the children were written on a flip chart by the teacher. She noticed which colours and which parts of the body they knew and named. With the teacher's help the coats were sorted and classified, for instance into parkas, duffel coats, those with hoods and those without. The children drew pictures of themselves wearing their coats. They later sat in a circle with the teacher and played a game of 'My coat is ...', in which they described their coats to each other, giving the teacher the opportunity to observe their skills in speaking and listening. 'Dressing up' in the home corner before taking the dolls for a walk reinforced the more directed work with the teacher.

If you were focusing upon a setting such as a playgroup, you may have observed similar principles underpinning adult practice – making sure that the children were learning by doing, playing and talking. You may have observed the children taking an active interest in a well-planned environment which was based upon the children's interests and concerns. The role of 'subjects' would probably be difficult to spot. You may have noticed a slightly different adult role, with perhaps less direct intervention in the children's activities, although the adult was still observing the children carefully to notice what captured their attention, so that this could be built upon in future planning. As an adult working in this setting you may have had opportunities to discuss and share ideas about appropriate ways of planning the environment to encourage independence. You may have helped to think about and devise ways of recording your observations of children so that their abilities were identified and promoted.

Early years educators

The quality of learning experiences offered to and encountered by children in early childhood centres is affected by the principles and beliefs of the adults working in these settings. Such adults need to understand and articulate what they are doing and why they are doing it. Working with young children requires a knowledge and understanding of how they learn best, what they should learn and the sort of environment which will foster this learning.

UNIT 3 WEEK TWO

You have seen from Week One that adults working in early childhood centres have different roles, responsibilities and training. I have used rather general terms such as 'early years educator' or 'early years practitioner' to describe the adult role in these settings. However, I agree with Cathy Nutbrown (1994) that this can lead to a lack of clarity. She uses the term 'professional educator' and defines what she means by this:

> I use the term professional educator to mean adults who have some relevant training and qualifications and understand something of how children learn, and who are active in their thinking and interaction with children in group settings. [p.x]

I think I prefer the term 'early years educator', but find her definition of the professional role of this adult a helpful one.

The report *Starting with Quality* (1990) lists the knowledge, understanding, skills and attitudes which adults working with young children need to possess, as you will recall from Unit 2. These include:

- understanding of the way children learn

- knowledge of recent research and understanding of its implications in relation to the provision of quality experiences for young children

- observational skills and effective recording, monitoring and assessment of the curriculum.

Such adults will be able to look at children's learning and see it with a professional and informed eye.

Approaches to looking at children learning

The work in this section builds on Unit 2 where you looked at the influences on your own learning and also the ways in which young children learn and develop. The focus will be upon the ways in which adults working with young children can collect evidence from their communications, behaviour and play, in order that they can understand better what young children know, feel and can do – to glimpse their understandings and insights. This 'evidence' can then be used as a basis for planning further learning and development.

Joan Tamburrini (in Bartholomew and Bruce 1993) helps to clarify the relationship between development and learning. She suggests that development is about children acting spontaneously within the general situation in which they function. An example is given of Mathew, who at two years old can run and jump, but cannot yet skip or hop. He loves to run across open spaces and jump to music. Tamburrini suggests that learning is not spontaneous, but provoked by another person or situation. Mathew is taken to run across a field with an uneven surface, so he is learning to run in a particular situation. He goes to a fair and learns to jump on an inflatable castle, which presents particular problems for him. Most learning happens in the course of children developing, and often we do not notice it happening. As you know from Unit 1, running and jumping is what two year olds need and like to do; usually they are with people who encourage this. However, if children are constrained from developing normally (the Romanian orphans confined to their cots are a recent example) their learning is seriously impaired.

Observing children learning

In working through the first two units you will have undertaken a number of activities which asked you to observe children learning. You will have discovered that observation plays a key role in planning for and providing opportunities for children to learn. You have already practised this skill in a number of the activities you have done so far where you have looked at different aspects of children's development.

In order to move children on from what they already know, understand and can do, early years educators need to know where children are in their learning and development. Observation is the key to this in the early years. Very young children cannot show what they know through paper and pencil tests, by answering obscure adult-led questions or through finished products, as we saw from Gita in Figure 3.5. They show what they know and can do through their spontaneous talk and questions, through their gestures and early communications, through their attempts to solve problems and to act out what they know about the world around them in their play. We all know what the infant wants as she vocalises, looks and points at a nearby toy. We sensitively observe and interpret her need from these outward signals and from the context. We respond by giving her the toy or encouraging her movements towards it, probably naming the toy in the process. In turn, she learns that her communication is successful, that she can perhaps get the toy independently of the adult, and that it is called 'ball'.

I want to invite you now to consider once more the important role of observation in looking at children's learning and to consider further ways of recording what you see.

■ Activity 3 B

Make a list of all the ways that you can think of to observe children. Then check your list against the one below.

- Just looking and listening

- Making notes of what the children are doing

- Writing down everything that is said

- Tape recordings

- Camera

- Collecting 'finished products' and talking to the children about what they have done

- Video recording

The rest of this activity will require you to carry out a planned observation. In Activity 4 which immediately follows you will be asked to evaluate the methods you used.

Use one or more of the above methods of observation with a child you wish to observe. Think about the following before you begin:

- What do you want to know? What do you want the observation to tell you?

- When will you do the observation?

- Where, in what context?

- Will the child be alone, with an adult, with other children?

- What methods will you use?

❏ Commentary

What you want to observe will help you to decide the best way of doing it. For example, talk may be best recorded in a running commentary, noting down what is said; however, you may find it difficult to write quickly. Alternatively a tape recorder may be used, but you will need to decide if you have time to listen to and transcribe the tape afterwards. You may wish to note how a child plans for and makes a model from waste materials, in which case watching, participating and making brief notes may be the best method. However, if you wish to keep a record of the product, then a photograph can be taken.

UNIT 3 WEEK TWO

You will remember from Units 1 and 2 that descriptive observation is not enough. The next important step is to *interpret* and *analyse* what you have seen. You will also remember the need to be *objective* and to try to be *unbiased* in your interpretations. This is where the skill of the 'professional educator' defined by Cathy Nutbrown (1994) becomes crucial. We need to make sense of what we see in order to inform planning and to support the child's development. However, the purpose of this activity is to encourage you to think about the different ways in which you can observe and record children's learning.

■ Activity 4 A/B

Having carried out your observation, now carry out a critique of your method, considering the following points:

- Did your observation tell you what you wanted to know? If not, what would be a better way of finding this out?

- What additional information would you like to collect to gain a clearer picture of this child? How will you do this?

- Is the information you gathered sufficient to help you to plan or support further the child's learning? If not, how will you obtain this?

- What have you learned about the provision being made for this child? (Consider the provision of equipment, experiences and adult involvement.)

❏ Commentary

You have just carried out a planned observation, using a method of your choice, to consider possible ways of finding out more about what children know and can do. You have approached it in quite a formal way using the professional skills and tools associated with observing children. Once you have developed these skills it is of course possible (and often more feasible) in a busy home or early childhood centre to carry out shorter unplanned observations as the opportunity arises.

You will remember from Week One that I pointed out the importance of catching 'the teachable moment'; Katie's mother did this when she explored the notion of chapters with her. To do this you need to be an alert child watcher. I return to Katie at the age of three years and five months as an example. This observation took about a minute to scribble down in a notebook; the analysis was carried out later and of course took more time.

Observation
Katie had found in a drawer the card game WHOT which was unfamiliar to her. She began to play with it. She pointed to the letters on the pack and said 'This says SNAP'. She then went on to 'read' the instructions from the game with comments such as '... and then you put the cards there ...'. [Miller 1996]

What does this brief observation tell us about Katie's learning?

Analysis/interpretation
Although Katie's guess (or hypothesis) about the name of the game was incorrect, she had formulated a reasonable alternative name on the basis of her previous experience with similar card games and print in other contexts. She also showed an expectation that the print associated with the game would have a meaning and a language that was associated with the game (i.e. gave instructions rather than told a story). It showed something about her attitude to learning that she was prepared to take a risk, have a guess about what the print meant. She was being active in her thinking. If you recall the areas of experience we discussed in Week One of this unit you will see that under the heading of 'Language and literacy' she has some understanding of graphic (written) representation and understands that written language takes different forms.

UNIT 3 WEEK TWO

Planning for learning

As a result of this observation I might decide that I would like to explore further Katie's knowledge about print and the forms it can take – perhaps through focusing upon her use of books and drawing her attention to print in the environment on labels, notices and street signs, for instance, to find out what she recognises. I would want to ask her parents about what she notices at home. If this observation had taken place in a group setting I might want to consider the provision made for looking at and sharing books.

A record of learning development

This one short, anecdotal (i.e. unplanned) observation has yielded quite a lot of information about Katie. Noting down this and similar observations and dating them begins to provide a *record* of learning and development. In one nursery school which I visit frequently these types of brief observations, both planned and unplanned, are recorded onto 'Post-it' sticky notes. If, at the end of the day or week, discussion with the nursery team or parent suggests they are significant in the context of a child's learning and development, they are then transferred to a more permanent record.

In another nursery each staff member has their own notebook to record events and behaviours which seem significant. The following example is taken from Bartholomew and Bruce's book *Getting to Know You* (1993), which as the title suggests is about getting to know children and their families better.

William's entry form for the nursery provides essential background information. It shows that he is just three years old, and has recently been in hospital for a minor operation. He is English speaking, but his speech is a little unclear. There is further information about his family, his likes and dislikes and current skills. Staff have added to this by writing on 'Post-it' sticky labels, which are then inserted in his file. For example:

> 7 January beige room. Parted from mother without any distress. Pushed shopping trolley. Put blocks inside. Moved blocks into house. Tipped out on to table. [p 77]

Other record sheets note William's progress in other areas such as science and mathematical experiences; some observations note his interest in volume and capacity, some blocks, earth and water in containers. The parents' record sheets also inform the staff's thinking. All this information is used to extend his learning in all areas of the curriculum.

In addition to such written observations, collecting and dating samples of children's drawing, emergent writing or photographs of their constructions, with relevant notes about *why* the work was collected, can all contribute to a *profile* or *portfolio* of their learning and development. These can be stored in a folder and discussed with parents at appropriate times.

Recording what has been observed is a major part of the professional role of the early years educator.

Frameworks for observation and record keeping

Records need to show what the adult observes and how the adult supports learning and development. In their book about record keeping in early childhood centres, Bartholomew and Bruce (1993) note the need at regular intervals to take stock of where each child is, in order to review the needs of the child and the family. They present a variety of formats used by staff and parents to 'get to know' children, some of which have been discussed above.

Frameworks for recording children's progress and development can take a variety of forms. Some are devised by staff in early childhood centres to meet their particular needs. These are often in the form of houses, animals, flowers or jigsaws, which are divided into sections representing different areas of learning and the development of specific skills. Others are developed and published by LEAs, for example the *Kensington and Chelsea Early Years Profile* (1992). Some of these published formats have explicit links with the National Curriculum. Sheila Wolfendale (1990) has developed a checklist in the form of a little book called *All About Me*, which is designed for parents of children with special educational needs, to help them note down and record from time to time their child's development and progress. It is a record for the family and gives parents a basis for discussing their child's progress with early years educators and other professionals.

There have also been developments involving even very young children in contributing to profiles and records of their progress and development. These take account of what they have to say about their skills, likes and dislikes. For example, there may be a page with a child in the centre saying 'I can', surrounded by circles containing statements such as 'do up my zip' and 'tie laces' (Wolfendale 1990).

Figure 3.6 shows the jigsaw sheet used with parents in the Sheffield Early Literacy Project. It focuses on three key aspects of early literacy development – sharing books, emergent writing and environmental print.

■ Activity 5 B

Complete as much as you can of the jigsaw record sheet in Figure 3.6 for a young child whom you know quite well. Complete the sheet by shading the jigsaw sections that the child has achieved. You may find it helpful to colour the different areas – sharing books, emergent writing and environmental print – in different colours. If you work in a professional setting, try to enlist the help of the parent or carer and note their comments. If you are doing this activity as a parent, you may want to share your findings with a professional early years educator.

Note the areas in which the child has shown most evidence of development. Discuss the reasons for this. Consider how other areas of development, not shaded in, might be encouraged. Keep a record of your discussion.

❏ Commentary

I have used this sheet with parents in a nursery school as a focus for talking about their children's literacy development. They were asked to shade in the areas in which they felt their child was developing. Here are some of their responses:

* Some were surprised to see the extent of their children's achievements

* One set of parents commented that their child was not keen to use pencils and pens, he preferred to do more active things

* Some had not thought about the importance of alerting children to the idea that books have authors or titles.

This information was of course very valuable to the nursery staff. It was entered into the children's records and was used to inform joint planning with parents (see Miller 1996).

I wonder which you think is more helpful for looking at children's learning and development – the observations you carried out in Activities 3 and 4, or this pre-planned framework?

You may have decided that such a checklist of skills can *limit* observations of children because only the items noted on the checklist are looked for and other important behaviours and events may be missed. The observation of Katie with the card game WHOT lends support to this view. Alternatively, you may have found it helpful as a means of *focusing* your observation. Bartholomew and Bruce (1993) suggest that the best use of frameworks for observation and record keeping may be as an 'aide memoire' to alert the adult to aspects of behaviour and development which may be important to record and as a record of children's progress.

UNIT 3 WEEK TWO

Figure 3.6 The Sheffield Early Literacy Project jigsaw sheet
Source: Weinberger et al (1990)

UNIT 3 WEEK TWO

So what's new?

I said in Week One that researchers, working alongside practitioners, are still looking for ways of finding out more about how young children learn. Research can help adults working with young children to look at learning and development with a fresh eye. Hopefully this will then lead to improved practice. I also made the point that adults working in early childhood centres need to keep abreast of such developments. The work of Chris Athey (1990) on schemas is a good example of how researchers, parents and practitioners working together have achieved important new insights into how children think and learn which have led to changes in practice and curriculum planning.

Schemas – patterns of learning

Chris Athey's research builds upon Piaget's work which you encountered in Units 1 and 2. From birth children show that they can use and develop schemas (patterns of behaviour) such as sucking or grasping. As they grow and develop these schemas increase in number and complexity and become co-ordinated with one another. Early schemas form the bases of the patterns of behaviour which children show between the ages of two and five. Athey describes a schema as 'a pattern of repeatable and generalisable actions which can be applied to objects or events' (Nutbrown 1994).

The main schemas identified by Athey (in Nutbrown and Swift 1993) are:

- *dynamic vertical*, e.g. flying a toy aeroplane

- *dynamic back and forth/side to side*, e.g. moving on a climbing frame

- *dynamic circular*, e.g. hopping round in circles

- *going over and under*, e.g. taking cars over and under a bridge

- *going round a boundary,* e.g. building a brick boundary around toy cars, taking the cars around it

- *enveloping and containing space*, e.g. wrapping a dolly in a blanket

- *going through a boundary*, e.g. building a brick boundary around toy cars, taking the cars through it.

Each schema can be considered under four headings:

- *Motor level*

- *Symbolic level* – action, graphic representation, and speech

- *Functional dependency relationship* – cause and effect

- *Thought level* – anything children can talk about without a reminder (i.e. internal representation).

Chris Athey observed children to see which schemas or patterns of learning they were engaged with, then supported, fed and extended their interests through visits (for instance, to a railway station), through providing materials with which they could experiment to represent their idea (e.g. painting, mark making) and through the support of adults.

As Cathy Nutbrown explains so clearly in her book *Threads of Thinking in Young Children* (1994), the actions and marks relating to these descriptions of movement can be identified in young children's drawing and mark making, in their play and in their thinking and language. For example, if a child is focusing upon a particular schema relating to roundness the child is working on a circular schema. The form is roundness, although the content can be anything which extends this form: wheels, a rolling ball, rotating machinery. These schemas provide the bases for later learning as they become assimilated into more complex concepts.

UNIT 3 WEEK TWO

To return to William for a moment, he became preoccupied with unacceptable forms of *trajectory* schema (biting, hitting). The staff in his nursery extended and diverted this interest by providing plastic bottles suspended from a washing line for him to hit with bats and balls. As they noted, this then furthered his development and learning in eye-hand co-ordination (physical and visual development), physical forces (scientific experience) and estimation of distances (mathematical experiences) (Bartholomew and Bruce 1993).

Having read about Chris Athey's work, I identified one of my own young daughters as a keen *enveloper*. She loved to cover herself over, put things in bags and envelopes, dress up and make parcels. She would build dens in her bedroom with her bedclothes, enveloping herself in a cosy nest. Perhaps you can think immediately of a child or children in whom these patterns can be identified? One early childhood centre, Pen Green in Corby, Northamptonshire, has developed a booklet to alert parents to their children's schemas, for instance covering up with a flannel in the bath or wrapping 'presents' in toilet rolls (Pen Green Centre, undated booklet). Curriculum planning guidelines and formats for observing and recording children's progress within this framework have also been developed (Bartholomew and Bruce 1993).

Now try Activity 6 to give you an idea of what this research tells us about young children learning. The example is taken from a collection of observations made by a group of Sheffield nursery teachers after they had followed a course led by Chris Athey (Nutbrown and Swift 1993).

■ Activity 6 A

Read the observation below and try to identify the schemas involved. Use Athey's schema framework listed earlier in this section.

Using the underneath of the climbing frame. Each child dressed in a cape and went underneath. They represented a TV character (e.g. Batman). In turn they marched round the frame and back underneath. William kept going in and out of the bars. Their explanations: 'We are in a cave', though William said 'cage', and 'We are on the lookout for enemies'.

❏ Commentary

The teachers concerned decided that the schemas involved were:

* going under

* enveloping and containing

* going round a boundary

* William – going through a boundary, in and out of climbing frame bars.

You can see that this research and the subsequent work by practitioners has led to fitting the curriculum to the child, rather than trying to fit the child into a curriculum framework. You can also see how observation of the child's drawings, play and language informs the planning of the curriculum. Discussion of the above observation by the nursery team will have led to planning learning experiences and activities which will build upon the current interests of William and his friend, and no doubt other children in the centre will share some of these schemas.

Effective Early Learning Research Project

Before ending this week's study I would like to draw your attention to just one more research project, the Effective Early Learning Research Project led by Professor Chris Pascal and Tony Bertram of Worcester College of Higher Education (Pascall et al., 1995) The project aims to raise the quality of early learning available to all three- and four-year-

UNIT 3 WEEK TWO

old children. A key focus of the research is to look at children's learning by attempting to observe and 'measure' the level of involvement in an activity. Levels of involvement are assessed by several factors, for example:

- the *energy* the child puts into an activity. For example, you will have 'seen' evidence of 'hard thinking' and activity in young children (and yourselves, I hope, during this course!) – the creased forehead, the tongue curled outside the mouth, pressing down hard on the paper, as a task is tried.

- *persistence* in a task, i.e. how well and how long a child concentrates

- *satisfaction*, i.e. how pleased children are with their achievements

- *language* – children saying how much they enjoyed an activity, and whether they ask for it again.

Adult intervention is a major focus of the project too. Adults are assessed for their sensitivity; the level of stimulation generated by the activity; and the degree of freedom given to the child to experiment, choose and express ideas. The emphasis, as you can see, is on the *process* of learning rather than *outcomes*. Like the Quality in Diversity Project described in Week One, this research is attempting to look at aspects of learning that are much more difficult to measure than answers to pages of sums. In a recent workshop which I attended, Chris Pascal reported how one infant teacher had changed her practice as a result of her observations. She had traditionally offered the children in her class more formal work in the mornings and play-based activities in the afternoon. In fact she found much higher levels of persistence, concentration and engagement in the afternoon sessions, which led her to make changes in her practice.

You might like to observe some children in your own workplace, or the one you are visiting, to see if the characteristics mentioned are present when children are engaging with activities and tasks.

Review of the week

As you near the end of this week's work I hope it has helped you to see that early years practitioners need to understand why they do what they are doing. I hope you have been able to see that observing and recording development and learning helps both parents and early years educators to note children's progress and to share valuable information. I also hope you have understood that, in order to plan for children's learning and development, you need to know what they can do now and what their interests and needs are.

Take some time now to think about the following questions:

- What principles underpin your practice/those of the early childhood centre with which you are familiar?

- Are there some approaches to observing and recording development and learning that you would now like to try out in your home or workplace?

- How will this week's study influence how you 'look at children's learning'?

- Is there some additional reading you would like to do?

Before moving on to Week Three, complete the review activity in order to consolidate the work in this section.

■ Review activity B

Either in your own workplace or in an early childhood centre that you know well, find out as much as possible about how the adults observe and record the children's learning, development and progress. Find out how they use this information in order to plan for children's learning and development and to plan the learning environment.

Try to make notes on the following:

- Methods of observation/information collecting

- Formats/frameworks for recording (note areas, skills covered)

- Parent/child involvement

- In what ways do observations and records inform planning?

- Do they take account of children from different cultural backgrounds or children with special learning needs?

- What happens to the information when the child leaves the centre?

If possible, obtain copies of checklists or other methods of observation, profiling or record keeping. In the light of your work so far in Weeks One and Two, take a critical look at what you have found out.

- What do *you* think about these procedures?

- What changes, if any, would you wish to make? Say why.

❏ Commentary

It may be helpful for you to know about how one student working in a nursery school approached this task. The main points are summarised below.

- She described how the parents fill in an information sheet for each child, covering background, personality and special skills. Copies were put in the appendix of her assignment

- She noted how the nursery teacher fills in the child's record form twice each term, based upon regular observations which are recorded. Examples were put in the appendix of her assignment

- She described how the record sheet is completed at the end of the year and passed on to the next teacher

- She explained how the records are used in planning for the children

- She discussed critically the fact that there is no parental involvement in this nursery

- She discussed the fact that the nursery is reviewing and improving its policy on assess-ment and record keeping.

Further reading

Bartholomew, L. and Bruce, T. (1993) *Getting to Know You: A Guide to Record Keeping in Early Childhood Education and Care*, London: Hodder and Stoughton

Nutbrown, C. (1994) *Threads of Thinking in Young Children*, London: Paul Chapman

There is a full list of references at the end of Unit 3.

Unit 3: Week Three
Linking home and early childhood centres

Objectives

In this third week of Unit 3 you will focus more closely upon the important role of the adult in young children's learning and development. By the end of Week Three you should:

* understand the differences and similarities between the role of parents (or main carers) as children's first educators and the role of professional educators

* have considered why parents and early years educators need to work closely together

* examined some ways in which parents and early years educators can work together

* have reflected upon parent/professional links in your own or another early childhood setting.

Activities

As in Weeks One and Two, the activities are planned to help you to understand more about the week's work.

This week you will need some time for a parent-professional discussion. The review activity will require you to spend some time carrying out a small-scale enquiry in an early childhood setting. The estimated time for this is about one and a half hours, plus time to write up your notes and comments about the information you have obtained.

About this week's study

You will be focusing on your own and others' roles as early childhood educators, and on the variety of ways in which parents and professionals can work together for the benefit of young children. Once again, evaluating practice in an early childhood centre is central to your study.

The role of parents

As the *Start Right* report (Ball 1994) states:

Parents come first. They are both the child's first educators – and the most important influence in the child's life. Their role is fundamental to successful early learning. [p 42]

The report offers the model of a triangle of support for the child, which involves parents, professionals and the community. I have illustrated this idea in Figure 3.7.

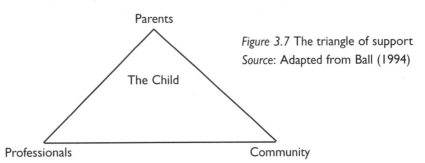

Figure 3.7 The triangle of support
Source: Adapted from Ball (1994)

Ball puts parents at the apex of this triangle of support for the child, where co-operation and collaboration with child care and education professionals is seen in the wider context of community. As the report goes on to remind us, it is from parents that children learn most in the early years. You will know from your earlier studies that the first five years of life are particularly crucial to learning and development. However, there is evidence from research showing that the nature of these early learning experiences and the involvement of the parents are of particular importance for children's subsequent development.

In the USA in the 1960s a great deal of money and effort were spent in developing so-called 'intervention' programmes, together known as Head Start. Head Start aimed to give a better start in life to children considered to be disadvantaged by poverty and home circumstances. These early childhood education programmes were an attempt to break the cycle of poverty with all its subsequent effects on children's life chances. The programmes were varied in terms of their setting, mode of delivery, staff involved and duration, so it is difficult to compare and evaluate them. However, evidence from one of the more carefully designed studies, known as the High Scope Perry Pre-School Project, showed that a high-quality curriculum plus good staff training and *parental participation* (in this case, usually the mother) showed the most striking results, particularly in the areas of greater commitment to school, better jobs and less anti-social behaviour as the children reached the teenage years.

In a review of two types of early intervention programmes, which were either home or centre based, an important factor appeared to be the interest of the mother and her direct involvement in the teaching process, that is, where mother and child were engaged in a common activity. The longer-term positive effects of this and other successful programmes were attributed to the fact that the main participants, here the mother and child, remained together once the programme had finished. This ensured continuity and also benefits for the younger children in the family. What is thought to happen is that a process of change takes place within the family whereby the initial effects of the intervention cause a change in the child's self-esteem and subsequently in the parent's view of the child's potential. This results in a positive spiral that leads to improved life chances for the child (Bronfenbrenner 1975; Sylva, in Ball 1994).

Children and familiar adults

It is known from other research that mothers (or major caregivers) tune into their babies' behaviour from birth. Reciprocal, interactive behaviours eventually develop, initially through the mother taking the lead role. She allows time for the baby to respond to her and she responds sensitively and contingently to the baby's gestures and signals (Schaffer 1977; see also Units 1 and 2).This helps infants to understand the crucial turn-taking aspects which lie at the basis of communication skills. Bruner's (1975, 1977) research has also shown how mothers help their infants to develop communication skills as a result of a shared activity around an object – for example, holding up for the infant and naming a brightly coloured musical ball so that the infant can touch the toy and cause it to play a tune. Bruner identified as particularly important the way in which the adult *scaffolds* or supports the child in the activity, for the baby could not cause the ball to move or make a noise without the adult's help in holding it. This framework for understanding the role of the familiar adult in children's learning and development stems from Vygotsky. As you will recall from Unit 2, Vygotsky suggested that children had two develop-mental levels:

- their actual development

- what they were able to do next.

The interchange between these two levels he described as the 'zone of proximal development' (ZPD). Figure 3.8 illustrates the concept.

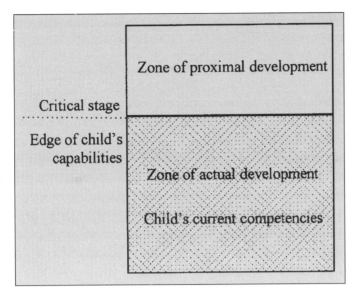

Figure 3.8 The zone of proximal development

Source: Adapted from Pascall and Bertram (1995)

In the ZPD the child is at the edge of her capabilities. The difference between the two levels is what the child can do alone and what she can do with the help and guidance of a supporting adult. Cathy Nutbrown (1994), citing Vygotsky, describes this as the child doing with assistance today what she will do by herself tomorrow. Within this framework, the adult helps the child to move forward in her thinking, skills and understanding from where she was before. As you will have understood from Unit 2, this emphasises the social context in which learning takes place and the important role the adult plays in this.

Before moving on to the next section, I would like you to think about your own role as a parent. Alternatively, you could draw upon the experience of another parent you know well, in order to reflect a little more about the notion of scaffolding and the ZPD.

■ Activity 1 A

Either drawing upon your own experience as a parent of a young child, or through discussion with a parent you know, list at least six examples of the ways in which parents extend and support their children's learning in and around the home setting.

Try to focus on incidents where you felt the child was at the critical point of almost being able to do something (that is, he or she was in the ZPD), but was in need of adult help in order to progress.

❑ Commentary

Here is my list, remembered from when my daughters were younger:

- reading a book aloud, pausing to let her have go at a familiar word

- supporting her spoonful of food until it almost reaches her mouth, then letting her manage the last stage

- supporting her bottom from behind on her first attempt to go up the stairs

- writing her name when she asked me to, as a model for her to copy

- going up the stairs, counting as we go

- helping her to find the Coco Pops pack on the supermarket shelf by encouraging her to look for the familiar background and logo, then reading it together.

The special role of parents

I hope your thinking has led you to see the unique position that parents occupy. They are able to support and extend their children's development in ways which are attuned to the child's social and cultural background. I could certainly see my role in scaffolding my own daughters' development and learning as I recalled the above events. Parents would seem to have three key advantages over the professional educator (Miller 1996):

- a unique knowledge of their child
- time for one-to-one interactions
- a natural context for learning.

Early learning in the home setting has been described by Munn and Schaffer (1993, p 64) as 'an *ad hoc* affair, with adults using opportunities to extend learning as they present themselves in the course of daily routines'. They go on to say that such learning is so effective because it is relatively unplanned and informal. In other words, it relates to what the child is interested in at that moment. A study which involved tape recording the conversations of four-year-old girls at morning nursery school and at home found that the mothers did a great deal of 'teaching' in the course of everyday events (Tizard and Hughes 1984). The researchers found that the children had an intense curiosity about the world they lived in which was reflected in their searching questions; the authors described these as 'passages of intellectual search' (p 131), as illustrated in the following extract (p 124):

Child: Is our roof a sloping roof?

Mother: Mmm. We've got two sloping roofs, and they sort of meet in the middle.

Child: Why have we?

Mother: Oh, it's just the way our house is built. Most people have sloping roofs, so that the rain can run off them. Otherwise, if you have a flat roof, the rain would sit in the middle of the roof and make a big puddle, and then it would start coming through.

Child: Our school has a flat roof, you know.

Mother: Yes it does actually, doesn't it?

Child: And the rain sits there and goes through?

Mother: Well, it doesn't go through. It's probably built with drains so that the water runs away. You have big blocks of flats with rather flat sort of roofs. But houses that were built at the time this house was built usually had sloping roofs.

Beth, the child involved, then goes on to explore with her mother what happens to snow if you have a flat roof. As Tizard and Hughes discuss, Beth pursues this abstract topic with penetrating logic. She counters her mother's explanation of water drainage with the example of her school roof and the fact that water does not seem to come through. Although not all the conversations were at this level, the study nevertheless points out some interesting contrasts between children's conversations in home and at nursery school.

There is no doubt that parents are, and wish to be, involved in their young children's learning and development. In a large-scale project in Sheffield which encouraged parents' involvement in their children's literacy development, parents were asked to describe some of the things they did to help their children. These included (Nutbrown 1994, p 89):

- pointing out signs when on the bus and in shop windows

- looking at the labels on tins, naming the soup, spaghetti, other packages

- playing the part of a character in the book after reading it together

- putting up an alphabet poster on their bedroom wall, looking at letters and saying them.

Adults in early years centres need to build on the intense interest which parents have in their children and on their resultant knowledge. As Vicky Hurst (1994) has said, parents are children's historians; they are the holders of their children's histories long before children begin any form of education or day care. Early years educators therefore need to find ways of sharing in their expertise.

The role of the early years educator

I have said that the role of the parent or main carer as educator is fulfilled naturally for most young children in the home setting. It is a unique role because it is attuned to the child's interests, culture and social context. Because of their intimate knowledge of their child, parents are able to respond intuitively to their learning needs and can give more time to the individual child than the adult in a group setting, even when home life is very busy. As you saw from Activity 1, parents can snatch opportune moments – they can catch the 'teachable moment' discussed in Week One. Interacting in this way is harder for adults in early years centres, where they are trying to meet the wide-ranging needs and demands of a larger group of children. In these settings adults will have a role which complements that of the parent, but it is not the same role. It cannot be carried out in the same way.

The High Scope curriculum offers a good example of how the adult's role might differ in early childhood centres. In planning daily activities the adult requires the child to *plan* what he or she wishes to do, to *carry out* the activity, then to *review* and *reflect* upon it. This is known as the 'plan, do, review' sequence, and it aims to encourage independent thinking and planning.

In early childhood centres time needs to be found to see what children are thinking, doing, saying and showing an interest in, so that learning and development can be planned for and supported in a way which puts the child at the centre of the curriculum. You can see, I hope, why informed observation is so central to the adult role. Play is of course the key vehicle for planning the curriculum in these settings (Bruce 1991). Involving parents in this process makes this task easier, even at the simple level of asking them what they have been noticing about their child that they would like to share.

I would like now to return briefly to Cathy Nutbrown's (1993) description of the role of the professional educator. The task of the early years educator is a demanding one; in fact it encompasses many roles. Some of these are similar to the role of the parent, as can be seen from the following descriptions:

The adult as model
The adult models or demonstrates many activities for the child: reading a book; writing a list or notice; carefully planting and watering seeds; cutting with scissors; being kind to others.

The adult as observer
The role of the adult in observing children from an informed perspective has already been stressed. It is through informed observation that assessment arises; it is how we find out what children know. It is how we evaluate what we do as educators.

The adult as provider
Adults provide children with carefully chosen equipment, materials and experiences to match their needs and interests. These will reflect the child's cultural background, including material to which all children can relate.

The adult as supporter
Provision of materials, although important, is not sufficient. The adult's role in drawing children into the meaningful use of materials is crucial. The adult as supporter of children's learning and development has multiple roles – interacting and intervening where appropriate, guiding, encouraging and instructing (Munn and Schaffer 1993).

UNIT 3 WEEK THREE

The adult as playmate

In order to respond to children's individual needs, adults need to make time to become involved in children's spontaneous play. They will sometimes, for instance, be invited to have tea in the home corner or shop in the greengrocer's shop. This offers a means of gaining insight into children's thoughts and feelings (Lally 1991). It may also be that the adult has to look for opportunities to be involved, but in a way that does not interfere with the child's agenda. This requires careful and sensitive listening and observation. Opportunities may then arise for extending and enriching the play through suggestions or additional props.

I would like to pause at this point to encourage you to think about these roles in the light of your own experience.

■ Activity 2 A

- If it is relevant, briefly describe the situation in which you are currently working with young children. Alternatively, draw upon a situation where you have interacted with young children, for instance as a parent, baby-sitter, childminder, playgroup worker or teaching assistant

- Reflect upon your roles in the situation you describe. You might find Cathy Nutbrown's description a good place to start

- For each main role listed above, briefly describe an incident which demonstrates how you took on the role

- Try to analyse what you did and how you think you helped the child concerned.

❏ Commentary

You may have been surprised by the number of roles you adopt in caring for and educating young children. You probably thought of others that were not listed above. The activity should help you to think more about when and in what situations the different roles are appropriate. For example, it can be hard to decide whether or not to join in (interact) when a child is engaged in an activity. This is where observing and listening come in. As noted above, in play it is important to stay with the child's agenda, not to impose your own adult one.

Organising a supportive environment

A factor identified by Munn and Schaffer (1993) in enabling early years educators to give sensitive and appropriate support to young children was the way the adults were organised in the nurseries they observed. A key worker system was used which enabled adults to form close relationships with 'their' group of children. You can see that this allows for a role relatively close to that of the parent. Adults working in reception or Key Stage 1 classrooms, with poor child-to-adult ratios, will find this idea difficult to implement. In a report on four year olds in infant classes Cleave and Brown (1991) noted the need for children of this age to have a sufficient number of adults in the classroom in order to feel secure and confident. Mary Jane Drummond (1995) reiterates this in her report on Hampshire's Early Admissions Programme.

I have stressed that young children need sensitive and responsive adults who are in tune with the individual needs of children, both in the home and in early years centres. I have suggested that the roles of the adults in these two settings are complementary, but different. A descriptive term suited to both roles might be that of a 'warm demander' (Ball 1994) who will take children gently forward into the zone of proximal development. What is important is that parents and early childhood educators work together to share their knowledge of the child, in order to provide continuity and progression in the child's learning and development.

Working with parents

We will now look in greater depth at why working with parents should be an integral part of early years provision (Braun 1992). This unit has so far suggested that this is a 'good thing', and we have explored some of the reasons for this. There is a wide range of literature covering the rationale for involvement and looking at different aspects. Parent involvement in reading has been a major sphere of activity in primary schools (Topping and Wolfendale 1985; Hannon 1995). More recently there has been growing interest in involving parents in their children's literacy development in the pre-school years (Miller 1996). Parents of children with special educational needs have been encouraged to become involved in the assessment and teaching of their young children (as you will explore more fully in Unit 4). Government reports, legislation and parents' charters have endorsed the collaboration of parents and professionals and have strengthened parents' rights to be involved in their children's education (Wolfendale and Wooster 1995).

It is, however, easy to be confused by the plethora of descriptive terms surrounding working with parents and to be unsure what these mean on a day-to-day basis. You are no doubt familiar with some of the following:

- partnership

- involvement

- collaboration

- contact

- parent help

- participation.

These terms suggest a *continuum* of work with parents ranging from a room for parents to use, through open evenings and parent consultations to home teaching projects such as Portage programmes where parents and professionals assess, plan for, and teach the pre-school child together. Sheila Wolfendale (1985) has attempted to define real partnership with parents by offering the following criteria:

- Parents are active and central in decision making

- Parents are perceived as having equal strengths and equivalent expertise

- Parents are able to contribute to as well as receive services

- Parents share responsibility, so they and professionals are mutually accountable.

Dorit Braun (1992) suggests that 'parental involvement' means staff finding and creating opportunities for parents to be involved in various ways. 'Working with parents' is a much broader term and implies an attitude to parents based on mutual respect. It can include very informal links and the taking of opportunities as they arise, as well as joint planned activities between parents and staff. This is perhaps a more realistic view of what is possible. As Braun notes, involvement is difficult for some parents. They may have commitments, may feel uncomfortable in some settings, or may be ill at ease with English. Non-attendance at events should not always be interpreted as lack of interest. A flexible approach to working with parents can build upon opportunities which present themselves, not just those that are planned.

UNIT 3 WEEK THREE

■ Activity 3 A

- List all the ways you have been involved as a parent in your child's/children's care/ education. If you are not a parent, find a parent you know well to share the activity with

- In what areas have you been involved (e.g. literacy, fund raising)?

- Note where these activities fit in relation to the above continuum

- Note whether you found them helpful or unhelpful to you and your child

- Do the activities you describe fit the criteria for partnership described by Sheila Wolfendale?

❏ Commentary

The following examples came to mind as I thought about my own experience.

Example 1. Reports from school

My daughter's primary school sends home end-of-year reports. As is common practice in many schools, there is a space for parental comment at the bottom and this is returned to the school. At the end of year 1 my younger daughter's 'English' report said that she enjoyed books, which she did, but went on to say, 'She is now using a cue system (e.g. using initial letter sounds to ìguessî words) and is reading more confidently.' As parents we in fact disagreed with this. We were quietly concerned about her lack of interest in reading. She was a very active child and, although she loved to be read to, she didn't want to do this for herself. She often declared that she hated reading, that she 'couldn't read' and that it was 'boring'. We saw little evidence of her using the strategies the teacher had described. We expressed our concerns on the return form, while praising all the positive developments which had happened over the year. However, no contact or response followed until we initiated it.

This type of incident, albeit an isolated one, pays only token respect to the notion of working with parents. It is a principle which in this instance was not realised in practice. I felt excluded from discussing and helping to plan for and support my daughter. I felt that my views and concerns were not important. Although helping her with her reading, I was not sharing responsibility with the teacher. My activity was parallel to what was going on in school, not collaborative.

Example 2. Playgroup committee member and voluntary worker

When my younger daughter began playgroup I was in a position to have some involvement, as I had decided to work part time for a period in my paid position. As a committee member, I felt that I was able to have a real influence on the day-to-day practice of the playgroup. Areas of concern raised by parents were discussed and addressed. For example, there was felt to be a need to improve the book area and the children's use of books. A book-sharing project involving the local library was begun and was well used by the parents. Concern was raised about the sparse outdoor play facilities. A permanent outdoor play area was created through lots of fund-raising by parents and the enthusiasm and hard work of young soldiers enlisted from the local army barracks. Because of my early years teaching background the playgroup was keen to use my skills and ideas as a voluntary worker.

In relation to the partnership criteria, I felt that I was active and central in making decisions which affected my daughter's education. My strengths and expertise were valued and used. I could contribute to as well as receive this service, and I shared responsibility for plans and decisions which affected my daughter's education.

Involving parents in planning and assessment

There is perhaps a failure in some early childhood centres to recognise just how much parents do achieve for their children (Braun 1992), as my first example indicates. The attitude of early years educators can sometimes militate against working with parents, despite good intentions. Attitudes to parents need to be examined and explored openly and honestly, as do attitudes relating to child rearing and issues relating to ethnicity and culture. Differing views about care and education need to be explored, for example views about teaching reading and writing, what utensils to eat with, what learning through play means. Some centres find it helpful to have staff whose specific role is to focus upon this area of work. In any work with parents Dorit Braun (p 181) suggests posing the question 'How will this benefit the children?'

The myth of the uninterested 'working-class' parent has been dispelled by a number of studies (Wells 1985; Tizard and Hughes 1984). Yet parents are often reticent and unsure about what they do and about communicating this to other adults who are working with their children. In the words of one parent interviewed by Hannon and James (1990) in a study about how parents helped their children with literacy, 'You don't want to learn them wrong and then find out when they go to school that they don't know what they're talking about' (p 265). One head teacher in the same study, when asked about parental involvement said, 'You won't find much of that in this area' (p 266). It is not surprising, therefore, that the parents in the study were reluctant to approach nursery teachers for help.

In contrast, the staff of one nursery school with whom I have worked closely have been keen to involve parents in planning and assessment. For example, parents were asked to note their child's responses to environmental print around the home. Some of the parents brought the child's favourite food packet into school and told the staff what their child had said about it. Lucy's comments reproduced in Figure 3.9 provided valuable information about her literacy development. She recognises some capital letters and even more lower-case letters, and can read some familiar words. She has some strategies for reading print: she guessed the word 'children' as 'Christopher', possibly from the initial letter sound or, as the parent suggests, from the shape of the word. This information was entered into Lucy's record form in the section for parents' contributions and the packet and comments were put into her portfolio. The staff could focus their planning around this new information. They became more alert to the print Lucy was noticing in the nursery school. (Miller, 1996)

■ Activity 4 A

If it is relevant, draw upon your own experience of working with parents, or of being a parent. Work through the statements below (taken from Wolfendale 1985; Braun 1992), seeing which you agree or disagree with. Give your reasons why. If possible, discuss them with someone else. You could add some statements.

- Parents can give vital information.
- Children will learn better if parents and early years educators work together.
- Parents are experts on their own children.
- Parents are too busy with their own lives to be involved.
- Professionals know best what is right for children.
- Parents have the right to be involved.
- Mothers should stay home to look after their children in the early years.
- Parents should be involved in decision making.
- Parents can be highly effective teachers of their own children.
- Children are the responsibility of the family, not society.
- The responsibility for working with parents belongs to all staff.
- It is assumed that anything you do is good for parents.

Now complete this statement if you can:

'Working in a professional-parent partnership has taught me.......'

UNIT 3 WEEK THREE

Figure 3.9

Lucy's comments

Picked out 'round' faces with 'round' eyes and triangle 'nose'. Read 'HANSEL & GRETEL' as 'FACE MEAT' as this is her own familiar term for this favourite food.

Differentiated between all numerals and letters correctly. Named all numbers correctly. Including 6 (but 'pieces' instead of 'slices').

Told me that the meat cost 'two, one, O, C, T'.

Picked out the word 'NO' and read it. Knew no other words.

Named a few of the capital letters - A, S, E, L, F, C.

Named most of the lower-case letters but found the print very small.

Thought that 'children' said 'Christopher'. (Similar shape word?)

P.S. Enjoyed the guessing aspect of the activity and then insisted on eating most of the contents of the packet!

❏ Commentary

Working through this activity should help you to clarify your own ideas, beliefs and values about working with parents. Parental involvement in children's care and education is well established, as is the central role of parents in this. The interest and willingness of parents to be involved in their children's education in a range of early childhood centres is clearly documented. However, parents need flexible channels for working with early childhood educators which are accessible and non-threatening.

For some children, early childhood centres are very different and 'distanced' from the setting of the home. Working with parents can help to reduce the distance.

Review of the unit

You are now at the end of this week's study, which has focused upon the similarities and differences in the roles of parents and professionals working with young children. Take some time to look over the week's work and think about the following:

- What interested you most, and why?

- Are there any activities you would like to return to?

- How will this week's study help you to reflect upon your role in the context where you engage with young children?

- In what ways will it influence you within the parent-professional partnership?

- How will it affect parent/professional links in your own setting or workplace?

Now make sure you complete the review activity. It is intended to consolidate your learning so far and link this to your practical work as a parent or professional with young children.

■ Review activity AB

Focusing upon your own workplace or an early childhood centre that you know well, consider the ways in which parents and professionals work together. How are home-school links formed? The following checklist (adapted from Braun 1993) may help you.

How does the centre relate to parents generally?
- How are children introduced to the centre?
- How are greetings and separations handled?
- How is progress reported?
- How are events communicated, and to whom? (Parent may be grandmother.)
- How are parents' views sought and collected?

What opportunities are there for parents to be involved?
- Do parents help with the work?
- Do they contribute in other ways, e.g. talking about their jobs?
- Do parents influence thinking and practice?
- Do men and women, all ethnic groups get involved?
- Are other significant adults involved, e.g. childminder?

Home-centre links
- Are families visited at home?
- Are parents offered workshops/meetings to discuss practice in the centre?
- Is there a vehicle for home-centre communication, e.g. home school book?

As part of this review activity, consider what changes you would like to see in this centre. Would a home school booklet help, or a room set aside for parents? What is feasible, possible? Try to discuss this with a friend or colleague if you can.

❏ Commentary

The example below shows how one student who works in an early years unit in a primary school approached this activity. The main points she made are offered as a summary.

* The nursery teacher makes home visits in the term in which the children are due to start the nursery unit; thus the child and parents are seen on 'home ground'

* A parents' meeting is arranged at the school a few weeks before the new intake begins. The teacher takes the child's 'history' from the parent/carer

* Parents are encouraged to help in the classroom with listening to reading, cooking or craft activities. One benefit of this which the student wrote about was working with a parent of a child experiencing writing difficulties. She had been taught by her mother to write in capital letters as she could not form her letters easily. This was discussed, the reasons explored and alternative ideas suggested

* A Reception/Year 1 teacher holds an afternoon discussion group for parents called 'The Effective Parenting Scheme'

* There is an information booklet for parents

* There are regular consultation evenings

* This student would like to see the role of support assistants developed in working more closely with parents.

You have come to the end of this unit on Curriculum in the Early Years. Before moving on to Unit 4, look back through your notes over the last three weeks. Make a short list of ideas, theories or findings which have influenced your thinking about the curriculum in early childhood settings as an outcome of studying this unit.

Further reading

Ball, C. (1994) *Start Right*, London: RSA, Chapter 5, 'The home and the community'

Braun, D. (1992) 'Working with parents', in Pugh, G. (ed) *Contemporary Issues in the Early Years*, London: Paul Chapman/NCB

UNIT 3 WEEK THREE

Unit 3 References

Week One

Abbott, L. and Rodger, R. (eds) (1994) *Quality Education in the Early Years*, Buckingham: Open University Press

Athey, C. (1990) *Extending Thought in Young Children*, London: Paul Chapman

Ball, C. (1994) *Start Right*, London: RSA

Blenkin, G. (1994) 'Early learning and a developmentally appropriate curriculum', in Blenkin and Kelly (1994)

Blenkin, G. and Kelly, A.V. (eds) (1994) *The National Curriculum and Early Learning*, London: Paul Chapman

Blenkin, G.M. and Yule, N.Y.L. (1994) 'Profiling early years practitioners: some first impressions from a national survey', *Early Years*, Vol 15, No 1, pp 13-23

Bredekamp, S. (ed) (1987) *Developmentally Appropriate Practice in Early Childhood Programs Serving Children from Birth Through Age 8*, Washington, DC: NAEYC

Curriculum Council for Wales (1991) *Under Fives in Schools*

David, T. (1990) *Under Five – Under Educated?*, Milton Keynes: Open University Press

DES (1990) *Starting with Quality*, London: HMSO

Drummond, M.J., Lally, M. and Pugh, G. (1989) *Working with Children: Developing a Curriculum for the Early Years*, London/Nottingham: National Children's Bureau/NES

Drummond, M.J. (1996) *An Undesirable Document: Desirable outcomes for children's learning on entering compulsory education*, University of Cambridgeshire, Institute of Education Newsletter No.32, 1996.

Early Years Curriculum Group (1989) *Early Childhood Education: The Early Years and the National Curriculum*, Stoke-on-Trent: Trentham Books

Griffin, B. (1994) 'Look at me – I'm only two': educare for under threes: the importance of early experience', in Abbott and Rodger (1994)

Henderson, J., Ingram, I., Kilough, B., Matchett, M., Skelton, P. and Trues-dale, A. (undated) *Nursery Education: The Curriculum Guidelines*, NICC

HMI (1985) *The Curriculum from 5-16: Curriculum Matters*, London: HMSO

HMI (1989) *Aspects of Primary Education: The Education of Children Under Five*, London: HMSO

Hurst, V. (1994) 'Examining the Emperor's new clothes: nursery practitioners and the nursery curriculum in the post 1988 climate', *Early Years*, Vol 15, No 1, pp 37-42

Katz, L. (1995) 'Multiple perspectives on the right start', Paper presented at the Start Right Conference, Barbican Centre, London, 20-22 September

Kelly, V. (1994) 'A high quality curriculum for the early years', *Early Years*, Vol 15, No 1, pp 4-6

Leichter, H.J. (1984) 'Families as environments for literacy', in Goelman, H., Oberg, A. and Smith, F. (eds) *Awakening to Literacy*, London: Heinemann

Penn, H. (1995) 'Mission impossible?', *TES*, 3 February

Rouse, D. and Griffin, S. (1992) 'Quality for the under threes', in Pugh, G. (ed) *Contemporary Issues in the Early Years*, London: NCB/Paul Chapman

SCAA (1996) *Nursery Education: Desirable outcomes for children's learning on entering compulsory schooling*, DfEE

SCAA (1996) *Nursery Education Scheme: The next steps*, DfEE

Whalley, M. (1994) *Learning to be Strong: Setting up a Neighbourhood Service for Under-fives and Their Families*, Sevenoaks: Hodder and Stoughton Educational

Whitehead, M. (1994) 'Stories from a research project: towards a narrative analysis of data', *Early Years*, Vol 15, No 1, pp 23-30

Week Two

Allen, E. (1991) *The Concise Oxford Dictionary of Current English*, 8th edn, London: BCA

Athey, C. (1990) *Extending Thought in Young Children*, London: Paul Chapman

Bartholomew, L. and Bruce, T. (1993) *Getting to Know You: A Guide to Record Keeping in Early Childhood Education and Care*, London: Hodder and Stoughton

Bruce, T. (1991) *Time to Play in Early Childhood*, London: Hodder and Stoughton

DES (1900) *Starting With Quality*, London: HMSO

Early Years Curriculum Group (1989) *Early Childhood Education: The Early Years and the National Curriculum*, Stoke-on-Trent: Trentham Books

Early Years Curriculum Group (1992) *First Things First: Educating Young Children*, Stoke-on-Trent: Trentham Books

Kensington and Chelsea LEA Early Years Profile (1992) London: Kensington and Chelsea Education Department

Lally, M. (1995) 'Principles to practice in early years education', in Campbell, C. and Miller, L. (eds) *Supporting Children in the Early Years*, Stoke-on-Trent: Trentham Books

Lally, M. and Hurst, V. (1992) 'Assessment in nursery education: a review of approaches', in Blenkin, G. and Kelly, V. (eds) *Assessment in Early Childhood Education*, London: Paul Chapman

Miller, L. (1996) *Towards Reading: Literacy Development in the Pre-School Years,* Buckingham: Open University Press

Nutbrown, C. (1994) *Threads of Thinking in Young Children*, London: Paul Chapman

Nutbrown, C. and Swift, G. (eds) (1993) *The Learning and Development of Three to Five Year Olds: Schema Observations,* Sheffield: City Council Education Department, Early Childhood Education Centre

Pen Green Centre (undated) *A Schema Booklet for Parents,* Corby: Pen Green Centre for Under 5s and Their Families

Rodger, R. (1994) 'A quality curriculum for the early years: raising some questions', in Abbott, L. and Rodger, R. (eds) *Quality Education in the Early Years,* Buckingham: Open University Press

Pascal, C., Bertram, T, Ramsden, F,Georgeson, J, Saunders, M, Mould, C. (1995)*Evaluating and Developing Quality in early Childhood Settings: A professional development programme*, Amber Publishing Company

Weinberger, J., Hannon, P. and Nutbrown, C. (1990) *Ways of Working with Parents to Promote Early Literacy Development*, Sheffield: University of Sheffield

Wolfendale, S. (1990) *All About Me,* Nottingham: NES/Arnold

Wolfendale, S.(1993) *Baseline Assessment: A Review of Current Practices, Issues and Strategies for Effective Implementation*, Stoke-on-Trent: Trentham Books

Week Three

Ball, C. (1994) *Start Right*, London: RSA

Braun, D. (1993) 'Working with parents', in Pugh, G. (ed) *Contemporary Issues in the Early Years*, London: Paul Chapman/NCB

Bronfenbrenner, U. (1975) 'Is early intervention effective?', in Friedlander, B.S. (ed) *Exceptional Infants: Assessment and Intervention,* New York: Bruner/Mazel

Bruner, J. (1975) 'The ontogenesis of speech acts', *Journal of Child Language*, 2:1-19

Bruner, J. (1977) 'Early social interaction and language acquisition', in Schaffer, H.R. (ed) *Studies in Mother Infant Interaction*, London: Academic Press

Cleave, S. and Brown, S. (1991) *Early to School: Four Year Olds in Infant Classes*, Windsor: NFER/Nelson

Drummond, M.J. (1995) *In School at Four*, Hampshire County Council Education Department

Hannon, P. (1995) *Literacy, Home and School*, London: Falmer Press

Hannon, P. and James, S. (1990) 'Parents' and teachers' perspectives on pre-school literacy development', *British Educational Research Journal*, Vol 16, No 3, pp 259-272

Hurst, V. (1994) 'Searching for quality', Paper delivered at BAECE conference, Why Nursery Education?, Church House Conference Centre, Westminster, 29 September

Lally, M. (1991) *The Nursery Teacher in Action*, London: Paul Chapman

Miller, L. (1996) *Towards Reading: Literacy Development in the Pre-School Years*, Buckingham: Open University Press

Munn, P. and Schaffer, R.H. (1993) 'Evenements relatifs a la capacité de lecture, d'écriture et de calcul dans des contextes interactifs sociaux', *International Journal of Early Years Education*, Vol 1, No 3, pp 61-80

Nutbrown, C. (1994) *Threads of Thinking in Young Children*, London: Paul Chapman

Tizard, B. and Hughes, M. (1984) *Young Children Learning*, London: Fontana

Topping, K. and Wolfendale, S. (eds) (1985) *Parental Involvement in Children's Reading*, London: Croom-Helm

Schaffer, R.H. (1977) *Mothering*, London: Fontana/Open Books

Wells, G. (1985) *Language, Learning and Education*, Windsor: NFER/ Nelson

Whalley, M. (1994) *Learning to be Strong: Setting up a Neighbourhood Service for Under-fives and Their Families,* Sevenoaks: Hodder and Stoughton Educational

Wolfendale, S. (1985) 'Overview of parental participation in children's education', in Topping and Wolfendale *op cit* (1985)

Wolfendale, S. and Wooster, J. (1995) 'Supporting children with special educational needs: inclusion for all', in Campbell, R. and Miller, L. (eds) *Supporting Children in the Early Years*, Stoke-on-Trent: Trentham Books

Unit 4:
Supporting children with learning difficulties and disabilities

Alice Paige-Smith

Contents

Unit 4: Week One
Integrated education

Objectives

This week's study will introduce you to different approaches to the education of children with learning difficulties and disabilities. By the end of Week One you should:

* be aware of the different approaches: inclusive education and special education

* understand how children's needs can be assessed, including the statementing process

* have explored some of your own ideas about the education of children with learning difficulties or disabilities

* be able to understand parents' perspectives on their children's education.

Activities

This week you will need to arrange about half an hour for discussion with the co-ordinator of an early childhood centre or the Special Educational Needs Co-ordinator (SENCO) in a school, plus time to write up your notes. This is a shorter amount of time than usual. Next week you will need about two hours for observation and reflection, as most of your observations are concentrated in the second week of study in Unit 4.

About this unit

In this unit we shall be considering the experiences of pre-school and school children who experience difficulties in learning or have disabilities. The unit will examine how these children can be supported in the home and in early childhood centres. The views of their parents will be explored in relation to the experiences they have with professionals who administer the services and the assessment procedures for their children.

In Week One we will consider the different approaches to educating children with learning difficulties or disabilities, which may vary from a mainstream school or nursery to a special school. As you read in Unit 3, the different forms of provision may be influenced by what is on offer within the area where the child lives and the views of the child's parents. The experiences of Michael, who has Down's Syndrome, will provide an example of how parents may become actively involved in the education of their child from an early age.

In Week Two the perspectives of parents will be explored in more detail. How do parents feel when they find out that their child has a learning difficulty or a disability, and what is the role of professionals who work with parents – can they be their 'partners'? Approaches to early intervention and assessment in the form of the 'Portage programme' will illustrate how parents and professionals can collaborate on the early education and care of the young child. This section will draw on the examples of how the Portage programme was put into practice for Bob and Ellen.

This is followed in the third week of study by an example of how a nursery teacher in an inner London school monitors the progress of all the children in her class, using the 'key worker' system. The assessment and identification of children with learning difficulties or disabilities is also considered and related to the statementing process and the Code of Practice on the Identification and Assessment of Special Educational Needs (1994). In this section I have tried to examine how the assessment and statementing process of children who experience difficulties can prove problematic. Finally we consider how professionals – and parents – can support children in the classroom by looking at the roles of teachers, learning support assistants and learning support teachers. A case study of a child in a primary school will be presented in this final section.

Some important issues

Before we begin to explore the different types of school and early childhood centre experiences children may have, I would like to introduce you to some of the controversial issues which surround a particular group of children who may have a label on them such as 'Down's Syndrome' or 'cerebral palsy', 'learning difficulties' or 'special educational needs'.

One of the difficulties in describing provision for pre-school and school children is the lack of uniformity around the country between each nursery, playgroup, school, local authority and health authority. I have tried to overcome this by providing examples of children, parents and local authorities which illustrate the different dimensions and approaches to supporting children who experience difficulties in learning or have disabilities.

Who are children with 'special educational needs'?

While the 1993 Education Act and the Children Act (1989) identify policies which should be followed, these are open to interpretation by local authorities, schools, professionals and parents. These Acts not only provide procedures to be followed and duties to be fulfilled; they also provide interpretations of children who are 'in need' and who may be considered to have 'special educational needs'.

The concept of 'need' in education and care is closely tied to provision; a child considered to have 'special educational needs' may for example have Down's Syndrome, and may 'need' support from an assistant in the classroom or early childhood centre, or from a home liaison teacher, to encourage his/her communication skills.

This unit will consider how perceptions of children's 'needs' may differ and, at times, come into conflict with each other. Identifying children's needs is usually carried out as a part of an 'assessment' procedure conducted by professionals and involving parental contributions – if parents are asked to contribute, for many parents, in particular those from ethnic minority groups, may be unaware of their chance to participate (Rehal 1989).

How to assess 'needs'?

From birth, children who have been identified as having 'special educational needs' may go through an assessment process under the 1993 Education Act, resulting in an official document called a *statement*. This process identifies the 'needs' and 'provision' for the child and can be the source of conflict between parents and professionals who may have different attitudes about where and how children should be educated. Approximately 2 per cent of the school population have a 'statement' which identifies their special educational need. Another 18 per cent of the school population may be considered to have 'special educational needs':

> Pupils with special needs range from those who may have a short-term difficulty in learning, to pupils with profound handicaps. It is estimated that 20% of pupils will have a special educational need at some time during their school life. [Audit Commission 1992, p 1]

The proportion of school pupils estimated to have 'special educational needs' during their school life may be smaller or larger than you expected, or you may be aware of this figure, which was first cited in 1978 by the Warnock Report. You may notice as you work your way around this unit that the term 'special educational needs' is considered to be problematic. Instead of using this term I prefer to refer to difficulties children may experience in learning, or how they have a disability. This is because disabled people or people who experience difficulties in learning prefer these terms. You may have noticed, however, that the above quotation from the Audit Commission report uses a mixture of terms to define children's difficulties – including the category of children who may be considered to have 'profound handicaps'.

Including all children?

The concept of the *integration* of children into their communities, pre-school centres and schools has developed primarily due to the demands of parents and a shift towards the principle of 'comprehensive education' since the 1960s (Vislie 1994). Including all children in mainstream provision has been acknowledged in policy documents such as the Guidance and Regulations issued alongside the Children Act (cited in Potts 1992, p 14):

> Generally the development of young children with disabilities or special educational needs is more likely to be enhanced through attending a day care service for under fives used by all children.

■ Activity 1 A

Try to list all the different labels that you have used to describe adults or children with learning difficulties or disabilities. Which labels do you feel most uncomfortable about using, and can you think of any labels that you have heard other people or children use to describe children who experience difficulties?

Can you think of an occasion in your working experience when you have heard a friend or colleague, or a child, refer to someone by using their 'label' rather than their name? Write about how you dealt with this situation. Did you say anything? Did you feel uncomfortable?

❏ Commentary

These labels seem to be in common use:

*   'special needs children'
*   'SEN'
*   'developmental delay'
*   'retarded'.

I am sure you have heard others.

I recently had a conversation with a teacher about a child who receives support in mainstream school because he has cerebral palsy. I was trying to think of ways the teacher could work alongside the mother of this child because she was not satisfied with the work he was doing in school and was considering educating him at home. The teacher kept referring to the child's mother as 'Mum': 'Mum wants more homework', 'Mum is never satisfied'. I referred to the mother as 'his mother' or used her name and I felt the term 'Mum' used like this was categorising the mother as a person who was not a professional, but was 'just a Mum'. This mother happens to be a teacher and perhaps the term 'Mum' was not recognising the importance of her view, as a mother or a professional teacher?

We have considered some important issues in this section which support the work of the rest of this unit. You have been introduced to some of the different ideas about the experiences of the children who will be described in this unit. In the next section we will be considering ideas about inclusive education and you will have a chance to consider your own views on equal opportunities for children with learning difficulties and disabilities.

Exploring definitions: from special schools to inclusion

By the end of this section you should be more familiar with the terms 'integration', 'segregation' and 'inclusive education', and understand how the concept of 'equal opportunities' applies to children who experience difficulties in learning or have disabilities. You will then go on to read about the experiences of Michael, a young child with Down's Syndrome, and how his parents have ensured their 'choice' of educating him in a mainstream school.

'Inclusive education' has been used to describe the ways in which children and young people who experience difficulties in learning or have disabilities can be included in nursery, primary and secondary schools, as well as early childhood centres. The term 'inclusive education' originated in North America in the late 1980s and has been adopted by voluntary organisations which campaign for the education of children with learning difficulties or disabilities in mainstream schools (organisations like Parents in Partnership and the Integration Alliance). A number of books have appeared in this country which use the notion of inclusive schools and inclusive education (Potts *et al* 1995; Jupp 1992; Clark *et al* 1995).

The term 'inclusive education' has not been used in Education Acts or the Children Act to describe provision for pre-school and school-age children. The Children Act (1989) refers to how services should be provided that are 'appropriate to children's needs' (Children Act 1989, Section 17 [1]). Often this refers to children under five who may otherwise be taken into care (Potts 1992). The 1993 Education Act (which replaced the 1981 Education Act) can secure education for children under five years old if they are considered to have 'special educational needs'. The 1993 Act (Part III, Section 156) considers that:

> A child has 'special educational needs' if he has a learning difficulty which calls for special educational provision to be made for him.

The provision these children receive may take the form of special schooling. In one inner London education authority, for instance, there is a wide range of different special schools for pupils with emotional and/or behavioural/social difficulties, profound deafness, physical disability, moderate learning difficulties, or profound and multiple learning difficulties. Many special schools have nursery classes which admit pupils from the age of two (Potts 1992). The attendance of children at these schools has been described as their exclusion or 'segregation' from mainstream schools since they are taken away from their local community school and educated in a school according to their 'special educational needs'.

Some children may receive support in mainstream schools, nurseries and playgroups as they are 'integrated'. Integration has been described by Tony Booth (Booth and Swann 1987, p 1) as 'a process of increasing the participation of children and young people in their communities'. Camden education authority, for example, provides a Primary Learning Support Service for children excluded from Key Stages 1 or 2 of the National Curriculum. This education authority claims in its policy of special educational needs that it supports integration 'for those pupils who are likely to flourish in a mainstream setting' (Camden LEA 1994, p 4).

Education policy and equal opportunities

The Special Education Policy Statement of the London Borough of Newham refers to the desegregation of special education and how it is the 'first step in tackling prejudice against people with disabilities and other difficulties' who, Newham education authority suggests, have been omitted from previous equal opportunities initiatives (Jordan 1992). Developing integration in this local authority is based on the policy commitment which recognises how all children will benefit:

It is also the right of pupils without disabilities or other difficulties to experience a real environment in which they can learn that people are not all the same and that those who happen to have a disability should not be treated differently. [Jordan 1992]

This London borough showed a commitment to integration by producing a policy statement about integration and setting up a Learning Support Team which included a pre-school team to support children with learning difficulties or disabilities in mainstream pre-school provision (Wolfendale and Wooster 1992).

In the 'Further reading' section at the end of this week's study you will find another account which describes the way that the London Borough of Islington tried to address the issue of early integration (Boushel *et al* 1992).

Inclusive schools?

Two American educators, Susan and William Stainback, describe what they consider to be an inclusive school:

> An inclusive school is a place where everyone belongs, is accepted, supports, and is supported by his or her peers and other members of the school community in the course of having his or her educational needs met. [Stainback and Stainback 1990, p 3]

Their book describes different ways schools can increase the participation of all children, including:

- peer support
- children helping each other
- professional collaboration
- teachers work closely together supporting individuals or groups of pupils.

The American educator Mara Sapon-Shevin has written about inclusive communities (Sapon-Shevin 1990). She considers that inclusive communities are caring and effective, and that the members of these communities feel as though they belong. A school can be an inclusive community if it represents a wide variety of diversity: different religions, cultures, economic circumstances and family differences. However, while some schools may appear 'inclusive' because children and young people with disabilities and learning difficulties are educated there, the same schools may also 'exclude' pupils who have been given the label of 'behaviour problems'.

A recent article in the *Times Educational Supplement* ('Tolerance declining for disruptive pupils', 1995) notes how the exclusion of pupils is increasing and occurring at an earlier age and that schools seem to be growing less tolerant of pupils with behavioural problems.

■ Activity 2 A

1. List the reasons why children should have the opportunity to be included into their local community early childhood centre or school. You may wish to use a highlighter pen to identify the points made in the previous section, then ask yourself whether you agree with these reasons.

2. Can you remember any school experiences which made you feel 'excluded' or which involved the exclusion of other children? For example, did your school stream, set or band the children?

❏ Commentary

1. Here is a list I have made. Compare it with your own:

Equal opportunities

- The right to be a part of your local community

- To go to nursery, playgroup or school with your brother or sister

- To benefit other children who may be fearful of disability

- To develop tolerance and acceptance of all children

- To learn alongside peers

- To get support from the local community

- To have fun with friends

2. A specialist teacher assistant (STA) gave this account:

I come from a large family in which I have one brother who actually detested going to school. I can remember him crying and pleading with mum each day as she left him there, and her tears as she walked away. He says that at the time he felt (and was told by the teacher) that he was totally useless at school because he could not read. He found writing very difficult and could not do the work set for him. In fact he became so traumatised that his writing gradually became illegible and he ended up going to a remedial school which he left as soon as he could.

In later years he was diagnosed as dyslexic. He became a conservation volunteer and met his wife through that work. With her help and encouragement and the use of a word processor he has just passed a degree course in Social Studies.

The memory of seeing him standing at the school door heartbroken has stayed with me to this day. It has made me determined to help and encourage any child I meet who is having difficulties so that their school days are happy ones.

Perhaps you can remember a school experience like mine. When I was on my first teaching practice at a primary school the class teacher told a child with learning difficulties to do her English and Maths work under the teacher's table. I was not sure why this practice was carried out; perhaps the teacher thought she could monitor what the child was doing, or else she was trying to make sure the child was not distracted by the other children. This child was excluded from her peers within the classroom.

Michael's experiences: a case study

In the previous section we considered some different approaches to education and care in the community. In the present section we shall be exploring the experiences of one child and how his family have tried to ensure his integration into mainstream nursery and primary school.

I became involved in supporting parents who want their children to be integrated into mainstream schools when I took up my post as a 'support teacher'. In the following case study I have been representing Michael and his parents. Their experiences are not unusual, and they represent an example of how parents and professionals may come into conflict over perceptions of how and where a child may receive education and care.

Introduction and background

By the age of seven Michael, who has Down's Syndrome, had attended a nursery class in a primary school, a special school for children categorised as having moderate learning difficulties, followed by a mainstream first school (the local education authority where he lives has a system of first, middle and upper schools).

Michael's experiences show how his parents wanted him to be included in the same school as his twin brother, but because of Michael's 'special educational needs' this choice of school was hard to ensure. Michael's eventual integration into the same school as his brother came about through a process of the parents making their views known and the education authority agreeing to fund a learning support assistant.

Michael's experiences also raise questions about whether parents have choices of schooling for their children. What is the 'best' type of school for children who experience difficulties in learning, and who decides where children should be educated – parents or professionals?

Transition from home to nursery

Michael's parents wanted him to attend his local nursery. When they approached the headteacher they felt her attitude was not welcoming. She was adamant that he could not be accepted at the nursery until he was 'potty trained'; she thought that changing his nappy would be 'inconvenient'.

Michael's mother went to visit the headteacher of another school which had a nursery class. This headteacher was 'very welcoming', according to Michael's mother, as there was already another child with Down's Syndrome at the nursery. This headteacher agreed to register Michael and his twin brother at the nursery. At the same time she asked their mother to request support, in the form of a learning support assistant and a learning support teacher, from the local education authority. Michael had received support from a home liaison teacher who was based at an 'opportunity playgroup' and had visited Michael at home for one hour each week. They wanted this to continue while he was at nursery.

However, when Michael's mother rang the school the term before he was due to start she discovered that his name was not on the list of children who had places in the nursery. The headteacher and school governors did not feel they could give Michael a place at the school unless the education authority confirmed that they would provide a learning support assistant and a support teacher for him. This situation was resolved, and Michael did start in the September with his brother at the nursery school. He was provided with a learning support assistant for a few hours each week.

Transition from nursery to special school

When Michael was five years old he was assessed by an educational psychologist in different areas of his development, such as his play and cognitive skills. A report was then issued by the local education authority recommending that he attend the special school for children categorised as having moderate learning difficulties. This report was Michael's 'statement' of his special educational needs, which outlines how a child's 'special needs' can be met.

Part B of *The Code of Practice on the Identification and Assessment of Special Educational Needs* (DfE 1994, pp 27-29) provides an example of a statement which is filled in by the education officer from the child's local education authority.

Parents have the chance to contribute their opinions, which may or may not be included in the statement. For instance, the parents may choose a school to be specified on the statement; the education authority may agree or disagree with the parents' choice, and the final 'choice' of school on the statement rests with the professionals. Parents have the right to appeal against their decision. Have a look at Part B of the *Code of Practice* now. You will find it reproduced over the next three pages.

PART B

STATEMENT OF SPECIAL EDUCATIONAL NEEDS

Part 1: Introduction

1. In accordance with section 168 of the Education Act 1993 ('the Act') and the Education (Special Educational Needs) Regulations 1994 ('the Regulations'), the following statement is made by [*here set out name of authority*] ('the authority') in respect of the child whose name and other particulars are mentioned below.

Child

Surname ....   Other names ....

Home address ....

....   Sex ....

....   Religion ....

Date of Birth ....   Home language ....

Child's parent or person responsible

Surname ....   Other names ....

Home address ....

....   Relationship to child ....

....

Telephone No. ....

---

2. When assessing the child's special educational needs the authority took into consideration, in accordance with regulation 10 of the Regulations, the representations, evidence and advice set out in the Appendices to this statement.

PART 2: SPECIAL EDUCATIONAL NEEDS

[Here set out the child's special educational needs, in terms of the child's learning difficulties which call for special educational provision, as assessed by the authority.]

PART 3: SPECIAL EDUCATIONAL PROVISION

Objectives

[Here specify the objectives which the special educational provision for the child should aim to meet.]

Educational provision to meet needs and objectives

[Here specify the special educational provision which the authority consider appropriate to meet the needs specified in Part 2 and to meet the objectives specified in this Part, and in particular specify –

(a) any appropriate facilities and equipment, staffing arrangements and curriculum,

(b) any appropriate modifications to the application of the National Curriculum,

(c) any appropriate exclusions from the application of the National Curriculum, in detail, and the provision which it is proposed to substitute for any such exclusions in order to maintain a balanced and broadly based curriculum; and

(d) where residential accommodation is appropriate, that fact].

Monitoring

[Here specify the arrangements to be made for –

(a) regularly monitoring progress in meeting the objectives specified in this Part,

(b) establishing targets in furtherance of those objectives,

(c) regularly monitoring the targets referred to in (b),

(d) regularly monitoring the appropriateness of any modifications to the application of the National Curriculum, and

(e) regularly monitoring the appropriateness of any provision substituted for exclusions from the application of the National Curriculum.

Here also specify any special arrangements for reviewing this statement.]

PART 4: PLACEMENT

[Here specify —

(a) the type of school which the authority consider appropriate for the child and the name of the school for which the parent has expressed a preference or, where the authority are required to specify the name of a school, the name of the school which they consider would be appropriate for the child and should be specified, or

(b) the provision for his education otherwise than at a school which the authority consider appropriate.]

PART 5: NON-EDUCATIONAL NEEDS

[Here specify the non-educational needs of the child for which the authority consider provision is appropriate if the child is to properly benefit from the special educational provision specified in Part 3.]

PART 6: NON-EDUCATIONAL PROVISION

[Here specify any non-educational provision which the authority propose to make available or which they are satisfied will be made available by a district health authority, a social services authority or some other body, including the arrangements for its provision. Also specify the objectives of the provision, and the arrangements for monitoring progress in meeting those objectives.]

_____ .   _____

Date   A duly authorised officer of the authority

From special school to integration into mainstream school

When Michael was six years old and had been in the special school for a year his parents decided they wanted him to transfer to the same school as his brother. They thought he was not making significant progress in the special school, and they also wanted him to be in a mainstream school environment. They wanted an 'independent' assessment of him in his special school, and I carried out the following observations one Monday morning.

Observations

Michael is in a class 2 which has ten pupils aged six years old. The ten children in the class were doing the following activities:

Table one: tape recorder, two headphones, two children

Table two: sequence activity; three/two children/welfare assistant

Table three: puzzles; two children/welfare assistant

Table four: teacher/one child/news book; Fantasy Box; one to two children.

10.10

I sat at a table where three children were doing puzzles with one welfare assistant. Michael sat at another with two other children and a welfare assistant. They were looking at sequence activity cards. They placed these in the correct sequence as a group with the prompting of the welfare assistant.

10.15

Sequence activity finished and Michael went over to the table where I was sitting. He chose a puzzle. He picked up the puzzle and said, 'I see an ooo'. He finished this wooden form board puzzle of approximately twenty pictures of objects after five minutes. He then looked closely at some of the pieces and moved them between his fingers, his head resting on his arm which was on the table. The welfare assistant gave him another puzzle to do. The teacher was working one to one with pupils, calling them over for their turns to draw a picture in their news books. She wrote a sentence and used rebus signs.

10.20

Ben went to the toilet. Teacher asked him to sign toilet.

Michael finished his second puzzle in less than one minute. He did this one again. It was of five cars which were different sizes.

10.30

Michael left the puzzle table and went to the large wooden toy car in the corner where two boys were playing (I found out later that this is called the 'Fantasy Box'). He went over to play with the box and was smiling at his friend who was playing noisily and banging bits of wood into holes (these were the wooden 'keys'). The teacher told Michael's friend to be quieter. Ben still had not returned, I think he was in the adjoining class of year one pupils.

The teacher called Michael over to do his news book. She said that she knew he had had a busy weekend because 'Daddy' had written in the home book that he had gone for a walk. She wrote a sentence in his book and asked him to draw a picture. He drew what looked like a face and then scribbled over it. While he was looking at the rebus figure he was leaning close to his book and saying what sounded like 'Daddy'. The teacher was attending to someone else who had entered the class to show his work to the class teacher.

10.35

The class were told to get ready for playtime. They went to the toilet and fetched their coats. Michael was on the toilet and the welfare assistant was standing at the door of the toilet. I could not see if he put his coat on by himself or if he fetched it from his peg.

Playtime

Michael walked to the play area for class two, a fenced-off tennis court which is part of the larger playground where all the pupils are outside (the school has secondary age pupils).

The gate was closed behind this group. Each time a new pupil came, the door was opened and closed by the welfare assistant on duty. I asked her if there was anything for the pupils to play with, she said that she didn't know, that she was new this term and that she had been there for lots of wet play times (which meant they were indoors). Then some play equipment arrived and the children rushed to take a ball or a hoop. Michael strolled around the playground contentedly. He was following a line around the edge of the tennis court.

11.00

Story time. I went in at about five past eleven; the story was just ending. Michael sat on a bench with his class. He was listening attentively to the teacher, he was looking at her and at the pictures of the story book. When the story was finished two children spoke about 'slugs' – 'My mummy eats slugs' said one boy. Michael made some sounds quietly, three utterances, which could have been sentences, involving the word 'I...'. I could not hear as I was not next to him.

11.10

Michael was told by the teacher to play with the Fantasy Box with one other child. He was happy to play with the box and was smiling at his friend. From what I observed they were almost playing together, there certainly was co-operative play happening: they both were playing with the wooden keys at the same time. When Michael was in the driving seat the other boy wanted to sit there. Michael happily moved over and sat on the floor to play with the keys. They played quietly. The rest of the class continued with the puzzle table, the sequence table and writing their 'news' stories one to one with the teacher.

Interpreting observations

■ Activity 3 A

- Make a list of the activities Michael undertook with help from a teacher or a learning support assistant

- List the activities which Michael did on his own

- List the activities which Michael did with his classmates

- Using the lists you have made, try to say which activities required a special school setting and which activities could be carried out in any classroom.

❏ Commentary

On his own, Michael

- did some puzzles
- went to the toilet
- strolled round the playground

With his classmates, Michael

- did sequence activity
- played with Fantasy Box
- listened to a story

With help from an assistant or teacher, Michael

- did sequence activity
- worked on news book.

Your lists may highlight that some of the activities are more directed and supported than others, which would suggest that the low child-to-adult ratio in a special school might be more appropriate.

UNIT 4 WEEK ONE

On the other hand, Michael could have been provided with more activities to choose from, apart from simple puzzles which he completed quickly.

You may also have noticed that Michael required supervision when he went to the toilet – not always convenient in a primary classroom with one teacher. Michael did not interact with his peers in the playground or play with the equipment, which was perhaps surprising given the special school setting, where adults are meant to encourage such social interaction. Michael was happy in the class and wanted to play with his peers, and he had the opportunity to do this when he played with the Fantasy Box. He received one-to-one attention from the teacher when he did his writing. The interaction could have been more lively if more children were involved, although this may have distracted Michael from his task. I am not sure that a special school setting made any difference to Michael's learning experiences here.

Parent participation and Michael's statement

Michael's parents were presented with a copy of these observations and also a set of recommendations for activities that he could be encouraged to follow. On reading these observations Michael's parents were concerned about the isolation of their child during playtime, and they also felt that he needed the stimulation of other children's conversation and interaction that he would get in a mainstream classroom.

Michael's parents wrote a letter to the LEA's Special Educational Needs Officer explaining that they wanted Michael to attend the mainstream school that his brother attended. They asked for the school which was named on his statement of special educational needs to be changed and that he should receive support from a welfare assistant in the classroom.

A meeting was arranged with the Special Educational Needs Officer. The parents put forward their point of view and I supported them by representing their views. By the end of the meeting, which was over an hour long, the education officer agreed that Michael would be provided with part-time support from a learning support assistant in the mainstream school his parents wanted him to attend. Prior to this meeting the parents had met with the headteacher of the mainstream school and had agreed that Michael would need a high level of individual support from a learning support assistant in the classroom.

Michael started at the primary school in the January. This school has three classes for less than 100 pupils aged between five and nine, and is in a small village on the outskirts of a New Town.

Two terms after he began at his mainstream school an 'annual review' of his progress was conducted. The parents, his class teacher, the headteacher, an educational psychologist, the special education officer and I attended this meeting. Michael's statement of his special educational needs was also discussed at this meeting as it required updating in accordance with the regulations of the 1994 Code of Practice on the Identification and Assessment of Special Educational Needs published by the Department for Education. His last statement was made while he was in nursery school and his parents wanted his new statement to include the provision of a learning support assistant for twenty hours each week at the primary school that he was now attending.

The meeting was lengthy and the discussion focused on the progress Michael had made at his school. This was summarised as follows by the headteacher, who sent a letter to the education officer responsible for special education:

> Michael has made recognisable progress and many steps towards increasing independence since his transfer to Highlands First School.

Advice for the new statement was agreed between the parents, teachers, psychologist and education officer. Notes taken of the meeting by the headteacher were then sent to the special education service. Here are some of the main recommendations:

UNIT 4 WEEK ONE

Special Educational Needs
- To develop expressive language skills and to continue to improve listening and general comprehension

- To develop early literacy and numeracy

- To encourage his creative and imaginative development including imaginative play

- To encourage self-help skills and greater independence, particularly taking part in school routines with decreasing support.

Special Educational Provision
- Access to a rich social and language environment together with daily adult support in small-group games and activities

- Access to individual and small-group work with regular adult support in order to help with cognitive skills, size, shape, knowledge of early number, names, sequencing and representational skills

- Maintain current level of adult support in order to ensure this provision is possible (20 hours a week).

When the parents received a draft copy of Michael's new statement from the education service, however, they were surprised to read that the draft statement was virtually unchanged from the original statement issued when he was at the end of his nursery education. The only alteration was to the section on 'Appropriate school or other arrangements' which had been changed from 'a special school catering for a child with moderate learning difficulties' to 'a mainstream school with appropriate teaching and welfare support for a pupil with moderate learning difficulties'.

The parents wrote a lengthy response to the draft statement as, under the 1993 Education Act, they had 15 days in which to reply. They were hoping they would be able to ensure that the support from an assistant was written into his statement of 'special educational needs'. This document becomes an important legal document for parents who want to ensure that their child is integrated into a mainstream school. However, the LEA did not agree to include a specific amount of hours of support on Michael's statement. His parents may now go through the appeal process and are considering whether they may have to take their case to the Appeal Tribunal which has been set up since the 1993 Education Act.

The *Independent* on Saturday 5 August 1995 carried an article on how other parents, like Michael's, have to represent their views on the education of their children who experience difficulties or have disabilities. The article was entitled 'Campaigners for special needs children face jail', and it focused on the action of an educational psychologist and a higher education lecturer who were refusing to pay fines after they held a sit-in at the offices of an education authority. They were protesting about the authority's decision to send two children to special schools against the wishes of their parents, who want them to be integrated into mainstream schools.

Parent action

■ Activity 4 A

Cameron and Sturge (1990) produced the following advice for parents on how to meet professionals on equal terms:

General advice	Reason
Build confidence in your ability.	Because you are an expert at being a parent.
Use your feelings rather than your emotions.	So you can use your tears and anger rather than being incapacitated by them. They can be a powerful tool.
Look out for what is not being said or written.	Leaving out information can be a way for people to manipulate situations.
Be persistent.	Because what you can achieve matters a great deal to you.
Find allies.	So you are not struggling on alone.
If necessary, go up the hierarchy.	If you have tried, but not got anywhere, with the professionals closest to you, consider going to the person with overall responsibility who may be in a better position to make a decision.
Be prepared and organised.	To avoid getting flustered, forgetting issues you intended to raise.
Work at what you want for your child and yourself.	Because it's your child, your lives, and you know what your needs are.
Ask, ask and ask again.	Because it's the best chance you have of finding out what you need to know.
Keep a list of all the people you are involved with, including their names.	To help you remember who is the most appropriate person to turn to in each situation.

- Tick off which pieces of general advice have been taken by Michael's parents. Choose one from the list of general advice and say in more detail how they have followed this advice

- What do Michael's parents consider his 'needs' to be?

- Write a possible solution to Michael's educational future from the parents' perspective.

❑ Commentary

- You may have considered that Michael's parents were well prepared and organised when they presented their case to the local education authority. They went 'up the hierarchy' when they made their views known to the professionals. They have also pursued their demands by taking action, writing letters, making phone calls and being persistent.

- Michael's parents consider his needs to be centred around maintaining friends and family connections, which are seen as supporting his social development. They wanted Michael to attend his local nursery and to go on to the same primary school as his brother. They would also like the continued support of a home liaison teacher.

- The solution to Michael's educational future could be that he continues to receive support in mainstream school, and that this support is provided by the local education authority. Michael's needs will change when he progresses through his schooling, especially when he reaches secondary school age. He may experience difficulties in learning, but the curriculum could be adapted to meet his needs, with appropriate support and teaching methods.

Review of the week

The case study of Michael and the experiences of his family illustrate the lack of choice parents have over their children's schooling. The case study also illustrates how Michael's parents used his 'statement' to ensure his provision and how parents' 'choices' in education can be restricted by the power of professionals to disregard their views. Michael's is one example of how parents may find an integrated placement for their child who has a 'label' such as Down's Syndrome difficult to ensure.

Perhaps the difficulty arises because the parents' request for integrated education is unreasonable; special schooling may be the 'best' form of schooling for the child. Or maybe professionals' decisions should be more influential than the views of parents when it comes to children's schooling. How do you feel about these issues?

■ Review activity B

If possible, obtain copies of policy documents about children with 'special educational needs' from (a) your local school and (b) the early childhood centre you are visiting, or that you work at. Read through each document, then answer the following questions:

- Is each policy document 'inclusive' for all children?

- How does each policy document refer to children with learning difficulties or disabilities?

- How does each policy document refer to parents?

- Write a list of positive and negative aspects about each policy document. What is good about the policy and what could be improved? What differences do you notice between the school's document and that of the early childhood centre?

You should be able to obtain a policy document from a school. Every school should have a special educational needs policy and a school governor who is responsible for this issue. Every school should have a copy of *The Code of Practice on the Identification and Assessment of Special Educational Needs* (DfE 1994).

Many early childhood centres, though not all, will have devised their own policies. For example, most pre-school playgroups will have followed the advice given in the Pre-School Playgroups Association document, *Learning for All* (1992). Other centres will be following the advice of their local authority. It will be interesting to see what policy document, if any, your early childhood centre is using.

❏ Commentary

You may find policy documents difficult to read and understand – I know I have had to read some documents two or three times before I have fully comprehended the ideas expressed. Sometimes I write notes as I read through documents; this helps to interpret the meaning of the document in a way which highlights the points that are being made.

You may wish to discuss the policy document with the person who is responsible for putting it into action in the school or early childhood centre. (In the school this will be the special educational needs co-ordinator and the school governor who has responsibility for special educational needs. In the early childhood centre the person responsible will usually be the head, the co-ordinator or the play leader.) This will raise your awareness of how the policy is put into practice and its effect on the children and staff of the centre or school.

You may wish to focus on an aspect of the policy such as:

- early intervention

- partnership with parents

- assessment.

Try to speak to a parent from the early childhood centre and school from which you have obtained the policy documents. See if the parent has had a copy of the policy and ask them what they think about it.

I have been supporting a parents' group in my local area that has been asked for their views on the local education authority's policy on special educational needs. The group has had a three-hour meeting and has produced three pages of comments. These comments will be a part of the consultation process, during which parents' views will be considered, but they may or may not be included in the final policy document. Nonetheless, the consultation process is one way in which parents' views can be incorporated into education policy.

Further reading

Wolfendale, S. and Wooster, J. (1992) 'Meeting special needs in the early years', in Pugh, G. (ed) *Contemporary Issues in the Early Years*, London: Paul Chapman and National Children's Bureau

Boushel, M., Debenham, C., Dresner, L. and Gorbach, A. (1992) 'Attempting to integrate under fives: policy in Islington, 1983-8', in Booth, T. et al (eds) *Policies for Diversity in Education*, London: Routledge

You will find a full list of references at the end of Unit 4.

UNIT 4 WEEK ONE

Unit 4: Week Two
Understanding parents' perspectives

Objectives
By the end of this week's study you will have explored:

- early intervention and assessment for children with learning difficulties and disabilities

- the role of professionals and parents in early intervention programmes, including the Portage programme.

Activities
This week you will be asked to spend up to two hours observing children and evaluating practice in an early childhood centre or school, plus time to write up your notes.

About this week's study
During this week's study we will consider parents' perspectives in more detail. I begin by outlining forms of early intervention and assessment procedures which may be initiated by professionals who are responsible for monitoring, evaluating and guiding the learning and development of the child who has been referred to them from either the health or education services.

An example of how the assessment process begins in one London borough leads to the discussion of the idea that children with disabilities experience different attitudes when they come into contact with the health and education services. The notion of professionals as 'partners' to parents when they work with children has been emphasised. We explore how professionals can be partners by examining parents' experiences and views. This is especially important in the example of the Portage programme of early intervention which requires a close partnership between parents and the Portage home visitor.

The assessment process has become a tool of professionals working with children who experience difficulties in learning or have disabilities. We will be taking a close look at how the process of assessment is encapsulated in education policy which relates to children categorised as having 'special educational needs'. Finally, we will consider assessment in a nursery school context and approaches to supporting children within a nursery school.

Early intervention: professionals and parents
Parents may become aware of their child's difficulty at birth or during their early years. In the London Borough of Newham the parents of children whose disabilities or learning difficulties are identified from birth will be referred to the Child Development Centre on leaving hospital (Wolfendale and Wooster 1992). A senior medical officer will visit the parents at home and provide advice, information and a referral to a physiotherapist. The 'assessment' of the child is initiated at this early stage by professionals from the medical field, including doctors and health visitors. Next, when the child is aged between three and six months another assessment will take place, and a 'broad-based multi-disciplinary team' will continue to monitor the child until he/she is five. Figure 4.1 illustrates the professionals who may be involved with a child who has been identified as having a learning difficulty or disability from birth:

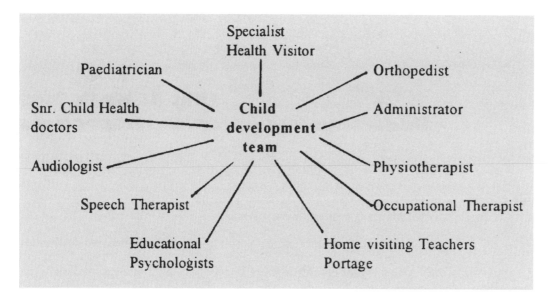

Figure 4.1 The child development team in the London Borough of Newham
Source: Wolfendale and Wooster (1992, p 130)

These professionals will continue to provide advice and monitoring on the child's progress. For some children, who are considered to need support from a speech therapist or an occupational therapist, a referral would have to be made through the child's doctor or pre-school centre. If the provision is available then the child may visit the therapist at her or his workplace, or in some cases the therapist may visit the child in an early childhood centre or school. However, children referred from school will be the responsibility of the Newham Learning Support Team rather than the Child Development Centre.

This Learning Support Team has 154 pre-school pupils on roll, with 15 on their waiting list; there is a pre-school co-ordinator, a senior Portage worker, seven teachers and nursery nurses. The members of this pre-school team provide home visits and long-term support to children in nursery. They run programmes consisting of training and support activities, including 'advice on individual children, information on assessment and curriculum' (Wolfendale and Wooster 1992).

The value of early intervention

Chris Goodey (1992) is the parent of a child with Down's Syndrome. His partner, Linda Jordan, wrote about her experiences of an early intervention programme carried out in partnership with a professional – in this case the Portage teacher. I will describe the Portage model in the next section.

Before we go on, I would like you to think about the issue of early intervention. In Unit 3 you considered some of the advantages of parental involvement in early childhood education as well as care. Linda Miller discussed how this can be made possible in early childhood centres and schools. Many would argue that these issues become even more important in the case of families where a child is experiencing learning difficulties or has a disability.

■ Activity I A

Make a list of reasons why it is important for parents and professionals to work together if the child with learning difficulties or disabilities is to receive all the support they need.

❏ Commentary

Compare your notes with the points made by Garry Hornby (1991) about the importance of early intervention and the involvement of parents. Hornby outlines the advantages of parents becoming involved in supporting their children, with advice from professionals:

- Without the active involvement of parents the developmental progress made by children will typically be reduced

- Unless the intervention has some impact on parents themselves it is unlikely that gains which the children make will be maintained in the long term

- The needs of parents for support and guidance must be a major consideration.

Hornby suggests (p 210) that the early needs of parents of children with disabilities are as follows:

- having the diagnosis of disability communicated to them in a sensitive and constructive manner

- obtaining information about the child's disability or learning difficulty and suggestions on facilitating the child's development

- receiving emotional support and help in understanding feelings and reactions

- meeting other parents of children with similar disabilities.

Most of these needs can be met by an early intervention programme known as the Portage programme. This originated in 1969 in the small town of Portage in the United States of America. The next section will discuss this model in detail.

The Portage programme

The idea behind the Portage model was that parents 'with instruction, guidance and support ... could teach their own children to grow and develop to their maximum potential' (Shearer and Shearer 1986). The Portage approach involves parents in the teaching of their children in their own homes. The family is visited weekly by home teachers who teach parents how to follow an activity programme designed for individual children's skills.

This section describes how the Portage programme was used to help two children, Ellen and Bob, and their parents.

Ellen's experiences

Linda Jordan has described how Portage was used for her daughter Ellen, who has Down's Syndrome (Jordan and Wolfendale 1986).

A checklist was produced by the Portage home visitor, and the activities which Ellen could already do were ticked off. Together the mother and the Portage home visitor decided that they would work on Ellen's ability to turn her head to sound. An activity chart was provided, and Ellen had to do six 'trials' each day – she would be encouraged to turn her head to a sound six times each day, for a week. Once she had achieved this the activity might change, say from turning her head to an unfamiliar sound to turning at the sound of her parents' voices.

> For the rest of the week my husband or I did the trials each day and although it may not sound very significant ... we gained tremendous satisfaction from carrying out these small tasks with Ellen. When she turned her head for the first time it was wonderful and by the end of the week Ellen turned her head every time we rang the little bell. [p 14]

The benefits of the Portage model are that parents and the teacher can see progress being made by the child as realistic targets are set. The use of structured record keeping of daily trials mean that parents are working with their children for at least ten minutes a day which, according to Linda Jordan, 'helps to avoid the guilt' that parents often feel about not helping their children enough.

UNIT 4 WEEK TWO

Over a period of 18 months Ellen received over 60 home visits; each target set was achieved within one, two or three weeks and was recorded on activity charts and record sheets. Targets were set for Ellen in the areas of Language, Language/Cognitive, Social and Self-help, and Motor Skills. Here are some examples in the area of language and cognition:

- to point to herself when asked 'Where's Ellen?'

- to identify (via touch or point) two body parts, 'mouth' and 'eyes'

- to identify on a person 'hair'

- to point to her own nose on request

- to bring a named object (out of three) on request (cruising, not walking, at that stage).

Parental involvement and early intervention

■ Activity 2 B
- Why was early intervention so important for Ellen and her parents?

- As parents, carers and early childhood educators you will work with young children on a one-to-one basis for at least part of the day, so the following task should be easy for you to arrange.

  - Choose a learning activity you might do with a child. This might be something like painting, doing a puzzle, writing a story, reading a book – or maybe teaching a skill like washing hands or throwing a ball

  - Divide up the task or activity into small steps, writing down each step. Think about each step involved in learning the task, as in the Portage model

  - Carry out the activity

  - How did the Portage model help you? How did it help the child?

❏ Commentary
- Early intervention was important for Ellen because her learning was encouraged to progress. Her parents were given guidance on how to become involved in her learning.

- Here is an example given by a key worker in a day nursery. He wanted to teach three-year-old Andrew to clean his teeth after lunch. The key worker first of all broke this task down into small steps, or what Portage workers call 'component skills'. He then considered the order in which the skills should be taught.

  Component skills in 'cleaning teeth'
  - Pick up toothbrush
  - Turn on tap
  - Wet brush under tap
  - Unscrew toothpaste tube
  - Squeeze toothpaste onto brush
  - Screw top on toothpaste
  - Brush teeth with brush
  - Rinse brush under tap
  - Pick up cup
  - Fill cup under tap
  - Rinse mouth with water
  - Turn off tap

When it came to considering the order in which these component skills should be taught, the key worker decided to group them like this:

- All the skills involving the tap and water

- All the skills involving grasping

- All skills involving squeezing and turning

- All skills also associated with awareness of the mouth.

The key worker and Andrew's parents chose one group of skills to focus on each week. This helped Andrew to gain an increasing sense of achievement, until he could do the whole operation of cleaning his own teeth.

The learning activity you chose may have been quite different, depending on the age and point of development of the child, as well as the particular early childhood setting you work in. My guess is that the same principles apply, in that breaking down a task into manageable steps makes things easier for the child and for the assistant trying to teach them something.

Bob's experiences

This section will illustrate this process of task analysis, or breaking a task down into small, manageable steps.

Bob is a year old and has been receiving support from a Portage teacher since he was six months old. The local education authority where he lives has an Early Stimulation Project based at a nursery school, where one part-time and two full-time Portage teachers provide support for 40 children. Bob's mother had heard about the Portage programme and was very keen for her son to begin. When she found out about the Early Stimulation Project she rang them up for information and asked them when they could begin visiting her son. She had to be persistent with her demand and eventually she was provided with a Portage teacher for Bob when he was six months old. This teacher visited him at home for one hour each week to stimulate Bob and to talk with his mother, and at the end of each session she provided a checklist of skills for Bob and his mother to follow. Goals were set to last for one term. His first goals were as follows:

Name of child: Bob
Date: February 1995

SOCIALISATION
Smiling and vocalising to his mirror image

SELF-HELP
Eating strained food fed by parents
Eating mashed table foods fed by parents

COGNITIVE
Removing objects from different open containers

MOTOR
Turning from stomach to side, maintaining position 50% of the time
Putting down one object to deliberately reach for another offered to him

LANGUAGE
Vocalising in response to attention
Babbling (series of syllables)

Here is a record of the activities he did during his first session made by the Portage teacher and given to Bob's mother at the end of the session.

Name of child: Bob   Date: March 30

ACTIVITIES INCLUDED IN THIS SESSION:

Looking at the rattles held in his hands

Helping him to crumple up paper held in his hands

Moving a cloth from his face for Peep-Bo game

Touching him from behind to encourage him to turn

Placing toys of different feel and weight on his chest

as he lies on his back – to get his hands up to feel

Grasping a dangling ring

The arrangements for carrying out the activities were less structured than for Ellen as Bob's mother would be given this list to refer to during the week. Each week new targets were set for Bob and his mother to follow. During the Easter holidays Bob received a different sheet of activity suggestions which included a picture of a rabbit:

EXTRA SPECIALLY HAPPY EASTER

Activity suggestions: Bob

Lots of hand clapping games and songs

Putting his hands into containers to find objects

Pressing the pads, to activate the fan and the buzzer

Lots of work on his tummy

Hand held to wave to everyone

At the end of June, after a few months of the Portage programme and nine visits, Bob's home visitor prepared a report on his progress. The report evaluates whether Bob has achieved the aims set for him over the term; the date was recorded alongside the activity when he was able to do the task, next to the date the activity was started, so the time it took for Bob to achieve each task was made available. These tasks related to the original goals selected each term in these areas:

- Socialisation
- Self-help
- Cognitive
- Motor
- Language

Teaching objectives were then set in the light of his progress. Here is the section in the report which covers the area of Bob's socialisation:

Bob: July	**PORTAGE PROGRESS**	(DATES)
AREA	TEACHING OBJECTIVES	
Socialisation	Seeks eye contact when attended for 2-3 mins	
	Responds to own name, by looking/reaching to be picked up	
	Manipulates toy or object	
	Shakes/squeezes object in hand, makes sound unintentionally	
	Vocalises to gain attention	
	Reaches for and pats at mirror image or another infant	
	Holds and examines offered object for at least a minute	
	Squeezes or shakes toy to produce sound in imitation	

Bob had achieved all these objectives by July, a few months after he had started his Portage programme. Four months later his weekly objectives had progressed to include more play activities:

Name of child: Bob   Date: October 30

ACTIVITIES INCLUDED IN THIS SESSION:

Take the man out of the car

Putting the squeaky birds into the container with help

Turning pages (several at a time)

Holding his hand to 'scoop'

Stacking bricks for him

Looking at named familiar objects
(taking him round the house to look and touch the objects
as you name them: light, door, table)

Since Bob had started on his Portage programme his activities in the areas of socialisation, self-help, cognitive, motor and language had all progressed. The advantages to Bob, his mother and the home visitor of using this programme were that his development was clearly supported by structured activities and his progress was monitored. As Bob has Down's Syndrome his 'developmental milestones' may be different to those of other children, and the structured activities carried out by the home visiting teacher showed his mother how to encourage his development. Bob's mother is delighted with his progress and appreciates her contact with the home visiting teacher, whom Bob greets when she arrives for their weekly sessions. These meetings are more than intensive periods of working with Bob as they also provide a chance for his mother to talk about her concerns and Bob's achievements with the home visiting teacher. The observation that follows illustrates this point well.

Observation of a Portage session with Bob

One of Bob's sessions, when he was one year old, began when the home visiting teacher arrived for his weekly session. She took off her shoes in the hallway and greeted Bob enthusiastically as she entered the sitting room. His mother immediately placed him in his wooden chair (provided by the service) and strapped him in. The 'matching' table fitted comfortably around him so that he was at the right level to play with objects, using his hands. His mother commented on how his feet now touched the ground whereas when he first had the chair and table his legs were splayed out. His mother told Ann, the home visiting teacher, that she was pleased because he had started drinking from a cup. Ann responded by saying, 'Yes, he went straight from a bottle to a cup.' She then asked where his bus was, the toy she had left for him to play with last week. Ann then sat on the floor opposite Bob, as close as she could get to him, face-to-face, in order to maximise their eye contact and overall communication together. Ann asked his mother if he had made any attempt to put the wooden toy men back into the holes in the bus during the week. Bob's mother replied that 'he seemed to do things and then he goes back again'. Turning to Bob she said, 'Give it to mummy,' and he threw the toy man on the floor in her direction. 'I'm going to put this man in the car. Can you follow it? Do you want it?' Ann said to Bob. He took the man and tried to put it back in. His mother told Ann how she remembered how Robin, her older son, used to get pots and pans out from the kitchen at the same age as Bob and that maybe she should try Bob with the pots and pans. Ann continued to encourage Bob to put the toy man into the car for ten minutes; she showed him how to do it and then sang 'The wheels on the bus go round and round' while moving the car up and down the table. She then took out another toy from her bag and Bob anticipated his next toy excitedly by waving his hands up and down, making babbling noises and smiling while looking at the bag.

A plastic toy with three dolphins which squeaked when they were pressed emerged from her bag. 'This toy can be used for colour matching,' Ann told Bob's mother, and said that she didn't know the Makaton sign for dolphin [Makaton is a form of signing which can be used to reinforce language]. Bob's mother said that she had enrolled for a class to learn Makaton signing and they discussed the pros and cons of using signs. 'Apparently Pam is against using signs and says that she never used them with her son who is now seventeen years old. But I suppose it's worth trying – if it works,' said Bob's mother. 'In', said Ann when she placed the dolphin in its hole, and she made it squeak three times. Bob reached out to touch her hair and smiled at her. Ann leaned further towards Bob and showed him her hair 'Hair, eyes, nose, clap hands,' she said to him as she touched her features using his hand and then touched his and helped him to clap his hands, finishing off with the action rhyme 'Round and round the garden, like a teddy bear …'.

By this time twenty minutes had passed and Bob picked up the dolphins and banged them onto the table. 'Bang, bang, bang,' responded Ann. She then took out some Stickle bricks from her bag and encouraged Bob to pull them apart, again reinforcing this action using the word 'pull' repetitively. 'Go on, Bob, get a good grip,' encouraged his mother, but Bob was more interested in exploring the toy by banging it on the table and tasting it; at the same time he was making lots of babbling noises: 'meh, meh, meh, meh, meh, ba, ba, ba, ba, aa, aa, aa, aa'. His mother then went to get him a bib because he had started to dribble. Ann commented on how it was unusual that he was dribbling, and his mother explained that he was teething. She then told Ann how she was really pleased that he had started to move from his stomach into a sitting *position and that this was a real achievement she was proud of. Meanwhile Ann had started playing peek-a-boo with a Stickle brick which she also turned into a camera and started to take pictures with. 'He really explores things, doesn't he?' she said to Bob's mother. 'Oh yes,' she replied, 'he turns them all over, bashes them to see how they work.' 'Oooooo, eeeeee', was Bob's response.*

'I'm not sure how to tell his brother that he's got Down's Syndrome,' Bob's mother said to Ann (Robin was at playgroup). She spoke to Ann about how Robin had begun to notice that other children the same age as Bob did not have a standing frame to help them to stand up. He had recently been at a friend's house who had a young child the same age as Bob and he asked his mother why this baby did not have a standing frame. 'I don't know what you should say,' said Ann. 'I know that there has been some research on how to deal with siblings, and we asked someone to come and give us a talk on the subject, but I expect each family finds their own way of telling their children.' She then took out a small cardboard book of photographs of common objects and gave this to Bob; as she turned the pages she pointed and named the objects and encouraged him to try to turn the pages. When they got to the picture of a train Bob smiled and looked excitedly at the picture and made an 'oooo, ch' noise. Ann left the book, the dolphin toy, the Stickle bricks and the weekly activity chart with Bob's mother, and suggested that she made sure that she pointed to objects in the room and named them: light, door, table, etc.

Working with the Portage programme

■ Activity 3 A

You have now read about how Portage has been used for two children, Ellen and Bob. Make some notes in answer to the following questions:

*   What methods did you notice the Portage teacher using? How did the Portage teacher work with Bob's mother?

*   What significant achievements has Bob made since he started his Portage programme? How do you think Bob's progress was being enhanced by the Portage programme?

*   What are the advantages and disadvantages of this way of working with children and parents?

❏ Commentary

When I observed Bob's session with his Portage teacher I was impressed by the relaxed atmosphere and the way his mother was encouraged to participate in the development of his learning. The Portage teacher took off her shoes when she entered the house and sat on the floor working with Bob, at his level. She talked *to* Bob and very rarely *about* Bob. This illustrated the respect she held for him. She also supported Bob's mother by asking her lots of questions and providing helpful, but not too prescriptive, answers – for instance, how she could deal with his older brother's questions about Bob's disability or differences from other children.

The advantages of this way of working are the close contact and the development of the mother-child relationship, both of which are directed by activities. Hence Bob's mother, who is a trained nurse, is given information about how to 'teach' her son in a directed way. She has also had to learn about how to access resources for her son because she comes from New Zealand and is unsure of how the support services operate in England.

The small steps of progress provide a sense of achievement for both mother and child. The main areas of progress may be considered to be that Bob and his mother have fun playing together; the development of Bob's fine motor and gross motor skills; and his enjoyment of books.

UNIT 4 WEEK TWO

Assessment and children with learning difficulties and disabilities

Assessment is a central part of the Portage programme. Gaining an accurate picture of the child's present achievements helps the Portage worker to decide which tasks to turn to next. This seems very important in the early years if children are to make appropriate developmental progress.

'All About Me'

The psychologist who worked with Ellen and her parents, Sheila Wolfendale, went on to design national guidelines in the form of a checklist for parents about their child aged two to six years, which could then be used to contribute towards their assessment under the 1981 (replaced by the 1993) Education Act. *All About Me* (1990) is a checklist for families to complete about their child, so that they then have a profile of their child's development and learning and can formulate plans to support the child's progress. The idea behind the checklist is that it is a means of sharing information between the home and the early childhood centre or school. It is written in the first person so that parents can say what the child can do. In the section on Language, for instance, the parent can fill in sections like:

- When I made my first sounds
- Now I can name parts of my body
- Playing and learning
- Doing things for myself
- My physical development
- My health and my habits
- Other people
- How I behave
- My mood and feelings
- Future plans.

The checklist is written and presented in a style which is accessible for parents who can use the English language, and emphasises parents' skills of observing, assessing, predicting, describing, reporting and recording their child's experiences. This information can then complement the reports produced about the child by professionals, including teachers and nursery staff. The trial of *All About Me* was carried out with 130 children around the country, and it was found that mostly mothers filled in the checklist (Wolfendale 1990).

'Special educational needs'

Once children approach school age, assessment forms the basis of a statement of educational need. The 1978 Report of the Committee of Inquiry into the Education of Handicapped Children and Young People, often referred to as the Warnock Report, established that 'the concept of special educational needs should be broadened to encompass a wider range of pupils and young people with learning difficulties' (Croll and Moses 1985). The Warnock Report (DES 1978) recommended the changing of the specific labels of 'severe' and 'moderate learning difficulties' to 'special educational needs'; the 1981 Education Act sanctioned this all-encompassing term. The report attempted to reduce the classification of pupils according to the nature of the disabilities or learning difficulty by introducing a term which focused on the 'needs' of the pupils. The concept of 'special education' was broadened to include a larger proportion of the school population – about one in six children at any time. Up to one in five children may require special educational provision at some time (Croll and Moses 1985).

The 1981 and 1993 Education Acts describe a child with 'special educational needs' as having 'significantly greater difficulty in learning than the majority of children of his age' or 'a disability which either prevents or hinders him from making use of educational facilities of a kind generally provided in schools ... for children of his age'. Informing the categories of pupils are factors such as the child's IQ, behaviour and medical 'needs'. A group of professionals including educational psychologists and possibly teachers, occupational therapists, physiotherapists and doctors identify the child's learning 'needs' to produce a formal statement. As you learned earlier in this unit, this document, outlining the child's 'special educational needs', can involve a contribution from the parents if they are asked to outline their perception of their child's 'needs'.

On the one hand, the statement may protect the child's right to provision and was intended to take the parents' views into account, providing an important document for the child, the parents and the professionals. On the other hand, it has been criticised for not achieving these objectives. The procedure has been intensely criticised for not respecting parents' views (Goacher *et al* 1988). In a study of parents' experiences and the statementing process Cornwell (1987) found that parents felt 'anger and distress'. Most parents wanted:

> understanding, personal contact and kindness. They wanted people above all to listen to them, not just a token invitation to give their views, but to have their opinions about their own children valued and respected. [p 54]

In 1992 a Government report which described provision for pupils with special educational needs in England and Wales resulted in a handbook which presented detailed practice for schools and local education authorities. This handbook, called *Getting in on the Act*, suggested that the statementing process should:

- allow parents the right to express a preference for their child's school

- provide a shorter assessment process

- regulate the time taken to complete assessments and statements.

These suggestions were incorporated into the 1994 Code of Practice on the Identification and Assessment of Special Educational Needs, and there was a recommended limit of six months on the statementing process.

A closer look at assessment

■ Activity 4 B

For this activity you will need to consider the assessment procedures for a child you know who may be experiencing learning difficulties or have a disability. The child may be at the early childhood centre or school where you work or where you are visiting. There are several ways you could approach this task.

- You could carry out your own informal assessment of a child, observing them participating in a number of different activities, then use these observations as data for your assessment. (It may be that you could use some of your observations from previous units if this is appropriate.) Remember, as usual, to gain permission first, and to observe the rules of confidentiality.

- You may have access to a child's statement of their special educational needs.

- There may be a child with whom you work who has a less formal assessment of their learning and the support they require.

Consider the assessment in the light of the following questions:

1. Who has written the assessment?

2.   Who has contributed towards the assessment: parents, professionals, the child?

3.   What does the assessment tell you about the child?

4.   What is the learning support provision outlined in the assessment? (This may or may not be specified. If not, what would you recommend?)

5.   How would you feel if you were the parent of this child reading the assessment (or perhaps, how would you feel if this report was about your learning)?

6.   Make a list of further activities which would help develop the learning of the child in a positive way.

If you are unsure how to proceed with this activity, have a look at the example which follows.

❑ **Commentary**

Here is an example contributed by a learning support assistant. (The names have been changed.) You can ask the same questions of this assessment. Compare it with your own example.

Summary assessment by the Learning Support Assistant

Claire came to the Reception class unable to converse freely with adults and peers. She was shy and withdrawn. Her writing skills were very immature. She was unable to commit to paper even the simplest of shapes. Her reading ability was good but her comprehension and her ability to internalise information was poor. Claire had difficulty in controlling her bowel movements. This caused comment among her peers in the class.

Claire was observed in school by an educational psychologist and in subsequent meetings with parents, teachers and social workers it was agreed that she receive 10 hours a week supported learning assistance.

I was appointed as her learning support assistant, which was a real challenge for me. Under the guidance of her class teacher I worked with Claire, gaining her trust and encouraging her to do more and more things for herself. The sense of achievement when she did produce a piece of writing or a drawing was immense. She loved to have the class teacher praise her or have her show her work to the class and receive a clap. So did I!

I worked with Claire for four years, either one to one or in a small group. She eventually came to enjoy our conversations and even initiated them at times. Most satisfying for me was the transformation Claire underwent from a quiet, withdrawn child to a happy girl able to converse and make friends with her peers.

Townsford Nursery School: assessment on entry

A caring but at times rather muddled single-parent family – has little contact with father. Claire was affected badly by her parents' divorce when she was two and a half years old and her behaviour regressed at this time. Family then attended Brownham Family Centre but progress was very slow.

Since coming to this nursery at age three and a half (beginning part-time, then moving to full-time place) there has been great progress. Staff feel she could manage in mainstream primary education as long as she receives support. It was recommended by a multi-professional assessment team that she attend her local primary school, with 10 hours learning assistance support per week – for the first two terms, to be reviewed – and that she continue with speech therapy.

Blogshire first screening schedule (on entry to primary school)

Name		D.O.B.	
School			

Parents' information		**School observation in first term**	

1. Speech and language

Delay in speaking	Yes/No	Failure to speak in class	Yes/No
Difficulty in articulation	Yes/No	Limited language development	Yes/No
		Poor articulation	Yes/No

2. Vision

Concern re: sight	Yes/No	Screws up eyes	Yes/No
Colour discrimination	Yes/No	Peers at objects	Yes/No
History of squint	Yes/No	Fails to look at pictures	Yes/No

3. Hearing

Any concern re: hearing	Yes/No	Any concern re: hearing	Yes/No

4. Behaviour

Difficult at home	Yes/No	Poor relationships with children	Yes/No
Difficulties with toileting	Yes/No	Marked anxiety	Yes/No
		Hyperactive	Yes/No

5. Motor co-ordination

Difficulty in movement	Yes/No	Difficulty in PE	Yes/No
Clumsy with a pencil	Yes/No	Poor pencil control	Yes/No

Further activities for Claire suggested by the Learning Support Assistant
Making books – *to help develop her creativity and imagination, as well as language skills like sequencing and sentence structure. Important for her to have an end product too.*
Play board games – *in a group setting Claire can extend her conversational skill and mix with other children.*
Cutting and sticking – *extending her own interests and developing fine motor skills, perhaps making a topic book.*

It may be that in comparing your own comments with this example you were able to understand more about the difficulties of accurate assessment, as well as the obvious advantages of collecting information. Did you notice a discrepancy, as in the example, between parents' and professionals' perceptions of the child? Would you be happy reading a similar assessment of your own child? Or of yourself as a learner? Thoughts like this can help us all to be a little more careful about the way we describe children and their families.

UNIT 4 WEEK TWO

Claire's mark-making (first two terms of primary school)

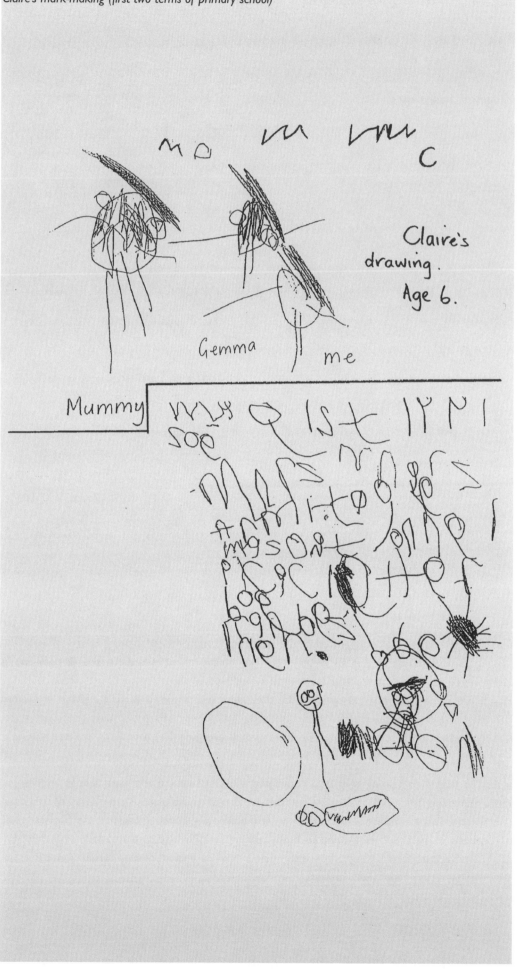

The Code of Practice

I am sure that many interesting comments will result from this activity. Perhaps you have been surprised at the amount of assessments of a child, or even the lack of assessments for a child, who is experiencing difficulties. Since the introduction of the Code of Practice (DfE 1994) in schools in September 1995, children who experience difficulties in learning are identified as having 'special educational needs' and there are 'school-based stages' which are procedures whereby schools place children from stage 1 to stage 3. Children who are considered by the school's special educational needs co-ordinator to be at stage 2 require an individual education plan: 'the plan should build on the curriculum the child is following alongside fellow pupils and should make use of programmes, activities, materials and assessment techniques readily available to the child's teachers' (DfE 1994, Section 2.93, p 28). Children who are considered to be at stage 3 require support from the local education authority through a statement.

The introduction of these stages has led to an increase, in some primary schools, of children identified at stage 1 – as having 'special educational needs'. Their parents become involved in this process when they are asked to contribute their views and perceptions of their child's performance at school. You may wish to consider the Code of Practice stages in more detail. You could ask to look at a copy at a school, or speak to the school's special educational needs co-ordinator, or else you could request a copy from the Department for Education and Employment.

Assessment in a nursery school

As young children may not go through the statementing process until they are of school age, even though the process can start from birth, many teachers monitor and evaluate the progress and activities of all pupils all the time. You may recall links with Unit 3 here, where you worked through the section on observation and record keeping. Here is an account showing how a nursery teacher called Zelda describes how she assesses the children in her Inner London nursery school:

I have thirty children in my class and two nursery nurses. We each take ten children and we are responsible for keeping all their examples of work. We also carry out observations of them. We record any liaison with parents or outside agencies. As the class teacher I am responsible for ensuring that the records are kept up. We call this the 'Key Worker System'.

We are able to fill the records out from our observations. As we observe a child demonstrating particular skills or evidence of particular understandings within the broad areas of development (i.e. language, maths, science, social skills, motor skills, etc) we write these down, date them, then collate them weekly or bi-weekly so we can see where there are gaps or if there is anything we should be concerned about.

We plan our activities daily so if there are any children we need to help in a specific area or we're not sure about a specific area, we write that into our daily plan.

If a child is causing us concern because they're not progressing well, we then follow our Special Needs Policy and Procedures. This consists of contacting parents, making specific strategic plans, reviewing them and moving on to outside agencies if necessary.

Very few children get a statement completed while they are at our nursery. Occasionally we are able to get an assessment started. This may be because children are only with us for five terms and they are so young. It takes a couple of terms to weigh up our concerns about developmental delay – whether it is due to the child's experiences or immaturity – before we decide a child would benefit from an assessment. By the time all the information is collated and collected it's time for a child to start in a primary school. At least extra support is usually sorted out by that time. Our educational psychologist actually said we are a 'holding ground' when she talked to us about the new Code of Practice (1994).

UNIT 4 WEEK TWO

We hardly ever get children who already have a statement – two in the five years since I've been at this school. The local education authority has an assessment nursery where most children with recognised disabilities or learning difficulties are sent. Although we have approached our local health visitors, explaining that we would welcome children with special needs, very rarely are we approached.

The nursery school has a policy on record keeping which states:

> It is the aim of the school that each child will have a record of development throughout her/his time in the nursery, resulting in a cumulative record of achievement which is transferable to the child's next stage of schooling.

This policy outlines how the organisation of the records is the responsibility of the class teacher, whereas all the members of staff maintain the ongoing information on each child. Team meetings are held at the end of each day in order for staff to evaluate the events of the day and to plan 'to meet the needs of individual children, or those of a group within the class'. Parents are invited to share the child's progress with a member of staff twice during the child's period in school. When the child transfers to reception class a summative record of their progress is shown to the parent.

The purpose of the records is to gain a picture of the child's all-round development, to enable staff to pass on knowledge to others, for parents to share in the development of the child and to enable staff to plan learning situations for the children's interests and abilities.

Over the page is an example of a record sheet called a Child Profile which is filled in six weeks after starting the nursery by the child's key worker.

After each term a record sheet is filled in for each child, which includes a section on 'Intellectual development' in the areas of language and literacy; science; mathematics; and creativity. The child's emotional and physical development is recorded as well as parental involvement. The strategies or action taken are documented. The method of record keeping includes written and pictorial observation such as pieces of work which are considered to 'show progress', such as drawings of people, first marks or writing. All work is dated and should be accompanied by a written explanation or a quote. If there is concern about the child's progress, a team meeting would be initiated with the head teacher.

Not all nurseries follow such rigorous guidelines in monitoring, assessing and observing their children. They may have more informal ways of documenting the progress of the children. In another Inner London nursery school the key worker is responsible for ten children and has to make sure that they keep information about each child in the form of pieces of work. On the wall of the nursery at each activity corner are folders in which the teacher or nursery nurse can place their comments, or the child's work if they consider it to be a good example. The key worker is then told about this work or informed about any concerns, and this is recorded in the file for each child they are responsible for.

Assessment

■ Activity 5 B

1. List the main methods of assessment used in these nursery classes.

2. How do these compare with the context you work in, or the early childhood centre you are visiting? You may be able to use notes from work done in Unit 3 for this comparison. Otherwise, just list the methods of assessment in use, and comment briefly on them.

❑ Commentary

You probably identified a variety of methods. Perhaps there is already an assessment system set up in your early childhood centre or school. You may wish to find out more about this system and reflect on your role within this system. Could it be improved, and are there any difficulties with the way it is implemented?

UNIT 4 WEEK TWO

CHILD PROFILE (6 weeks after starting)

Name   D.O.B.   Date completed

Date of admission

How well did the child settle in?

Easily/with difficulty?

Relationships (any one in particular)

With staff: With peers:

Type of play

Observing: Parallel:

Solitary: Associatively:

Group time (story or other organised times)

Does s/he enjoy this?

Concentrate/follow activity?

Speak up at this time?

Does the child 'appear' confident/ shy/ anxious/ insecure? (Circle one.)

How are they really?

Can child follow instructions?

1 or 2 part directions?   More complex instructions?

Is the child able to make needs known verbally or non-verbally?

Is the child's speech clear?

Is the child monosyllabic or using full sentences?

Use of curriculum/favoured activities/rituals

To be completed after discussion with parent

Parent's comments on settling, etc

Is the child ready for a full-time place?

If not, what has been done about this, e.g. postponed or given a trial period?

Pertinent points or comments that you have gained from conversation with parent

Any other comments

UNIT 4 WEEK TWO

Review of the week

During this week we have explored approaches to early intervention which enhance the learning of children who experience difficulties or have disabilities. We have also considered the importance of the role of parents working with their children in early intervention programmes. And we have focused on the assessment of children during the early years – especially children with learning difficulties or disabilities.

Acknowledging parents' experiences and perspectives has been suggested as a formula for professionals to work to in a partnership relationship. This may entail professionals understanding the way in which attitudes towards disability and learning difficulty can influence the experiences of parents and children. For instance, some parents have attempted to redefine what it is like to parent a disabled child. They accept and support their child, rather than being in a state of 'shock' because their child experiences difficulties. Involving parents in assessment has been emphasised, although parent participation in the statementing process has been found to be problematic. Nevertheless, the procedures for assessment used in one nursery school have highlighted how professionals monitor all children and shown that all children can be included into a nursery environment with support from professionals.

Before moving on to the next week of study, make sure you complete the following review activity.

■ Review activity A

Take some time to look back over the work you have done this week.

*   What interested you most, and why?

*   How will this week's study influence your ways of caring for and educating young children?

*   Have you time for more reading on a topic which interests you?

Further reading

Department for Education (1994) *The Code of Practice on the Identification and Assessment of Special Educational Needs*, London: DfE

Jordan, L. and Wolfendale, S. (1986) 'Experiencing Portage: an account by a parent and a home teacher', in Cameron, R.J. (ed) *Portage: Pre-schoolers, Parents and Professionals*, Windsor: NFER-Nelson

There is a full list of references at the end of Unit 4.

Unit 4: Week Three
Supporting children in early childhood centres

Objectives

This week you will be focusing on the nature of professional support for children with learning difficulties and disabilities. By the end of the week you should:

- understand how the professional's level of self-awareness can influence children's development

- recognise a variety of different strategies useful in organising support for children with learning difficulties and disabilities in the school situation as well as in other early childhood centres

- have an increased understanding of the range of professional roles undertaken by support assistants.

Activities

This week you will need time to evaluate your own methods of supporting children. There are no more set observations this week but you may want to supplement your existing data to develop your understanding of the key issues.

About this week's study

By the end of this section you will be exploring how children can be supported in the classroom. This will be discussed in the light of Solity's (1995) argument that we need to have a critical level of self-awareness in order to influence children's development in a positive way.

The final part of this section will provide an example of how a child with Down's Syndrome, 'Silvie', was supported in a mainstream primary school. This account has been written in the first person, as a 'reflective account' of the experiences of the professional who supported the child.

Supporting children

We will begin by examining the role of the professional who works with young children. I will emphasise the importance of understanding that how we work with children can be influenced by our own individual approach and how we 'interact' with others. This may entail exploring how we communicate with children, and developing an understanding of what their experiences are like. For instance, you might consider what happens to children during their first days at school.

The self-awareness of the professional

The importance of reflecting on experiences for those who work with children has been stressed by Jonathan Solity (1995). He argues that it is important to recognise how the background of the professional can influence the way that children, and events, are considered. He also argues that the views and behaviour of the professional can have an effect on young children's social and emotional development. This is an area you may remember exploring in Unit 1 Week Three, where we looked at the development of self-esteem.

Solity implies that there may be a need for professionals to explore their own personal histories; that is, their background and experiences in their family life, school life and so on. He points out how teachers often explain the difficulties children have as caused by the home and parents, or 'within child' factors (such as ability or aptitude), rather than by factors associated with the school. One suggestion he makes is that interactions with the child should be 'straight' rather than 'blaming, placating, being reasonable or irrelevant'. The key features of 'straight' interactions are considered by Solity (p 19) to be:

*   acknowledging and not discounting the feelings of children

*   asking for what we want and making expectations explicit

*   giving children permission to behave in ways which contradict potent family and societal messages

*   negotiation.

These 'straight' interactions contrast to the 'games' which may be played out between the educator and the child, often leading to frustration, anger and resentment from the child. One way to avoid these feelings emerging from the child is to involve adults in:

*   identifying children's emotions

*   labelling them appropriately

*   communicating this to children

*   giving them choices about their behaviour

*   being explicit about the behaviour consistent with displaying different emotions.

In communicating with children by using the 'rules', the adult is acknowledging the behaviour of the child rather than trying to control it. Solity suggests that professionals should develop a critical level of self-awareness and a way of 'straight talking'. He says this is important in order for educators 'to have a positive impact on their role in facilitating children's social and emotional development' (Solity 1995, p 21).

■ Activity 1 A

1. Do you agree or disagree with Solity's statement that we need to have a critical level of self-awareness in order to have a positive effect on children's social and emotional development? Why?

2. Describe an example of how you have dealt with a child's anger or frustration.

❏ Commentary

1. Here is what a reception class teacher said:

    I agree with Solity. Otherwise I may find myself blaming a child for something that, in fact, I do. I remember a teacher who screamed at the children all the time. She used to moan about the way children in her class 'shouted at each other constantly'!

    I wonder if thinking about this kind of incident helped you to see the need for your own self-awareness.

2. When I worked as a class teacher in a school for children categorised as having severe learning difficulties one of the children in my class was Marian who had 'autistic tendencies'. She was five years old and would get very frustrated and angry if any paint went on her hand during a

painting session. When she noticed that there was paint on her hand – which was very difficult to avoid – she would try to rub it off with her finger. However, this caused the paint to spread and she started to scream and ran around the room, as if trying to run away from the paint on her hand. She would run to the sink and try to wash it off. If she splashed herself and became wet, she screamed even louder and tried to dry her clothes with a towel. She was usually jumping up and down fairly quickly, at the same time as trying to clean and dry herself.

My reaction was to ensure that the other children in the class remained calm and were attended to by the support assistants so that I could comfort Marian and reassure her until she calmed down. This usually took about ten minutes to half an hour. I remained with her and helped her to dry her clothes and wash her hands. She would get more frustrated and angry if her actions were not acknowledged. Occasionally this situation would cause disruption to the other members of staff and pupils in the class who would be upset by Marian's screaming. When she became calm I would suggest she joined the other children, or else I involved her in another activity.

The influence of 'personal baggage'

As discussed in Unit 2, the 'baggage' which you bring with you from your background enters into your work situation. It can influence your role as a professional – how you work with other professionals and parents – and it may affect how you see your role, your aspirations and interactions within the system or institution in which you work. One memory most people can recall is their first experience at primary or nursery school. The following study by John Shostak (1987) illustrates how observation and analysis in the classroom can reveal the different aspects of pupil-teacher relationships such as power and control.

Shostak carried out an observational study of one classroom during the children's first days at school. He describes the experiences of the children and the role of the teacher – how she exerts her power over the children in order to maintain control in her class. At first the teacher and welfare assistant greet each child in a friendly way and the children wander around the classroom so that they feel 'comfortable'. The twelve new children then meet the rest of the class who have been there for two terms. The register is taken with all the children organised on the mat, facing the teacher. She rewards each new boy or girl who says her name correctly when asked with a 'good boy' or 'good girl'. Shostak considers this to be a 'training of response' which moulds the children into becoming 'pupils'. The teacher continues her authoritarian role as she 'leads, organises, and commands'; she creates her 'audience' of children (p 9):

> The teacher takes on the attributes of censor, judge and motivator. She must find strategies to inhibit some behaviours, advocate others and gradually bring about the behaviours she desires.

Reinforcement was discussed in Unit 1 in the context of behaviourist models of child development. The following simple example of the way the teacher uses reinforcement as a way of correcting behaviour is given by Shostak (p 9):

> *Girl: 'Can I paint now?'*
> *Teacher: 'Pardon?'*
> *Girl: 'Can I paint please?'*
> *Teacher: 'That's better. I like that magic word.'*

Shostak identifies this type of interaction between the pupil and the teacher as 'micro-manipulation'. He reveals what goes on in the classroom during the children's first days at school by observing and then describing what happens. He includes examples of conversations between the children and the teacher which illustrate how the teacher exerts her power over the children. He goes on to describe how the teacher deals with a conflict situation by socialising the children. In the final instance her most powerful asset is that she can 'detain the children against their will'. When a child sang during story time she told the class that they would have to sit on the mat until home time. In contrast to this the children cannot say to the teacher, 'I've had enough of this' or 'I'm not going to look at you any more' (Shostak 1987, p 10).

Learning to be a 'pupil'

Shostak's description and analysis of children's first days at school is fascinating to read because he provides an account of what happens and then interprets these events. You may agree or disagree with his interpretation of events, but accounts of this type do provide 'a window' into children's experiences in the classroom.

Children who experience difficulties in learning or have disabilities may require support from their peers, an assistant or a teacher in order to access the curriculum and become a 'pupil' in a mainstream classroom. A disabled child who uses a wheelchair would require access to the classroom and around the school in order to become a 'pupil'. Solity's work indicates how communication and interaction between adults and children are an important aspect of how children can be supported, and he provides an insight into the power relationships between adults and children.

Many children who experience difficulties may receive support from a learning support assistant or a support teacher. One disabled child I knew wrote a job description for her assistant. At times the child, Linda, said she felt overpowered by their one-to-one relationship and did not want a 'shadow' following her around and getting in the way of her friendships with her peers. This direct communication helped Linda and her support assistant to work out a more appropriate way for Linda to be supported in school.

Approaches to supporting young children in mainstream schools

Support for children with learning difficulties and disabilities may come from their family and from professionals who work with the child and the family. In Week One of this unit we considered how Michael's family had support from a parent advocate and the teachers in his mainstream school. His parents also supported him by putting forward their wishes for him to attend a mainstream school alongside his brother. In Week Two we considered how Ellen and Bob received support from their Portage teachers, who also worked alongside the parents. In the section on partnership with parents we looked at how parents may want to have a lot of information about their children when they first discover that their child has a learning difficulty or a disability. In some cases parents felt supported by professionals, while in others they felt that the professionals presented their own views in preference to the views and knowledge of the parents.

Support for children with disabilities or learning difficulties may come from a variety of professionals employed by the health service, social services, voluntary organisations and the education service. They may be specialist teachers, health visitors, doctors or social workers. In this section we shall be exploring how children are supported in mainstream classrooms by teachers and learning support assistants. This approach of supporting children in mainstream schools may vary from support in the class to withdrawal from classrooms; the child may be taught on a one-to-one basis or else in small groups. Will Swann (1992) points out how withdrawal teaching was carried out in the 1970s to improve pupils' numeracy and literacy skills, and was known as 'remedial education'. He also notes that by the 1980s there was a shift away from 'remedial education' towards support in class from support teachers. However, he also points out that this shift is difficult to generalise about and that changes have occurred at different rates around the country.

UNIT 4 WEEK THREE

In 1985 the Inner London Education Authority produced a report entitled *Equal Opportunities for All* reviewing the authority's special education provision in the light of the 1981 Education Act. The review established a support service for pupils in mainstream schools with statements of their special educational needs. In 1986-87 the Education, Science and Arts Committee met at the House of Commons to hear evidence and report on *Special Education Needs: Implementation of the Education Act 1981*. In Volume I the committee recognised how extra teaching hours can be allocated to schools in order to provide for pupils' 'special educational needs'. The committee noted that they were impressed with the allocation of teaching hours in Denmark and Sweden:

> The flexible use of these hours seemed to reduce the demand for complex assessment procedures which allocate resources to individual children. It is possibly in the establishment of appropriate staffing levels for a school as a whole that the most effective contribution can be made to providing for those with special educational needs. [Education, Science and Arts Committee 1987, Section 31, p xv]

The committee went on to recommend that the Department for Education and Science should produce a Circular on staffing as they had identified that support for schools in the form of extra teaching hours was 'best practice'. In Nottinghamshire in the early 1990s an educational psychologist interpreted Circular 11/90 guidelines for staffing levels in a way which released surplus money from special schools and reallocated over £1 million in financial support towards supporting pupils with special needs in ordinary schools (Audit Commission 1992a, p 64).

The Audit Commission's report *Getting the Act Together* (1992b), which contained recommendations for changing practice, recognised the importance of centralised support services maintained by local education authorities, and suggested that this would ensure that schools did not divert support to other purposes. However, when we considered the experiences of Michael we saw that his parents have found it difficult to ensure support for him in his mainstream school, despite the fact that he has a statement of special educational needs.

Despite recommendations from the Education, Science and Arts Committee (1987) and examples of 'good practice' for providing support for children in mainstream schools, the practice of support may be different around the country, and indeed between individual education authorities and schools.

The support teacher's role

Glenys Andrews (1989), who was head of a support service in a London borough as well as an advisor and trainer, stresses the description given in 1978 by Her Majesty's Inspectorate (Scotland) of the role of the learning support teacher as involving consultancy, direct tuition, co-operative teaching and temporary support.

Consultancy	For pupils, class and subject teachers, school management teams, parents and external agencies to include individual pupil needs, curriculum, organisation, teaching methods and resources of whole class or whole school
Direct tuition	Providing one-to-one support for children
Cooperative teaching	Teaching alongside the class teacher, following the pedagogy of the class teacher and adapting the curriculum for individual and small-group tution
Temporary support	For the pupil in the class, and for the class teacher, supplemented by a learning support assistant

UNIT 4 WEEK THREE

Each of these aspects of support teaching is an important part of the support teacher's role, and if possible they should be equally balanced. However, the support teacher is accountable to the parents of the child and bound by the written details on the child's statement. Consequently, the support teacher should work closely with the parents, gaining their approval of her or his way of supporting the child and to provide feedback on the progress of the child. The support teacher should also provide the type of learning experiences identified on the child's statement of special educational needs.

Glenys Fox (1994) asked 80 special needs assistants to define their supporting role. Their responses fell into three main categories (p 9):

- supporting the pupil
- supporting the teacher
- supporting the school.

The same assistants identified their supporting role as having the following characteristics:

- promoting independence
- inspiring confidence and trust
- valuing the child
- fostering peer group acceptance
- encouraging and giving rewards
- developing listening skills
- enabling the child
- knowing the background
- finding out about the special need
- keeping confidences
- being 'in tune' with the child's physical needs.

■ Activity 2 B

Choose a child that you have contact with on an individual basis. It may be that they have been identified as having 'special educational needs'.

Using Glenys Fox's three categories, make some notes about how you offer these three kinds of support. For instance you might say:

- *Supporting the child*: Spend 10 minutes each day sharing a book.

- *Supporting the teacher*: Contribute to the child's records of achievement based on my observations of them at play and at work.

- *Supporting the school or other early childhood centre*: Attending meetings with parents and other professionals where the child's progress is discussed.

You might also find it helpful to look at the above list of characteristics of the support assistant's role, as identified by the assistants themselves. How might they influence your involvement with this child?

❏ Commentary

Clearly, the role of the support assistant involves a variety of strategies for working with the child and the school. Presumably 'knowing the background' and 'keeping confidences' would have brought the assistant into contact with the child's parents. However, most of the supporting role could be identified as 'child centred'. Fox also makes the point that only when the class teacher works closely with the assistant alongside an effective learning programme will the child achieve 'success'.

The readings listed in the 'Further reading' section this week include more examples of ways of offering support.

UNIT 4 WEEK THREE

Supporting Silvie

One piece of research I have conducted has included a reflective account of my experiences and observations when I worked as a support teacher (Paige-Smith 1994). I had wanted to write about what went on in the classroom as a part of a case study on a particular child. I found this case study difficult to write, and I had a struggle to acknowledge the importance of my experiences, even though I recognised that they had shaped me as a 'professional' in the workplace.

I was appointed as Silvie's support teacher in January 1987, after her first term at primary school, when she was five and a half years old. I worked with her for one and a half days each week for three years. I came with a label, too: a trained teacher for pupils categorised as having 'severe learning difficulties'.

My role as a support teacher was not clear cut. I was there to support Silvie, and within that role I had the freedom to decide the best way of doing that. I had to stop working with individual programmes written down for the welfare assistant or teacher to refer to. This practice was common in the special school system but was not appropriate in a mainstream school. The welfare assistant ignored the plans, as did the class teacher. Silvie's work in the classroom was either with the whole class or with small groups. I compromised by providing a written list of aims and objectives for every half term so that we all knew what stage Silvie needed to work on in each curriculum area. Her mother was consulted on this programme and she referred to it at home.

At times I taught the whole class so that the class teacher would have time to work with Silvie. I also relieved the class teacher during story time so that she could get on with other things. This gave the class teacher time to be with Silvie and to observe her with the rest of the class. It also gave me the chance to experience how Silvie was responding within the whole class situation, whether she was listening, paying attention and understanding what was happening.

Often I would sit on the mat with her and act as her interpreter. I would tell her what the class teacher had said in a simpler form as her understanding of language was weaker than some of her peers. The teacher would ask the children to talk about something – say, food – as part of a project. She might have said, 'What do you like eating for dinner?' I would then hold Silvie's face, meet her eyes and whisper 'Nice food? Chapatis, apples, chocolate?' Silvie would then choose one of these. I would then yank up her hand really high in the air, the class teacher would ask Silvie what she liked eating for dinner, and 'chocolate' was the reply. She received mountains of whispered praise from me. A lot of non-verbal communication went on between the class teacher and me. It was important to make sure that Silvie was always participating with her class. She needed positive reinforcement from the teachers so that she felt a sense of achievement and success.

The lesson I learned from being Silvie's support teacher was that her inclusion in a mainstream school was beneficial to her both educationally and socially. Her inclusion had also changed the school. There was an increased understanding of other pupils in the school who experienced difficulties in learning. As Silvie had the label of Trisomy 21, so-called 'Down's Syndrome', she was expected to have difficulties in communicating and learning to read, write and count. Yet there were other pupils in her class who were not progressing as well as Silvie. Silvie's inclusion challenged the prejudicial assumptions in society and schools about Down's Syndrome once she started to progress educationally and socially (Paige-Smith 1994).

Learning support

■ Activity 3 A

The previous activity invited you to analyse the nature of the support you offer, focusing on one child. Now make a list of further activities which could develop this child's learning in a positive way.

Finally, consider the following questions:

1. How has your background influenced your approach to caring for and educating young children?

2. What do you value about your approach to supporting children?

❏ Commentary

It will help you to talk with a colleague or friend about this activity. Questions may have arisen during this activity which have led you to consider why you decided to become a parent or work with young children. You may have known that this is what you have wanted to do from a very early age; an experience, or something someone has told you, may have reinforced this decision. Did you have any other career opportunities? If so, why did you not go down another path? Were your decisions based upon the opportunities you had as a child, young person or adult?

Finally, do you feel valued in your work, and how do you achieve job satisfaction? Often I find that just watching young children playing or involved in an activity can be very satisfying. Do you agree?

Review of the unit

This unit has introduced you to different aspects of the education and care of young children who experience difficulties or have disabilities. In your role as a parent, carer, or as a professional worker at an early childhood centre or school, you may find you notice that a child requires extra support. I hope this unit has contained useful information which has equipped you to explore and understand what provision can be made available and how important it is to encourage parental involvement.

Further reading

Alyson, C. (1992) 'Chris Raine's progress – an achievement to be proud of', in Booth, T. et al (eds) *Curricula for Diversity in Education,* London: Routledge

Ellis, M. (1995) 'An inclusive curriculum within a nursery school', in Potts, P. et al (eds) *Learning Teaching and Managing in Schools,* London: Routledge

UNIT 4 WEEK THREE

Unit 4 References

These are the readings mentioned in Unit 4:

Week One

Audit Commission (1992) *Getting in on the Act*, London: HMSO

Booth, T. and Swann, W. (eds) (1987) *Including Pupils with Disabilities*, Milton Keynes: Open University Press

Booth, T., Swann, W., Masterson, M. and Potts, P. (eds) (1992) *Policies for Diversity in Education*, London: Routledge

Camden Local Education Authority (1994) *Special Education Policy,* London: CLEA

Cameron, J. and Sturge, L. (1990) *Under Fives Project*, London: MENCAP

Clark, C., Dyson, A. and Millward, A. (1995) *Towards Inclusive Schools*, London: David Fulton

Department for Education (1993) *Education Act*, London: HMSO

Department for Education (1994) *The Code of Practice on the Identification and Assessment of Special Educational Needs*, London: DfE

Department of Education and Science (1978) *Special Educational Needs* (The Warnock Report), London: HMSO

Jordan, L. (1992) 'Integration policy in Newham, 1986-90', in Booth *et al* (1992)

Jordan, L. and Wolfendale, S. (1986) 'Experiencing Portage: an account by a parent and a home teacher', in Cameron, R.J. (ed) *Portage: Pre-schoolers, Parents and Professionals*, Windsor: NFER-Nelson

Jupp, K. (1992) *Everyone Belongs*, London: Souvenir Press

Potts, P. (1992) *Right from the Start,* Unit 5, E242, Milton Keynes: Open University

Potts, P. et al (1995) *Learning Teaching and Managing in Schools,* London: Routledge

Rehal, A. (1989) 'Involving Asian parents in the statementing procedure: the way forward', *Educational Psychology in Practice,* Vol 4, No 4, pp 189-192

Sapon-Shevin, M. (1990) 'Student support through cooperative learning', in Stainback and Stainback (1990)

Shearer, D. and Shearer, M. (1986) Foreword in Cameron, R.J. (ed), *Portage: Pre-schoolers, Parents and Professionals*, Windsor: NFER-Nelson

Stainback, S. and Stainback, W. (1990) *Support Networks for Inclusive Schooling*, Baltimore, MD: Paul Brookes

Vislie, L. (1994) 'Integration policies, school reforms and the organisation of schooling for handicapped pupils in Western societies', in Clark, C. et al (eds) *Towards Inclusive Education*, London: David Fulton

Wolfendale, S. and Wooster, J. (1992) 'Meeting special needs in the early years', in Pugh, G. (ed) *Contemporary Issues in the Early Years,* London: Paul Chapman/National Children's Bureau

Week Two

Audit Commission (1992) *Getting in on the Act,* London: HMSO

Cornwell, N. (1987) *Statementing and the 1981 Education Act,* Bedford: Cranfield Press

Croll, P. and Moses, D. (1985) *One in Five,* London: Routledge

Department for Education (1994) *The Code of Practice on the Identification and Assessment of Special Educational Needs,* London: DfE

Department for Education and Science (1978) *Special Educational Needs* (The Warnock Report), London: HMSO

Ellis, M. (1995) 'An inclusive curriculum within a nursery school', in Potts, P. et al (eds) *Learning Teaching and Managing in Schools,* London: Routledge

Goacher, B. et al (1988) *Policy and Provision for Special Educational Needs,* London: Cassell Educational

Goodey, C. (1992) 'Fools and heretics: parents' views of professionals', in Booth, T., Swann, W., Masterson, M. and Potts, P. (eds) *Policies for Diversity in Education*, London: Routledge

Hornby, G. (1991) 'Parent involvement', in Mitchell, D. and Brown, R. (eds) *Early Intervention Studies for Young Children with Special Needs*, London: Chapman and Hall

Jordan, L. and Wolfendale, S. (1986) 'Experiencing Portage: an account by a parent and a home teacher', in Cameron, R.J. (ed) *Portage: Pre-schoolers, Parents and Professionals*, Windsor: NFER-Nelson

Rehal, A. (1989) 'Involving Asian parents in the statementing procedure: the way forward', *Educational Psychology in Practice,* Vol 4, No 4, pp 189-192

Shearer, D. and Shearer, M. (1986) Foreword in Cameron, R.J. (ed) *Portage: Pre-schoolers, Parents and Professionals,* Windsor: NFER-Nelson

Wolfendale, S. (1990) *All About Me*, Nottingham: NES Arnold

Wolfendale, S. and Wooster, J. (1992) 'Meeting special needs in the early years', in Pugh, G. (ed) *Contemporary Issues in the Early Years,* London: Paul Chapman/National Children's Bureau.

Week Three

Andrews, G. (1989) 'The management of support services: conflicts and tensions in the role of the support teacher', in Bowers, T. (ed) *Managing Special Needs*, Milton Keynes: Open University Press

Audit Commission (1992a) *Getting in on the Act*, London: HMSO

Audit Commission (1992b) *Getting the Act Together,* London: HMSO

Clare, A. (1992) 'Chris Raine's progress: an achievement to be proud of', in Booth, T., Swann, W., Masterson, M. and Potts, P. (eds) *Policies for Diversity in Education,* London: Routledge

Croll, P. and Moses, D. (1985) *One in Five*, London: Routledge

Education, Science and Art Committee (1987) *Special Educational Needs: Implementation of the Education Act 1981*, House of Commons, 3rd Report, Session 1986-87, London: HMSO

Fox, G. (1994) *A Handbook for Special Needs Assistants*, London: David Fulton

Inner London Education Authority (1985) *Equal Opportunities for All*, London: ILEA

Paige-Smith, A. (1994) 'Choosing inclusion: the power of parents in special education', Doctoral thesis, Open University

Shostak, J. (1987) 'As you mean to go on: first days at school', in Booth, T. and Coulby, D. (eds) *Producing and Reducing Disaffection*, Milton Keynes: Open University Press

Solity, J. (1995) 'Psychology, teachers and the early years', *International Journal of Early Years Education*, Vol3, No1

Swann, W. (1992) 'Difference and distinction', in Unit 8/9, E242, *Learning for All*, Milton Keynes: Open University

A last word

We hope you have found this self-study book enjoyable and helpful to you in your involvement with young children. If you have any comments on your experience of using the book, or if you are interested in using it to gain a qualification: the University of Hertfordshire's Certificate in Early Childhood Education and Care, please contact:

The Admissions Officer
University of Hertfordshire
Wall Hall Campus
Aldenham
Watford
Herts. WD2 8AT
Tel: 01707-285766